Old Media
New Media

Old Media
New Media

Mass Communications in the Information Age

Third Edition

Wilson Dizard, Jr.

 **LONGMAN**

An imprint of Addison Wesley Longman, Inc.

New York • Reading, Massachusetts • Menlo Park, California • Harlow, England
Don Mills, Ontario • Sydney • Mexico City • Madrid • Amsterdam

Editor-in-Chief: Priscilla McGeehon
Acquisitions Editor: Michael Greer
Marketing Manager: Megan Galvin
Full Service Production Manager: Patti Brecht
Project Coordination, Text Design, and Electronic Page Makeup:
Pre-Press Company, Inc.
Cover Design Manager: Nancy Danahy
Cover Designer: Keithley and Associates
Senior Print Buyer: Hugh Crawford
Printer and Binder: The Maple-Vail Book Manufacturing Group
Cover Printer: Coral Graphic Services, Inc.

Library of Congress Cataloging-in-Publication Data

Dizard, Wilson P.
    Old media, new media / Wilson Dizard, Jr. — 3rd ed.
        p.   cm.
    Includes bibliographical references and index.
    ISBN 0-8013-3277-X (alk. paper)
    1. Mass media—United States—Technological innovations.   I. Title.
    P96.T422U634   1999   99-29688
    302.23'0973—dc21   CIP

Please visit our website at http://www.awlonline.com

ISBN 0-8013-3277-X

2345678910—MA—020100

For Ithiel de Sola Pool (1917–1984),
who saw it all coming

Annotated Contents

U.S. mass communication patterns are changing radically these days with the introduction of the Internet and other advanced technologies along with shifting social and economic conditions. The result is a competitive mix of old and new media together with a different agenda for the role of information and entertainment resources in our personal and working lives.

A primer on multimedia computers, telecomputers, and other advanced information machines: what they are, what they do, and how they are influencing both old and new media.

A technological revolution in the ways information resources are distributed electronically is profoundly affecting the media industries. A review of the new networks and how they work.

The United States is the testing ground for the development and application of a wide range of new media technologies. The reasons for this are rooted in both First Amendment traditions and the practices of an entrepreneurial media sector. The changes in media patterns are the result of the convergence of political, economic, and technological forces.

Foreword

Everette E. Dennis

Distinguished Professor
Fordham University
Graduate School of Business

Any true understanding of mass communications in the modern age requires unusual sensitivity to technology and change, as well as deep knowledge of history, economics, politics, and sociology, for a start. Essential also is grounding in technology and technological change—not simply in what Arthur C. Clarke called "voices from the sky" in the future tense but also in the sometimes anachronistic system of communication as expressed in today's media. Only a person of unusual intellect, experience, scholarly capacity, and communications savvy could manage such a task. That, however, is just what Wilson Dizard—diplomat, technology and communications expert, scholar, and commentator—has done here.

At the heart of this book is an explication conveyed in overt and subtle tones of media convergence—that condition signifying a united state of media wherein all media forms and instruments come together by virtue of computers and digitization. Even as all media are blurring and blending together into what is really a single system or set of interrelated systems, so are individual media accentuating their distinctiveness. The world Wilson Dizard presents in *Old Media New Media* connects long-standing, traditional communication media with those only imagined today by futurists. It is this rich weave of durable media forms—along with those currently under siege and still others now being conceived in laboratories—that makes this a unique and valuable source of intelligence for students, media researchers, professionals, and the public.

Correctly recognizing that the future of communications lies at the confluence of old and new media, Professor Dizard has produced a book rich in its range and scope of the present and future shape of mass communication and deep in its understanding of the process that will, in fact, define and determine the kind and nature of media that people will experience in the twenty-first century. All books are a product of the experience of their authors, and Wilson Dizard has observed and participated in communications around the world, both in developing nations and in industrial societies. His understanding of the process and framework of the old media of print and broadcast technologies—including publishing, film, and television—connects and overlaps with his expertise about information networks and various new media technologies and data systems.

The story of old and new media cannot be told in technological terms alone, involving only relationships between people and machines, but it must be seen also through the prism of politics and economics, which grant permission for new entries, such as satellites and computers, to be on the media stage and sometimes allow old-timers, such as newspapers, to stay a bit beyond their prime.

Part of the concern of this book is with the pace of new media determined by the forces of invention, creativity, market demand, and regulatory freedom. The discussion speaks in broad policy terms and zeros in on new and evolving industry segments, such as cable. It is buttressed by an assessment of old media, such as newspapers and the movies, that are undergoing a remodeling process as they struggle to survive and flourish in the new information age.

All this helps to explain why good ideas and feasible technologies that could liberate people by providing massive information sources and up-to-the-minute graphics and retrieval do not always get transformed into reality. The interceding human factors, as they are called, are catalogued and analyzed effectively by Professor Dizard, who understands that even the finest technological innovation or the most brilliant new media form will not advance from the R&D lab unless market demand, cost-effectiveness, and the political-regulatory climate are favorable. When we hear predictions about the media room of the future or about the prospects of a given media industry, we often forget that pure logic and the magic of invention are not enough to make new media happen. For those reasons and others, this book also makes us appreciate old media, quite ingenious themselves, even more, and it also explains why seemingly obsolete media such as radio have gotten new life even in the face of television expansion.

Here is the story of the media family, etched against the backdrop of the whole communications system and confined not to a single country or culture but viewed with a global perspective. Old players or "media family" members are observed at various stages of development and appreciated for their contributions both ephemeral and lasting. Gracefully written, this solidly researched book is an exquisite consumer's guide to the future of communications media and has the rare distinction of connecting memories of the past with the present and future. Wilson Dizard can and does hold his own with world policymakers (and has been one himself), debating with technical experts on such issues as cross-data border flow and the future of radio while arguing about what system should govern a given old technology or technological innovation. Mr. Dizard's book is not giddy about the new "toys" on the block, yet it does not underestimate their potential. At the same time, the author appreciates the prowess and staying power of the conventional media and makes sense out of great complexity while offering a coherent theme and framework for unified understanding of mass communication in the information age.

Avoiding the jargon of engineering technology or of policy wonks, the book is eminently practical in its patient explanation of the juxtaposition of economics and politics as determinants of the changing media scene. Neither seduced by the new machines nor underestimating the power of technology both as a societal force and as a metaphor for change, the book is a masterful examination of society's central nervous system and its communication infrastructure, which are presented in a highly accessible form. It will, no doubt, be greeted with enthusiasm by all who are students of the media and of communication, whether they are just entering the field or have long occupied the executive suite. Once again, Wilson Dizard has given us an important treatise that is a sensemaker extraordinaire.

Preface

The transformation of the American media has accelerated steadily in the three years since the second edition of this survey appeared in 1997. This revised edition is designed to arrange the changes into a coherent pattern, detailing the media's continuing transformation as it adjusts to information-age realities.

My focus is primarily on the mass media—print, broadcasting, and film. For shorthand purposes, the discussion is divided between the *old media* and the *new media*—that is, the traditional forms and the new challengers. A partial list of the latter includes multimedia computers, laser discs, advanced facsimile machines, handheld data banks, electronic books, videotext networks, intelligent telephones, direct-to-home broadcasting satellites and the Internet with its new multimedia capabilities. The shared link in each of these services is computerization, a technology that is erasing all of the old distinctions that have separated each of the media services in past years.

Changes in the media sector are taking place at three levels—technical, political, and economic. Technologically, all media are adjusting to the new prospects opened up by the digitization of their traditional products. Politically, new laws and regulations at the federal, state, and local levels are reducing the barriers that limited media organizations in taking full advantage of the new technologies. Economically, two trends dominate. At one level, there is the continuing consolidation of power into larger media conglomerates. Opposing this is the rise of smaller, new enterprises that are challenging the conglomerates in both product innovation and in marketing savvy.

Then there is the Internet, whose astonishing growth is influencing all of these trends. In the past decade, the Internet has been transformed from the province of a small group of computer buffs to a mass-consumer resource available to tens of millions of Americans. Moreover, the Internet has evolved from being a simple text channel to a provider of digitized print, video, and audio services. In the process, it represents a challenge to the ways in which the entire mass media sector produces and markets its products.

The Internet's influence on the American media industry is in its very early stages. This survey will describe its initial impact as well as examine its potential role on media patterns in the early years of the new century. It is no exaggeration that how we deal with the new media environment created by the Internet and other new technologies will define the shape and direction of U.S. postindustrial society.

These media developments are part of a larger shift in American communications. Digital technologies are pushing us toward a national information utility. The result will be networks based on computers and advanced circuits that will make information available in any form—voice, print, or video—almost anywhere, just as we now tap into electricity or water utilities. The U.S. information utility is now about half completed, radically changing the ways in which business and government operate. The next decade will see the consumerization of the utility affecting most American homes.

This will not be a smooth transition. Technological options have to be translated into political and economic realities. There are as many powerful forces opposed to changes in the status quo as there are those who support them. The debate is marked by many dissonant voices. In industry, professional cheerleaders see lucrative markets for glitzy new products and services. In public life at all levels, politicians worry about the impact on the governing pattern and, more directly, on their own careers.

Finally, there are the ultimate consumers of the new-media resources who, so far, have exercised commendable caution regarding the hoopla over technologies guaranteed to change their lives. There are real questions about how, or whether, multimedia computers and the other promised services will satisfy personal needs. What information do I really want? How much will it cost? What is missing? How much is enough? These questions have been pointedly summarized by media watcher Neil Postman: "Any fool can tell you what technology is good for. It takes real thought to figure out what computers will deprive us of." Too often the debate has been dominated by people who, in Evelyn Waugh's words, have never been troubled by the itch of precise thought.

There are, in short, no easy formulas. The ultimate question is how all these prospects can benefit us in a more complex postindustrial democracy. For over two centuries, our lodestar in defining information freedoms has been the First Amendment. Originally, it referred only to printed publications, but its protections have been expanded in recent decades to include the electronic media. Expanding its scope further will be increasingly difficult given the introduction of more complex media technologies.

There are disturbing signs that the new information resources could further strain the American social fabric. This shows itself in a growing division between the information rich and the information poor. If present trends continue, the former will dominate the information resources needed by all of us to survive and thrive, and the latter will become a postindustrial Lumpenproletariat, relegated to mindless entertainment and other trivia. The guarantee of equitable access to advanced information resources is the most urgent issue we face as we move into the new media pattern.

Acknowledgments

Many individuals helped me to prepare this study. I owe much to the counsel of the late Ithiel de Sola Pool, a teacher and scholar who inspired so many of us trying to make sense of the new-media environment. The title of his last book on information resources, *The Technologies of Freedom*, summarizes all that this study tries to express. My thanks go also to colleagues at the Center for Strategic and International Studies and at Georgetown University, in particular, to Diana Lady Dougan, chief of the center's communications policy program, and to Peter Krogh, former dean of the School of Foreign Service, both of whom gave me the space, time, and other resources to undertake this survey.

Among others who helped me were Elena Androunas, Walter Baer, Porter Bibb, Leo Bogart, Hodding Carter, Jannette Dates, Marcia DeSonne, Charles Firestone, Michael O'Hara Garcia, Henry Geller, William Garrison, Cheryl Glickfield, Robert Hilliard, Eri Hirano, Craig Johnson, Leland Johnson, Carol Joy, Montague Kern, Anton Lensen, Lawrence Lichty, Brenda Maddox, Robert Pepper, Marsha Siefert, Anthony Smith, Gregory Staple, John Vondracek, David Webster, Ernest Wilson, and George Wedell. I also want to acknowledge the courtesy extended by Dr. Eli M. Noam of Columbia University's Institute for Tele-Information, who allowed me to reprint, in an appendix, his imaginative "Principles for the Communications Act of 2034."

Finally, a heartfelt tribute, again, to my resident chief editor and thoughtful critic on works in progress, Lynn Wood Dizard.

Old Media
New Media

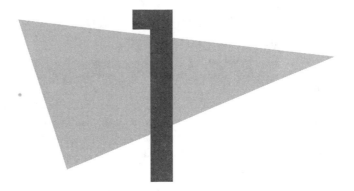

Mass Communications in the Information Age

The 1990s were a troubled decade for the Big Three television networks, NBC, ABC, and CBS. For the first time since they began keeping records on the subject, their combined prime-time ratings dropped below 50 percent. It was a rude shock for a business that had attracted viewers in over 90 percent of American households every night for over forty years. Now this dominance faced a serious threat. In 1998, cable TV channels beat the major TV networks for the first time in total viewers, ratings, and audience share during prime-time evening hours. It was a clear sign that television's role as the most successful mass medium in modern times was being transformed.

Television industry executives now recognize that the medium's audience losses are permanent: "We used to think that the possibility existed that the erosion was going to stop," ABC president Robert Iger declared in 1998. "We were silly. It is never going to stop."[1]

There are many reasons for this change, but the most important one is that television and the other older media are being challenged by the Internet and other technologies that offer an expanded range of information and entertainment services. The fragmentation of television's once solid national audience is only one example of this trend. Other media are similarly affected. For example, by the late 1990s, daily newspaper readership by adults had dropped from a post–World War II high of 78 percent to under 60 percent.

In this survey, we will explore the impact of today's emerging mix of old and new media in the United States. The transition has been under way for a decade or more, and it will accelerate in the coming years. Measuring the change is difficult. The American media industry is too large and diverse to fit into easy generalizations. It includes more than 1,500 television stations, 12,000 radio stations, 11,000 cable systems, and 15,000 newspapers and periodicals, among other resources. The industry stretches from the *New York Times*, offering "all the news that's fit to print," to station KPQD in Bighorn, Texas, bringing the best in country music to all those folks out in Radioland.

IMPLICATIONS FOR MEDIA CAREERS

The changes taking place in the media have a special importance for young people planning careers in the field. The old stereotypes are disappearing throughout the industry. One of them is the newspaper reporter—always a white male—with his hat tilted on the back of his head, yelling, "Get me rewrite!" as he phoned in the details of a six-alarm fire or a political scandal. The myths live on, but real life in the media world is totally different from those myths. When this author began his journalistic career in the city room at the *New York Times* over forty years ago, the technologies available to him were pencils, pads of paper, a rotary dial telephone, and an old typewriter that refused to type the letter *p*.

Today's city rooms are dominated by banks of computer terminals, fax machines, videorecorders, and other computer-driven devices. Many of these machines will be replaced in a few years by higher-tech versions or by completely new technologies that will even further change the workplace and demand more sophisticated skills.

Meanwhile, in the executive suites of media companies, the pace of technological change is forcing managers to adapt to a new business environment. The result, as we shall see, is a continuing round of mergers, alliances, buyouts, and downsizing of old-line media firms as they prepare for an uncertain future.

For students planning media careers, these changes offer an intriguing mixture of hopes and doubts. On the one hand, they will be entering a business—the production and distribution of information—that is expanding at an extraordinary rate. Old-line media will continue to play a critical role because of their longtime expertise in assembling and marketing information. However, there are also challenging opportunities in the newer, electronic media. Overall, the evolving electronics-based media environment promises more creative, rewarding careers than at any time since the first modern media technology—Gutenberg's printing press—was developed in the fifteenth century.

As men and women prepare for media careers, one of the few certitudes is that they will be dealing constantly with the impacts of technological change and with the demands for greater intellectual involvement and academic skills. This process is well under way now, and it will accelerate as we move into a new century. What will these changes be? Fortunes, and careers, will be made or lost on the answers. Microsoft Corporation's Bill Gates, who has already made his fortune on a good technological bet, predicted (in his book *The Road Ahead*) that people will get the information they want from wallet-sized computers linked to vast databases. Does this signal the demise, after a long decline, of the old-line media? Or does it suggest that newspaper, broadcasting, and film companies, among other present-day media operations, have a golden opportunity to thrive by applying their expertise to the new environment?

Bill Gates's wallet computer is only the beginning. Computers are already being sized down to near-wallet proportions. Meanwhile, other visionaries are proposing ideas that make Mr. Gates's pocket computer seem like a quill pen. Consider, for instance, the researchers who are looking at ways to expand human information processing by implanting microchips in the brain. As Professor Itiel Dror of the Cognitive Neuroscience Laboratory at Miami University of Ohio points out:

> The brain is an information-processing device. It can be expanded to increase processing capacity or memory just like you may add RAM or upgrade your C.P.U. on a personal computer. The brain also produces an output that is carried out via motor commands. So there is no problem—in theory—to connect machines directly to the brain so the output commands will go directly to the computer. . . .[2]

Today's media industries are not directly threatened by the possibility of microchip brain implants or by the more likely prospect of Bill Gates's wallet computer. It would, however, be imprudent for anyone planning to work in the media to dismiss the career implications of such technological developments. This book is not about brain implants or other futuristic ideas that may or may not change media patterns. It focuses on current and near-term developments, with particular attention to the political, economic, and technological factors influencing the ways the media industries will produce and distribute their products in the next few years.

Major changes have already occurred. Cable television, videocassette recorders, and the Internet are the most familiar examples of recent technologies that are currently reshaping media patterns. They are pulling audiences away from television broadcasting and other old-line services. In a relatively short time, they have become formidable parts of the media pattern along with TV, radio, film, and print publications.

The older media will be around for a long time as part of the American communications mix, but they will be different. The winds of change have swept away the comfortable assumptions that guided their operations in recent decades. The old media have a new agenda: Who will compete with what products for which audiences in a more complex marketplace? There will be many winners and losers in the industry shakeup now taking place. The survivors will be the organizations that adapt to changing technological and economic realities. The losers will be the corporate dinosaurs, large and small, that cannot or will not change—all candidates for mergers, takeovers, or plain, old-fashioned bankruptcy.

A NEW TECHNOLOGICAL GENERATION

The critical element in this new pattern is a group of advanced computer-based services that will compete in the entertainment and information industries. These services include the Internet, high-definition television, digital radio broadcasting, multimedia computers, handheld data banks, wireless cable systems, CD-ROM (compact disc–read-only memory) laser discs, direct broadcast satellites, advanced facsimile machines, intelligent telephones, consumer computer networks, portable electronic newspapers, and national videotext services.

The ultimate mechanism for delivering many of these advanced media services to homes may be the telecomputer, a fusion of television and computer technology in a single box. The telecomputer offers a full range of video, voice, and print services. (Each of these technologies is discussed in Chapters 2 and 3.) Corporate America is in a race to see who can develop and market a new array of technologically advanced multimedia services

Do these new services fit the definition of mass media? In the current dictionary sense of the phrase, they do not. Until recently, mass media has meant centrally produced, standardized information and entertainment products distributed to large audiences via separate paths.[3] The new electronic challengers modify all of these conditions. Their products often do not come from a central source. Moreover, the new media usually provide specialized services for many separate, relatively small audiences. Their most significant innovation, however, is the distribution of voice, video, and print products on a common electronic channel, often in two-way, interactive formats that give consumers more control over what services they receive, when they receive the services, and the form of each service. As economic analysts John Browning and Spencer Reiss point out, "Old media divides the world into producers and consumers: we're either the authors or the readers, broadcasters or viewers, entertainers or audiences, one-to-many communications in the jargon. New media, by contrast, gives everybody a chance to speak as well as to listen. Many speak to many—and the many speak back."[4]

DIGITIZED APPLES AND ORANGES

Purists argue that the new media are substantially different from the old. Confusing them with conventional media is mixing apples and oranges—traditional channels and the glitzy new electronics. However, the pragmatic fact is that the dividing line between the two is being smudged every day. How can telephones compete with cable systems? Compact discs with books? Facsimile machines with newspapers? In each case, they already do compete. The coming years will see similar changes as advanced media technologies erode the old media's operating styles and claim an increasing share of their audiences and their revenues. It will be critical for young people entering the media profession to understand these new technologies, how they differ from older practices and how they will affect our lives, personally and collectively, in a new kind of information-age society.

This transition is being driven by many intersecting trends—political, economic, and technological. Many observers agree that technology is, at least initially, the primary engine of change. The mass media are among the many communications sectors that are being transformed by new ways of assembling, storing, and transmitting information.

The common factor in this transition is the shift to digitized information. Print, voice, and video products are increasingly created and distributed as bits and bytes, the on-off codes manipulated by computers. The old pattern of distributing media products by separate channels is fading away. In their places are networks that makes no distinctions between the voice, video, and print information they transmit. Increasingly, these resources travel down a common digitized circuit.

One fiber-optic wire, for instance, can deliver the entire contents of a newspaper, a TV soap opera, or a Hollywood film simultaneously and at the speed of light. The information-carrying capacity of these circuits is extraordinary: A fiber cable, as thin as a human hair, can transmit the entire contents of the *Encyclopaedia Britannica* in less than a minute.

THE INTERNET FACTOR

In Chapter 2, we will take a closer look at this technological revolution as it affects American media. First, however, we will examine the Internet, the software technology that promises to dominate the digital-media revolution in the new century.

Until the late 1980s, the Internet was an obscure technological toy, used primarily by a small group of computer buffs. It has since become the fastest-growing network in the world, with an estimated 300 million PCs in over 150 countries linked to the Internet at the turn of the century, according to a Merrill Lynch survey.[5] The network expanded by 50 percent every year in the 1990s, spurred by the interest of ordinary computer users in the World Wide Web and other Internet features. (See Table 1.1)

A 1998 survey by the Princeton-based NEC Research Institute estimated that the Web contained more than 320 million pages of information and entertainment. The NEC study also noted that even the best Web search engines were able to identify fewer than one-third of them.[6] What is clear is that the Web supplies more sheer information than all of America's mass media outlets combined. Most of the Web's content is still in print-media formats. This limitation will disappear as new Internet voice and video services compete directly with present-day media channels.

The Internet's power lies in its ability to cut across barriers that have limited access to vast amounts of information for ordinary consumers. It is the all-purpose key to cyberspace and, moreover, a software hitchhiker on all lanes of the new electronic information highway—the phone system and cable TV, broadcasting, and satellite channels. The mass media make up only one small part of an information industry that is increasingly dependent on Internet resources to deliver its products.

The Internet is still in its infancy. Until recently, fewer than a quarter of American consumers had access to its resources, but this is changing rapidly. According to Forrester Research, a computer consultancy, by 2002, over two-thirds of the total U.S. population will be linked to the Internet.

This expansion has led Nicholas Negroponte, director of MIT's Media Lab, to measure the Internet's impact at "10.5 on the Richter scale of social change."

TABLE 1.1   Consumer Online Households and Household Penetration

Year	U.S. Households (Millions)	Computer Households (Millions)	Computer Penetration of U.S. Households	PC/Modem Households (Millions)	Modem Households as a % of Computer Households	Modem Households as a % of U.S. Households	Online Households (Millions)	Online Households as a % of Computer Households	Online Households as a % of U.S. Households
1988	90.9	16.2	17.8%	1.4	8.6%	1.5%	0.9	5.6%	1.0%
1989	92.1	18.3	19.9	2.2	12.0	2.4	1.1	6.0	1.2
1990	93.3	21.9	23.5	3.2	14.6	3.4	1.6	7.3	1.7
1991	94.3	23.4	24.8	4.1	17.5	4.3	2.0	8.5	2.1
1992	95.7	26.4	27.6	5.5	20.8	5.7	2.6	9.9	2.7
1993	96.4	28.5	29.6	7.3	25.6	7.6	3.3	11.7	3.5
1994	97.1	31.1	32.0	9.4	30.2	9.7	4.7	15.1	4.8
1995	97.7	33.2	34.0	12.7	38.3	13.0	9.4	28.3	9.6
1996	98.8	38.7	39.2	17.5	45.2	17.7	15.2	39.3	15.4
1997	99.9	44.0	44.0	29.0	65.9	29.0	23.0	52.3	23.0
1998	100.9	47.0	46.6	38.0	80.9	37.7	28.5	60.6	28.2
1999	102.0	49.0	48.0	42.0	85.7	41.2	32.5	66.3	31.9
2000	103.1	50.5	49.0	45.0	89.1	43.6	36.0	71.3	34.9
2001	104.2	51.5	49.4	47.5	92.2	45.6	39.0	75.7	37.4
2002	105.3	52.7	50.0	49.5	93.9	47.0	42.1	79.9	40.0

SOURCES: Veronis, Suhler & Associates, Wilkofsky Gruen Associates, Electronic Industries Association, U.S. Bureau of the Census, Odyssey Ventures, Find/SVP

For Microsoft's Bill Gates, the Internet promises a golden age of "friction-free capitalism." Novelist William Gibson, who coined the word *cyberspace*, describes the network as "the great anarchic event that defies conventional commercial exploitation."[7] Other Internet observers predict that it will eventually evolve as a common information utility, serving all businesses and households. It will be an "information pipe," as ubiquitous and necessary as present-day gas and electrical utilities.

THE MEDIA-INTERNET CONNECTION

For the media industries, the Internet opens up the prospect of delivering a wide range of advanced information and entertainment services to expanded audiences.[8] As noted above, the Internet in its early years could only supply print data, together with some graphics. This limitation is disappearing as the network becomes a multimedia resource, capable of handling a full range of video, voice, and print products.

Meanwhile, the Internet is becoming more user-friendly. So-called "push technology" makes it easier for users to call up the information they want directly, bypassing the complex steps that frustrated them in the network's early years.[9]

However, operating on the Internet is still daunting for many people. As Anthony Rutkowski, an Internet-industry pioneer, points out, "Using the network is still too complicated right now for anyone but moderately skilled geeks. What we have to do is almost reduce it to the ultimate no-brainer potentially anywhere in the world, over just about any medium."

New Internet capabilities are already having an impact on mass media patterns. A 1998 survey by the Washington-based Pew Center for the People and the Press showed that the percentage of Americans getting news reports from the Internet at least once a week had tripled in the previous two years, going from 11 to 36 percent.[10] One result of this shift is that the Internet now dominates strategic planning in the American mass media industries. All major media firms, and most of the smaller ones, are adapting their operation to Internet realities. It is not an easy transition. The old-line media companies must now compete among themselves for Internet customers. They also have to deal with other information providers who are newcomers to mass media production and distribution.

The most prominent example of this new competition in the late 1990s is Microsoft Corporation. "The Internet is the primary driver of all new work we are doing throughout the product line," Bill Gates has declared. "We are hard-core about the Internet." Since then, the company has spent billions of dollars acquiring media links into the Internet, including a major 1997 investment in Comcast Corp., a leading cable TV networker.[11]

Another formidable competitor of the traditional media is America Online, the country's largest Internet access provider. In the late 1990s, AOL began expanding its services beyond print data to include multimedia voice and video links to its more than 20 million subscribers.[12] Meanwhile, average household use of AOL increased to an average of forty-five minutes per day in 1998, up from nineteen minutes two years earlier. The most used services on the Internet are news and information resources and electronic mail (see Table 1.2). "Chat rooms" are also popular. Research studies indicate that, by 1999, AOL subscribers were spending 45 million hours a month chatting with each other electronically.

TABLE 1.2 Leading Online Activities

	Percent Using Application	
Category	1996	1997
News and Information	82.0%	87.8%
Electronic Mail	80.5	83.2
Research	69.1	80.5
Surf Web Sites	66.9	75.3
Play Games	23.8	33.7
Participate in Chats	25.3	30.8
Post to Bulletin Boards	39.3	30.0
Shop	14.9	17.8

SOURCES: Veronis, Suhler & Associates, Wilkofsky Gruen Associates, Advertising Age/Market Facts

The significance of this figure for the old-line media organizations is that it represents time spent *not* looking at TV, reading a newspaper or going to the movies.[13]

Microsoft and AOL are only two examples of nonmedia companies whose strategy is to deliver to consumers an integrated package of multimedia services via the Internet and other channels. This strategy received its ultimate expression in June 1998 when the nation's largest phone company, AT&T, announced a $48 billion deal to buy Telecommunications Inc. (TCI), the second-largest cable TV firm. AT&T plans to become the leading provider of voice, Internet, and video services delivered over its own facilities and TCI's cable lines.[14] More than any other event in recent years the AT&T/TCI merger highlights the challenge that old-line media companies face in the new information environment.

DIALING FOR INTERNET DOLLARS

We will take a closer look in later chapters at the long-term impact of these developments on each media sector. Here it is useful to summarize the problems, and opportunities, facing the older media organizations as they respond to changes posed by new technologies, particularly the Internet.

The most direct threat is to their economic base. Specifically, this involves the challenge new information providers pose to their advertising revenues, either directly or through the rapidly developing practice of direct sales of services and products on the network. Loss of this revenue is a critical issue, particularly for print publications and broadcasting. Typically, newspapers get three-quarters of their revenue from advertising; the ratio is even higher for TV and radio stations.

The Internet is the most formidable of the new economic challengers. Until the mid-1990s, the network carried almost no advertising or direct-sales channels. Now electronic merchandising ("e-commerce") is the fastest-growing activity on the network. It began slowly, with companies developing Web pages that in most cases carried institutional advertising. By the end of the decade, this pattern had changed as retailers shifted to direct merchandising on the Web. At first, it was a slow, tentative move. By 1998, the consumer online market was valued at about $8 billion. This market is expected to double to over $17 billion by 2002. (See Table 1.3.) By 2005, Net commerce could account for as much as 6 percent of U.S. gross domestic product, according to a Forrester Research study.[15]

Internet retailers are offering an ever-wider range of goods and services, as consumers become more accustomed to shopping on the Web. "People have voted with their mouse clicks that if you make it more convenient, they will come. There is a huge opportunity here," says Office Depot executive Paul Gaffney. By 1998, over 20 million U.S. households were dialing into the Web for goods and services, according to the Yankee Group, a Massachusetts-based research firm.[16]

This, however, was just a small slice of the $7 trillion U.S. retail market. The larger significance of the new online merchandising of goods and services is that it is expanding at a wildfire pace. Electronic merchandising, much of it carried on the Internet, will profoundly affect all aspects of the American economy, including the media sector.

TABLE 1.3   The Consumer Online Market ($ Millions)

Year	Online Access*	Consumer Spending on Content	Advertising	Total
1988	$ 350	—	—	$ 350
1989	407	—	—	407
1990	542	—	—	542
1991	675	—	—	675
1992	829	—	—	829
1993	1,019	—	—	1,019
1994	1,192	—	—	1,192
1995	2,200	—	$ 50	2,250
1996	3,235	$120	200	3,555
1997	4,816	230	906	5,952
1998	6,087	342	1,700	8,129
1999	7,094	423	3,100	10,616
2000	8,246	504	4,200	12,950
2001	9,330	585	5,400	15,315
2002	10,341	632	6,500	17,473

Sources: Veronis, Suhler & Associates, Wilkofsky Gruen Associates, Internet Advertising Bureau, SIMBA Information, Find/SVP, Jupiter Commnunications

*Includes cable modem access

BREAKING INTO THE INTERNET

As we shall see in later chapters, media companies have been generally slow to exploit the Internet and other electronic channels as a marketplace for their products. Film and television firms have used the network primarily to showcase their productions. Newspapers and magazines have made some of their editorial output available, usually at no cost. By 1998, there were over 1,600 U.S. newspapers with online Web pages, but only one of them was making a profit from the service:[17] It was the *Wall Street Journal's Interactive Edition*, with over 150,000 subscription-paying readers.[18] Other publications were less successful when they shifted from free access to subscriptions. When *Slate*, an online magazine supported by Microsoft, began charging a $20 annual subscription fee for what it had been giving away, its readership fell from 200,000 to 30,000.[19]

Book publishing has been the exception to the media sector's slow start in exploiting the Internet. It is an industry that is being transformed by electronic marketing. Only a few years ago, futurists predicted that the digital age would see the eclipse of printed books. They expected readers to bypass old-fashioned books in favor of downloading information from a central source on the Internet and other electronic channels.

These predictions have been turned on their head, largely by a single Web site called Amazon.com. Begun in 1994 as a risky attempt to sell books online,

Amazon became the hottest single retailer on the Web, with 1998 sales of about $400 million. It offers customers mouse-click access to more than three million book titles through a simple direct-ordering procedure that includes price discounts and a guarantee of quick mail delivery. By 1999, the Amazon Web site had expanded into videotapes and music CD sales.

Amazon was the third-largest book retailer in the country in the late 1990s. Its success forced large conventional book chains such as Barnes and Noble and Borders to set up similar Web retail sites. More recently, book publishers have begun direct retailing of their products on the Web. As a result, online book sales are now a billion-dollar enterprise.[20] Whether online sales can reverse the longer-term decline in overall book sales remains to be seen. For the present, however, the Internet has demonstrated its power to give one media sector an important economic lift.[21]

At the turn of the century, other parts of the media industry are becoming more aggressive in exploiting Internet opportunities. It is still a mixed record, with few breakthroughs on the Amazon model.

Internet marketing is still a trial-and-error process. Despite the network's rapid growth, media firms and other retailers have very little information about Internet customers as a guide to their marketing strategies. For most of the Internet's short existence as a marketplace, its users have been overwhelmingly young, white, educated males.

IDENTIFYING THE INTERNET AUDIENCE

Recent research indicates that this pattern is changing. One of the more reliable surveys of Internet use, conducted at Georgia Tech, found that women represented 40 percent of Internet users in 1998. More significantly, they outnumbered men among new Internet users for the first time. The survey also showed that the average age of Internet users was thirty-five, and that over 80 percent have had some college education.[22] These statistics are useful, but they fall far short of the kind of demographic detail that media marketers have relied on over the years.

Lacking such data, many companies rushed onto the Internet with badly designed strategies. In most cases, their mistake was in underestimating the difficulties in changing consumer buying habits. This was particularly true of older, more affluent customers who were not accustomed to doing business by mouse clicks.

There are other problems. The Internet audience, although growing by leaps and bounds, is still generally reluctant to do business on the Web. Many of them worry about the lack of privacy and security on the network. Most information on the Internet is available to anyone. Stories about privacy abuses are common, including the case of the Ohio sheriff who lost his bid for re-election when his opponent got access to online records of the sheriff's rental of pornographic videotapes. Another concern is fraud; Internet purchases usually require a credit card number. Although better safeguards against electronic fraud are becoming available, many consumers are still reluctant to supply credit information on an open network.[23]

THE NEW ENTREPRENEURS

Nevertheless, electronic commerce on the Internet is here to stay, and the media industries will be an important part of its expansion. The transition is largely in the hands of a new breed of media executives. The future of their companies rests largely on their ability to develop successful strategies for exploiting Internet resources. We will take a closer look at these entrepreneurs as we examine individual media sectors throughout the rest of this survey. First we will take a quick overview of their role in a rapidly evolving media environment.

The group includes such industry innovators as Rupert Murdoch of News Corp., Gerald Levin and Ted Turner of Time Warner, Michael Eisner of Disney, and Sumner Redstone of Viacom, among others. Cut from a different pattern than traditional media executives, their talents are in multimedia information packaging. Product synergy is their working formula. Each item in their packages—films, books, television programs, and so on—becomes part of a media food chain that may start out as a magazine article, is then fleshed out as a book, and then becomes the basis for a TV or film production which finally ends up as a videocassette. "These companies no longer make films or books. They make brands," says Chris Dixon, a media analyst at PaineWebber, the New York brokerage house. The goal, he notes, is to package the brand in new and more profitable combinations: News Corp.'s *The X-Files*, Time Warner's *Batman*, and Viacom's *Rugrats*.[24]

The idea is to win a marketing advantage over their single-media competitors; it is not a new strategy.[25] The Disney Company has been in the multimedia business for over sixty years, with operations that include films, television, theatrical productions, theme parks, books, magazines, toys, a cruise line, and Mickey Mouse watches.

THE DISNEY STRATEGY

In a very real sense, all the other synergists are trying to match the Disney strategy. Its essential elements include a reliance on "family value" entertainment together with up-to-the-minute technological innovation. As *Wired* magazine noted in a 1998 analysis of the Disney organization, "Part media giant, part marketing monster, the Mouse continues to write the book on intellectual property—how to create it, how to manage it, and how to leverage it to the hilt."

This formula boosted Disney sales in 1997 to over $22 billion. A good share of these profits was due to the enormous success of the *The Lion King*, the company's all-time synergy-strategy champion film. It was released in fifty-one countries and later became an award-winning Broadway musical. Overall, it generated 186 items of tie-in merchandise, from books to dolls to T-shirts. By 1999, *The Lion King* had earned over $4.5 billion in worldwide sales of movie tickets, toys and clothing merchandise, videotapes, and music CDs, with the prospect that Disney will continue to pull in a steady stream of revenues leashed to *The Lion King* for many years to come.[26]

For other firms, multimedia synergy has turned out to be an elusive goal, as we shall see when we look at the big American information packagers. They are not only competing among themselves, but they face new challenges in an increasingly globalized media market. The result is a steady expansion of American media operations abroad. It also involves competition from foreign media companies moving into the U.S. market.

Dozens of high-flying media executives have been shot down as a result of bad (and usually expensive) decisions on how to deal with these market changes. A well-known case was Time Warner's decision to develop an advanced interactive cable TV venture in Orlando, Florida, in the mid-1990s. The system promised customers access to a wide range of voice, video, and print services delivered to their TV sets. The project was technically successful, but Time Warner's managers had seriously misjudged customer tastes. The project was quietly shelved after attracting just four thousand subscribers.[27]

CONCENTRATING MEDIA POWER

Despite setbacks, synergy strategies now dominate the new media environment.[28] Media synergy is more than a clever marketing device. It can be a potentially dangerous tool for concentrating media power and wealth in the hands of a small number of big corporations. One of the major trends in the media industries in the late 1990s was the accelerated pace of such concentration in fewer information packaging firms, such as Time Warner, Viacom, and Disney. The trend toward consolidation is changing the media industry in ways that need to be understood by anyone planning a career in the field.

As noted earlier, the old and new media share one resource: a common path for delivering a variety of services. Advanced telecommunications networks relay massive volumes of voice, video, and print products along common digital circuits at very high speeds. Electronics are forcing the technical integration of old and new media, with major impact on the future shape and direction of the industry.

In the 1980s, the big media companies recognized that satellites, computers, and other new technologies opened new prospects for synergistic multimedia operations. Most of these companies, with some exceptions, had been single-media operations. By 1990, this had changed, largely as a result of mergers and acquisitions that involved every major media firm and many smaller ones. The most dramatic of these corporate mating dances occurred at Time Inc., best known for its magazine products. The company's $15 billion merger with Warner Communications in 1989 created Time Warner Inc., whose combined film, media, print, and cable TV operations made it the world's largest media company until overtaken by the $19 billion merger of Disney and Capital Cities–ABC in August 1995. Time Warner recaptured the title several weeks later when it took over Ted Turner's Cable News Network (CNN) and other Turner assets.

These mergers have redefined the U.S. media sector. However, they are only the beginning of a shift toward a new pattern for the industry. Combining multimedia information and entertainment software production under a single corporate roof was the first part of the new strategy. But top-to-bottom integration is still to come. After the merger spree of the past fifteen years, most media companies still do not control the necessary electronic networks to deliver their products to consumers.

THE SEARCH FOR FULL SYNERGY

These distribution networks are still the profitable domain of the telecommunications industry, beginning with the telephone companies. Full media synergy cannot be achieved, its advocates argue, until media resources and telecommunications channels are fully integrated. The gradual joining of these separate resources is transforming the corporate nature of American media. In recent years, the media and telecommunications industries have shifted to strategies that move each into the traditional business territory of the other. In a stunning reversal of roles, the phone companies and other networkers are becoming media providers, and the media companies are becoming telecommunications providers. It is a process that is critical to understanding the future of U.S. media in a postindustrial age.

The event that set the stage for this change was the breakup of the American Telephone & Telegraph Company (AT&T) in 1984. It was the result of the settlement of a long-running antitrust suit brought against the company by the federal government. The agreement had two major consequences, both of which affected the American media industry. Ownership of AT&T's local telephone companies was transferred to seven regional Bell companies. At the same time, the national network was opened to full competition in a wide range of activities beyond ordinary phone service. The overall effect was a major expansion of telecommunications products and services, making it the fastest-growing sector of the economy in the 1990s.[29]

The media companies were largely bystanders in the events that followed the 1984 AT&T breakup. At the time, they were going through their own process of rearranging their corporate identities and practices through mergers and acquisitions. There was little indication then that changes in the phone industry would, within a decade, further transform the ways media companies did business.

The media sector benefited from the more competitive telecommunications market created in the aftermath of the AT&T breakup. New services were introduced, and the costs of telephone and other network facilities fell. What was not foreseen was that the newly liberated phone companies would use their freedom to begin to move into the information business, often in direct competition with media firms. Even more surprisingly, media sector companies began considering moves into the communications business not only to control delivery of their own products but also to compete directly in telecommunications services. This, in fact, is what is happening—in ways that are transforming both industries.

MERGING TECHNOLOGIES

The driving force in this new deal making is the advanced technologies that make possible the merging of communications and information capabilities over an integrated electronic network. The telecommunications and information industries—including the new and old media—now have technical and economic interests in common. The trend that began in the 1980s with alliances within the media industries has now been expanded to include a dizzying variety of alliances between the two sectors, combining each other's strengths to provide end-to-end information services.

These arrangements involve more than delivering traditional products such as broadcast television or Hollywood films. New high-capacity circuits are opening prospects for entirely new services. The most important group of these is broadly identified as interactive media, or IM in industry shorthand. IM offers consumers access to a wider range of two-way services that allows them to control both the mode and timing of delivery. Essentially, IM is information and entertainment on demand. (The early, primitive example is the home shopping channels on cable TV.) It represents a significant shift from traditional media patterns with their centralized production and one-way distribution to large audiences.

Interactive media is the great hope of the media and telecommunications sectors as they restructure themselves to compete in the new mass communications environment. The concept is still fuzzy, with more promise than performance. Interactive media's ultimate goal—large-scale consumer acceptance—remains to be seen. Cable TV's pay-per-view channels, an early form of interactive media, have not been notably successful in attracting large audiences. More sophisticated IM services, such as the availability of hundreds of movies on demand on home TV screens, has been slow to develop, as are other services such as video games, advanced home shopping, and access to educational resources. The number of such services is increasing, as are households that have the interactive machines (advanced TV sets, computers, etc.) to take advantage of them. Overall, however, consumers have been generally reluctant to pay the extra charges for the new resources.

LOOKING FOR CUSTOMERS

This has not stopped the industry's plans for attracting mass audiences—and greater profits—for interactive services. For the present, one of the most hopeful indicators of IM's potential is electronic games. A generation of Americans has grown up learning how to deal with this technology. Nintendo and Sega, the two largest producers of these games, have sold over 65 million machines in the United States. The future of the interactive games industries lies is shifting from games played with cartridges to interactive gaming via cable TV or telephone circuits. The target audience is young adults who grew up as couch commandos, punching into the bloody adventures of *Mortal Kombat* and *Night Trap*. In the late 1990s, the first generation of interactive games delivered directly to TV sets made its debut on cable TV channels.

Many other kinds of two-way media will be put on the market in the next few years. As today's young couch commandos become tomorrow's prime consumers, billions of dollars will be spent to attract them to a full range of interactive resources, including home shopping, personal electronic banking, and direct access to educational and training opportunities, as well as entertainment and video games.

Every segment of the media and telecommunications industries is involved in this expensive gamble for consumer dollars. The phone and cable TV sectors in particular are competing to provide interactive services. The phone companies come to the contest with relatively little experience in this kind of programming. The big cable TV companies, on the other hand, have already developed successful production resources such as Home Box Office and the sports channels. Both the cable TV and the phone companies will need to draw on the expertise of traditional media companies for the vast amounts of program materials needed in the new interactive environment.

The prospect of supplying this programming is the reality behind all the public relations hype that the media industries are generating about the glories of the coming interactive information age. Lurking behind these cheery messages are the old-line companies' fears that they could be replaced, or marginalized, in what is potentially the biggest change in consumer media patterns they have ever had to face. The transition to an interactive environment is both disruptive and costly, complicated by continuing uncertainty about consumer acceptance of the new products.

POLITICAL AND SOCIAL IMPACTS

We are only beginning to understand the effects these changes will have on media patterns in the coming years. It is not simply that Americans will have more electronic access to a wider range of information and entertainment resources than ever before—there are larger policy implications. Who will control these electronic channels? Who will decide what information will be available, and what the cost will be to consumers? Will we create a new class distinction between the information rich and the information poor, between people who know how to exploit information resources and those who don't? Will the new media bring us together or divide us? Network television has had many faults, but it did create a national audience, one that shared news and entertainment from Maine to Hawaii in ways that created something of a common electronic culture. That same audience, however, is now being fragmented as large parts of it shift to new media such as cable TV, videocassettes, and the Internet.

The prospects opened by interactive media are forcing changes in the U.S. legal tradition of separating the producers of information (the media industries) and the electronic distributors (primarily the phone companies). In recent years, technology and economics have bent this principle out of shape. The convergence of advanced media services—for print, voice, and video—in a single electronic circuit has pushed the media and telecommunications industries into a new competitive relationship. A major obstacle has been government regulations that sharply limited the phone companies and other circuit providers in operating media and other information services.

MEDIA VERSUS THE PHONE COMPANIES

The pressure to modify, if not eliminate, these restrictions became the center of an intense political debate after the AT&T breakup in 1984. The phone companies campaigned to eliminate government regulations that prevented them from supplying entertainment and other information services. Their efforts were opposed by the traditional media companies who feared that the phone industry would overwhelm their role as information providers in the new electronic environment. It was not an unreasonable fear given the phone companies' economic and technical clout coupled with their overall plans to move into new lines of business beyond traditional phone service.

Both sides brought heavy pressure on the U.S. Congress to defend their respective interests. The result was the Telecommunications Act of 1996, passed in February of that year. It is a complex mixture of compromises that puts the legal stamp of approval on a new pattern of convergent relationships between the media and the telecommunications industries. Basically, the new law lifted most of the restrictions that prevented the two sectors from competing—or forming alliances—with each other to provide consumer media and information services. The result was a new round of mergers, this time between media and telecommunications companies. The 1998 linkup between AT&T and cable giant TCI set the tone and pace of this trend. We will take a closer look at the Telecommunications Act and its implications for the media in Chapter 4. Here it is relevant to note that the 1996 legislation has defined the ground rules for American mass-communications developments well into the new century.

The transition to this new media environment is in its early stages. Advanced information and entertainment technologies still play a relatively minor role in American media. How and when they will take on a larger role is still an open question, but it would be a mistake to underestimate the cumulative effect of these changes on how Americans will get the information they need to survive and thrive in the new century.

DEFINING THE NEW MEDIA

As suggested earlier, the new media are not simply a linear extension of the old. The old and the new both offer information and entertainment resources to large audiences, conveniently and at competitive prices. The difference is that the new media are dramatically expanding the range of resources available to consumers through the Internet and other channels. In particular, they are beginning to provide online interactive links between the consumer and the information provider. This capability adds a striking dimension to the present mass media pattern with its reliance on one-way products delivered from a centralized source—a newspaper, a TV station, or a Hollywood studio. The new media is increasingly interactive, allowing consumers to choose what information and entertainment resources they want, when they want it, and in what form.

Consumers can even bypass the old media structure by setting up their own electronic networks. The result can be a new kind of democratic communications environment that matches media guru Marshall McLuhan's vision of thirty years ago of advanced information machines that will make Everyman his own publisher.[30] McLuhan's concept is being realized in the rapid spread of electronic personal communications networks, including the tens of thousands of Internet news groups and bulletin boards that link millions of Americans. McLuhan aside, the trail from the old to the new media is already littered with the bones of academics, think tank consultants, and other self-appointed seers who have made wrong guesses about the so-called information revolution. Their instincts were right, but their timing was off. Their mistake was in underestimating how rapidly the technological, economic, and political forces would converge to bring the promise of the new media to reality.

These forces are now coming together in ways that change the role of information in our lives.[31] This is particularly true of how we use the mass media. A study by Veronis, Suhler & Associates, a New York investment firm, suggests that Americans spend more time dealing with the media than with any other activity, including work or sleep. The survey estimates that we allot, on average, about 3,400 hours in a year—9 hours a day—to media. Television viewing (both over the air and by cable) accounts for more than 70 percent of that total, with newspapers, magazines, home video, books, and films sharing the remainder. (See Table 1.4)

CHANGING AMERICAN MEDIA HABITS

These media habits affect the form and direction of American society. The essence of every society is captured in its folktales about itself and its origins. Throughout most of history, these tales have been passed down by human storytellers. The *Iliad*, the Bible, the Viking sagas, and the Hindu *Mahabharata* epic all began as spoken stories. Their telling defined nations and shaped civilizations for millennia. Only in the past 500 years was this pattern modified, beginning with the introduction of multiple-copy printed books.

In modern America, and most of the rest of the world, storytelling has been modified once again with the introduction of electronic mass media, particularly radio and television. Television is the most compelling teller of tales and shaper of folkways, with its mélange of Dan Rather, soap operas, *The X-Files*, Saturday morning cartoons, Oprah, and other electronic icons. Debates may rage over the extent to which television is eroding our cultural heritage by displacing the comfortable, old folk stories, but there is little doubt that television's way of telling stories influences the way we see ourselves and the world around us.[32]

The new media add a powerful dimension to this cultural pattern. Their capacities for creating and distributing information and entertainment are far greater than any we have yet experienced. Will these new resources serve to enhance our personal and communal lives? Will they reinforce the best parts of our

TABLE 1.4 Hours Per Person Per Year Using Comsumer Media

Year	Network-Affiliated Stations*	Inde-pendent Stations*	Total Broadcast Television	Basic Networks[†]	Premium Channels	Total Subscription Video Services	Total TV
1992	914	159	1,073	359	78	437	1,150
1993	920	162	1,082	375	78	453	1,535
1994	919	172	1,091	388	81	469	1,560
1995	836	183	1,019	468	88	556	1,575
1996	803	177	980	498	89	587	1,567
1997	748	178	926	537	98	635	1,561
1998	704	178	882	580	98	678	1,560
1999	670	172	842	620	103	723	1,565
2000	640	168	808	655	108	763	1,571
2001	616	162	778	690	109	799	1,577
2002	591	157	748	718	109	827	1,575

SOURCES: Veronis, Suhler & Associates, Wilkofsky Gruen Associates, Nielsen Media Research, Simmons Market Research, Interactive Digital Software Association, Paul Kagan Associates, Motion Picture Association of America, Recording Industry Association of America, Newspaper Association of America, Book Industry Study Group, Magazine Publishers of America, Software Publishers Association

*Affiliates of the Fox network are counted as network affiliates. Includes UPN and WB affiliates, 1995–2002.

[†]Includes TBS

[‡]Playback of prerecorded tapes only

Note: Estimates of time spent were derived using rating data for television and radio, survey research and consumer purchase data for recorded music, newspapers, magazines, books, home video, admissions for movies, and consumer online services. Adults 18 and older were the basis for estimates except for recorded music, movies in theaters, and video games, where estimates included persons 12 and older.

tradition? Will they reflect the swift demographic changes taking place, such as the emergence of the Hispanic community as potentially the largest ethnic group in the country? These are critical questions for an American society caught in the swift currents of political, social, and technological change.

A NEW AGE OF INDIVIDUALISM?

George Gilder, senior fellow at the Hudson Institute in Indianapolis, considers the transition to a new media environment a liberation:

> A new age of individualism is coming, and it will bring with it an eruption of culture unprecedented in human history. . . . The upsurge in artistic output will enhance the position of the United States as a center of video production and creation. We will discover that television was a technology with supreme powers but deadly flaws. In the beginning, the powers were ascendant; now the flaws dominate. The cultural limitations of television, tolerable when there was no al-

TABLE 1.4 *(Continued)*

Radio	Recorded Music	Daily News-papers	Consumer Books	Consumer Magazines	Home Video†	Movies in Theaters	Video Games	Consumer Online	Total
1,150	233	172	100	85	42	11	19	2	3,324
1,082	248	170	99	85	43	12	19	2	3,295
1,102	294	169	102	84	45	12	22	3	3,393
1,091	289	165	99	84	45	12	24	7	3,391
1,091	289	161	99	83	49	12	26	16	3,393
1,082	265	159	92	82	50	13	36	28	3,368
1,075	260	157	95	82	52	13	39	35	3,368
1,066	261	156	95	81	53	13	42	39	3,371
1,056	269	154	96	80	55	13	43	43	3,380
1,047	278	153	97	80	56	13	44	46	3,391
1,040	289	152	97	79	58	13	46	49	3,398

ternative, are unendurable in the face of the new computer technologies now on the horizon—technologies in which, happily, the U.S. leads the world.[33]

Even at this early stage, we can see the outlines of the new mass-information and entertainment pattern. In it old and new media overlap and compete. New technologies such as the Internet are already cutting into the traditionally strong position of older ones. There are, moreover, at least a half dozen other major media technologies jostling to enter the marketplace.

The competition between old and new media involves a process that was best characterized sixty years ago by Harvard economist Joseph Schumpeter in his analysis of capitalist economies. Capitalism's vitality came from the dynamics of what he called "creative destruction." Schumpeter defined this as the ability to adapt to changes in technologies and markets. Creative destruction is as handy a phrase as any to describe the adjustments the U.S. economy is undergoing these days as it deals with such information-age realities as an increasing number of information channels, audience fragmentation, a greater concentration of media ownership, a growing gap between the information rich and the information poor, and the prospect of fewer well-paying jobs as computers and other advanced technologies replace human labor. The pressures are both domestic and global as international trade competition increases. The media business has been slower than most in dealing with these changes. It has been generally content to cycle and recycle its highly successful formats. Product changes have tended to be stylistic—the equivalent of the auto manufacturers' flashy tail fins back in the 1950s. For years, large parts of the media industry were driven by the pervasive attitude that, in a phrase, you don't mess with success.

MISJUDGING EMERGING TECHNOLOGIES

This attitude—you don't mess with success—was reinforced in the 1970s and 1980s by a series of well-publicized failures involving new technologies. The most spectacular losses were suffered by Warner Communications in its attempt to become the leader in the emerging market for home entertainment computers. In 1975, Warner paid $75 million for the company that had developed the Atari computer, a machine that could program interactive game cassettes. By 1982, Atari accounted for more than half of Warner's revenues. Within a year, however, the Atari market had collapsed, resulting in a loss of hundreds of millions of dollars for the company.

Such formidable businesses as Time Inc., AT&T, CBS, and the Knight-Ridder newspaper chain also lost hundreds of millions of dollars during the 1980s in a series of failed ventures involving videotext networks, broadcast satellites, electronic publishing, and the like. In most cases, the mistake they made was jumping too soon into untested, expensive technologies, and they further compounded this misjudgment with poor marketing strategies. As a result, they and other media companies were a more reluctant lot when the next set of proposals for high-technology ventures came along.

There *were* some notable successes, including an inspired decision by the top managers of Time Inc.'s cable TV operations. They proposed to use satellites to distribute Hollywood films and other entertainment features to thousands of local cable systems across the country. They called their network Home Box Office. The cable industry originally depended on a simple technology: coaxial wires, strung from telephone poles, that could transmit a dozen or more channels into suburban or small-town homes. Such cable technology had already been in use for twenty years before HBO combined it with satellites to create a continental network. The industry was quickly transformed from an isolated collection of local mom-and-pop systems into groups of national cable operators dominated by a few firms.

HBO: BRINGING IT ALL TOGETHER

HBO's success was a textbook example of the convergence of technology, economics, and politics to create a new media resource. The shift to satellite distri-bution technology was a crucial part of the process. The second leg of the convergence triangle was economics. Banks and other lenders fell over themselves in the rush to give money to cable system owners and program distributors. The lenders' instincts were eminently sound. Satellite transmission of Hollywood films, sports events, and other attractions vastly increased cable's consumer appeal. Starting with fewer than 10 million customers in the 1970s, the cable industry now provides services to over 70 million U.S. homes and other outlets.

Politics completed the triangle. In its early years, cable television was hailed by many observers as a new form of mass, democratic communications. Its many channels would give citizens a new outlet for expressing their views, dealing with community problems and the like through "public access" cable facilities. This potential has never been fulfilled. Cable company operators were interested only in using their channels for profitable entertainment shows.

They prevailed—largely because their systems were monopolies. The awarding of cable monopolies in cities and towns was heavily political. (The process was labeled "rent-an-alderman," reflecting the often flagrant ways in which franchise seekers influenced local politicians.) At the national level, the cable industry successfully fought off most attempts by Congress and regulatory agencies to force cable companies to carry free public interest programming. The National Cable Television Association, the industry's trade organization, rapidly developed into one of the most powerful and well-funded lobbies in Washington.

The cable industry faces some long-term problems in maintaining its strong position in the media sector, as we shall see.[34] For the present, however, cable TV is profiting from the successful convergence of technology, economics, and politics in its operations. The industry's strategy has been a model for the rest of the U.S. media establishment as it copes with the introduction of new technologies.

Essentially, media firms have two choices. They can either embrace the new media technologies as an extension of (or replacement for) their present operations, or they can upgrade their present products to make them competitive in a more crowded marketplace. In many cases, they are doing both.

These choices involve massive changes in the present media pattern. The readjustment has been under way for some time. It was first documented by New York University sociologist Richard Maisel in a pioneering 1973 study of American consumer information and entertainment patterns. Maisel's findings confirmed that traditional mass media were losing out to newer, more specialized outlets. He concluded that "the rate of increase for consumer expenditures for radio, television, magazines and motion pictures has been far less than the rate of increase in consumer expenditures as a whole. . . . The mass media are actually shrinking in size relative to the total economy."[35]

Maisel's groundbreaking research has been confirmed by the media sector's performance since then. He argued, prophetically, that the media were becoming a broadened mix of general interest and specialized information and entertainment products. He called the latter the "new media"—possibly the first use of the phrase in communications research.

Neither Professor Maisel nor anyone else at the time could have predicted the stepped-up pace of new media applications in the past twenty years. Maisel's research antedated the introduction of personal computers, national cable networks, consumer videotext, high-definition television, and the World Wide Web. We now see the transforming impact of those technologies on the information and entertainment industries. Joseph Schumpeter's creative destruction is alive and well in the media business these days.

Predictions about the terminal decline of present-day broadcasting, publishing, and other mass media are, however, decidedly premature. Media managers are not going to self-destruct, lemming-like, at the thought that their products may be taken over by the new technologies. Most of them are acutely aware that a new mix of information resources is emerging, with many new players entering the field. They must adapt to the new environment or disappear. Their survival will depend on their ability to craft workable strategies for producing and marketing new high-technology services over the Internet as well as through their present channels.

MEDIA: "THE ALL-AMERICAN INDUSTRY"

The *London Economist* has described the media sector as the last, great all-American industry. It is no accident that the United States is the world's information bank. The source of this accumulated wealth goes back two centuries to the First Amendment to the Constitution, which prohibits government interference in the media. The First Amendment's reference point was the press, the only mass media technology available at the time. Since then, constitutional protection of information rights has been widened by law and tradition to include everything from computer data banks to rock music. Columbia University communications scholar Eli Noam now proposes an updated version of the First Amendment, which would protect the right of the people to assemble electronically (see Appendix).

The evolving mix of old and new media can be a powerful force for strengthening and expanding First Amendment liberties. The changes taking place open up choices about how, or even whether, the expansion will continue. The subject is now important enough to have a prominent place on the national agenda as politicians vie with one another in proposing "information highway" projects.

Despite such efforts, there are no guarantees that the new media mix will lead us to an information age nirvana of freedom and prosperity. Many signs point in other directions. Whatever their faults and failings, the older media have played a vital role in producing and distributing a critical mass of information. They have also served as agenda-setting establishments, helping to define national purpose and consensus.

NEW MEDIA AND DEMOCRATIC VALUES

Will the new mix of old and new media play a similar role? More specifically, will the vast proliferation of increasingly specialized information resources and channels be a clear benefit? Media critic Douglass Cater has more questions:

> Is the fractionalization of audiences a net social gain? . . . What happens when each minority group can tune in to its own prophets? When there are no more Walter Cronkites each evening to reassure us that despite all its afflictions the nation still stands?[36]

His questions are important in weighing the impact of current media changes. The new technology applications tend to segment and divide audiences. Are 200 cable channels a significant improvement over the 3 national television channels that have dominated media habits until recently? Probably yes but maybe no.

There is a dark side to the flood of new entertainment and information resources. Media critic Neil Postman suggests that it could result in a spate of trivialized products whose effect is to anesthetize us to realities rather than energize us to understand and act upon them. He and other critics see disturbing signs that the expansion of media channels, competing for attention in a crowded market, could be dominated by a narcissistic mélange of lightweight services. We could be "amusing ourselves to death," to use Postman's phrase.[37]

Another concern is whether the new technologies will widen the rift between the information rich and the information poor in American society. A U.S. Department of Commerce study several years ago found broad discrepancies in household computer ownership based on ethnicity. Asian American households had a 36 percent computer penetration; this ratio dropped to 28 percent for white households, 12 percent for Hispanic, and 9.5 percent for African American.[38] These gaps are slowly narrowing, but the problem of unequal access to computer resources remains.

Other surveys have documented the advantage that the information rich have in knowing how to use computers and other new resources for their personal and professional advancement. The information poor may opt increasingly for hyped-up entertainment diversions rather than personal enrichment in the form of educational and other cultural resources. There could be further fragmentation of community, an increasing sense of disengagement, and greater distrust of government and other institutions that need broad consensus to be effective.

Economist Robert Reich sees that fragmentation already happening. The top fifth of working Americans take home more money than the other four-fifths combined. This affluent group is composed largely of "symbol analysts," to use Reich's awkward phrase. In plainer English, they are the professionals who create or otherwise work with information. In the process, Reich adds:

> [They] inhabit a different economy from other Americans. The new elite is linked by jet, modem, fax, satellite and fiber-optic cable to the great commercial and recreational centers of the world, but it is not particularly connected to the rest of the nation.[39]

DECIDING WHO CONTROLS INFORMATION

In Reich's opinion, because of their control over information, these symbol analysts are the movers and shakers of the country, increasingly isolated from the rest of society. The ultimate scenario could be a sort of benign, information-based fascism in which the elite have effective control of the facts and figures needed to keep order in a disintegrating society. This danger was once caricatured, not wholly in jest, by Columbia University law professor Alan Westin, who envisioned a single national data bank center in Philadelphia run by an elite Establishment. The facility is attacked by democratic dissidents, the Fold, Staple, Spindle, and Mutilate movement. The dissidents are defeated, and the Establishment decides to program every event in every citizen's life to prevent further disruption. Professor Westin's scenario lets the dissidents win eventually but not without some sobering insights about the relevance of information to the democratic process.

These issues of information access are often pushed aside in the rough-and-tumble of changes taking place in the media and other information areas these days. Technology and economics drive most of the decisions. It is critical, however, that machines and markets be guided by a new social consensus on the role of information resources, a consensus rooted in First Amendment traditions. The central issue is whether the new media are going to make us freer and more competent, individually and collectively, to deal with the complex problems of postindustrial democracy.

MEDIA RESPONSIBILITIES IN A NEW AGE

More than seventy years ago, Walter Lippmann, a leading journalist of the day, dealt with a similar set of issues in his book *Public Opinion*, a trenchant criticism of the role of media in a democracy.[40] Lippmann was wary of claims that citizens base their political and social decisions on an objective study of the pertinent facts. Most of our decisions are based on what he called "the pictures in our heads"—that is, fixed perceptions and prejudices. The idea of informed public opinion deciding issues and actions, he argued, is largely a wishful fantasy; the business of running the country is done by elites. He was critical of American journalism in particular for failing to provide even the basic information needed to sustain a viable democratic society. Mass media can never do the job itself, Lippmann said, but it has a grave responsibility to serve both as an adequate information provider and as a watchdog of the public interest. He saw the best hope in a media sector that would identify and monitor what he called "the governing forces" as a check on the ruling establishment.

The questions Walter Lippmann raised over seventy years ago take on new meaning in the current transition to a more complex media environment. There is a quickened sense of urgency about them. Communications researcher Vincent Mosco points out that computerization—the common module for all the new media—is in its infancy: "There are still many degrees of freedom left on how to computerize. . . . Now is the time to ask hard questions, since some social options remain."[41]

Another media scholar, the late Ithiel de Sola Pool, summarized this imperative in his last book, *The Technologies of Freedom*:

> The onus is on us to determine whether free societies in the twenty-first century will conduct electronic communications under the conditions of freedom established for the domain of print through centuries of struggle, or whether that great achievement will become lost in a confusion about the new technologies.[42]

In the chapters that follow, we will examine the technological, economic, and social forces affecting the new media environment in which these choices will be made.

NOTES

1. "Corporate Menace to Society," *Washington Post*, 27 May 1998, p. A-17.
2. Quoted in "Patents," *New York Times*, 1 January 1996, p. 46.
3. For a discussion of the nature of mass communication, see Robert Escarpit, "The Concept of Mass," *Journal of Communications* 29, no. 2, Spring 1987, pp. 44–47.
4. "Encyclopedia of the New Economy," *Wired*, May 1998, p. 105
5. "The Surge in New Satellite-based Services," *Satellite Markets*, Summer 1998, p. 10.
6. "Internet Search Engines Inefficient, Survey Finds," *Cowles/Simba Media Daily*, 3 April 1998, p. 2.
7. For a general description of the Internet's evolution, see Wilson P. Dizard, *Meganet: How the Global Communications Network Will Connect Everyone on Earth*, Boulder, CO: Westview Press, 1997, pp. 143–163.
8. "Warp Speed Ahead," *Business Week*, 16 February 1998, p. 80.
9. "The Big Push," *Washington Post*, 11 May 1997, p. H-1.
10. "Internet News Takes Off," Pew Research Center biennial news consumption survey. Pew Research Center for the People and the Press, Washington, DC, June 1998.
11. "Microsoft Continues to Lay Cable Plans," *Interactive Week*, 22 June 1998, p. 17.
12. "Honey, What's on AOL Tonight?" *Business Week*, 2 June 1997, p. 131.
13. "From Online to On the Line," *Washington Post* business supplement, 26 October 1998, p. 22.
14. "Ma Bell's Convenience Store," *Economist* (London), 11 June 1998, p. 61.
15. "The Net Is Open for Business—Big Time," *Business Week*, 31 August 1998, p. 108. See also "More Shoppers Are Buying Online," *Washington Post*, 24 December 1997, p. C-1.
16. "The Virtual Mall Gets Real," *Business Week*, 26 January 1998, p. 90.
17. "Net Asset," *Washington Post*, 10 November 1997, p. B-9.
18. "A Challenge for the Printed Page," *Financial Times* (London), 12 December 1997, p. 11.
19. "No More Media Elite," *Washington Post*, 8 July 1998, p. A-17.
20. "Booking the Future," *Washington Post*, 10 July 1998, p. A-1.
21. "Falling Sales Hit Publishers for 2nd Year," *New York Times*, 6 July 1997, p. D-1.
22. The survey was conducted by Georgia Tech's Graphics, Visualization and Graphics Center.
23. "Security Fears Still Dog Web Sales," *Interactive Week*, 20 July 1998, p. 44.
24. "Size Does Matter," *Economist* (London), 23 May 1998, p. 57.
25. Multimedia information packaging is not a new idea. The original media packager was William Randolph Hearst early in this century. Beginning with a large chain of newspapers, he expanded his operations to include Hollywood films, newsreels, magazines, and other enterprises. See Leo Bogart, "The American Media System and Its Commercial Culture," occasional paper 8, Gannett Foundation Media Center, New York, March 1991, p. 4.
26. "Size Does Matter," *Economist* (London), 23 May 1998, p. 57.
27. "From Gurus to Sitting Ducks," *New York Times*, 11 January 1998, p. Bu-2.
28. Bronwen Maddox, "Headline Makers," *Financial Times* (London), 17 December 1991, p. 16.
29. For a useful survey of the impact of the AT&T divestiture, see Robert Crandall. *After the Breakup: U.S. Telecommunications in a More Competitive Era*. Washington, DC: The Brookings Institution, 1991.
30. McLuhan's prophetic views on the new media are scattered throughout his books, including *The Gutenburg Galaxy*. Toronto: University of Toronto Press, 1962, and *Understanding Media*, 2d ed., New York: New American Library, 1964.

31. The most extensive study of the new information impact on American society is U.S. Department of Commerce, *The Information Economy*, 9 vols., Office of Telecommunications Special Publication 77–12, 1977. See also "Too Many Words," *Economist* (London), 20 August 1983, p. 79.

32. For a useful discussion of this issue, see "Children and Television: Growing Up in a Media World," special issue of *Media & Values*, no. 52–53 (Fall 1990–Winter 1992).

33. George Gilder, *Life After Television*. Knoxville, TN: Whittle Direct Books, 1990, p. 36.

34. "Cable Networks See Dimmer Future," *New York Times*, 7 July 1991, p. D-1.

35. Richard Maisel, "Decline of the Mass Media," *Public Opinion Quarterly* 37, no. 2 (Summer 1973): pp. 159–170.

36. Douglass Cater, "A Communications Revolution?" *Wall Street Journal*, 6 August 1973, p. 18.

37. Neil Postman, *Amusing Ourselves to Death: Public Discourse in the Age of Show Business*, New York: Penguin Books, 1986.

38. "U.S. Study Finds Varying Access to Phones, PCs," *Washington Post*, 25 July 1995, p. C-1.

39. Robert Reich, "Secession of the Successful," *New York Times Magazine*, 20 January 1991, p. 16. See also "The Information Gap," a special issue of Journal of Communication 39, no. 3 (Summer 1989).

40. Walter Lippmann. *Public Opinion*, New York: Harcourt Brace, 1922.

41. Vincent Mosco, *The Pay-Per Society: Public Opinion in the Communications Society*, Norwood, NJ: Ablex Publishing Co., 1989, p. 67.

42. Ithiel de Sola Pool, *The Technologies of Freedom*. Cambridge, MA: Harvard University Press, 1983, p. 10.

New Media Technologies: The Information Machines

The scenario is a familiar one: predictions about the glittering role that advanced media services will play in our futures. They suggest an electronic Utopia where in the comfort of our homes, we sit at our multimedia consoles plugged into a world of vast information resources. It is a crisp, clean world, where every problem has a ready solution because we have full access to the facts.[1] The prospect is intriguing but decidedly premature. Dramatic changes are indeed taking place in mass communications, but the road ahead is marked with as many pitfalls as opportunities. In this chapter, we look at the information technologies that will determine the shape and direction of the mass media in the coming decade.

The current changes are the third major transformation in mass media technologies in modern times. The first took place in the nineteenth century, with the introduction of steam-powered printing presses and cheap pulp paper. The result was the first true mass media, the "penny press" newspapers and large-scale book and magazine publishing industries. The second transformation occurred with the introduction of over-the-air broadcasting: radio in 1920 and television in 1939. The third mass media transformation—the one we are now experiencing—involves a transition to computer-based production, storage, and distribution of information and entertainment. It brings us to the world of multimedia computers, compact discs, handheld data banks, national fiber-optic networks, advanced facsimile messaging, Internet Web pages, and other services that did not exist a twenty years ago.

This new media pattern is qualitatively different from earlier ones in several ways. One technology—computerization—is now the module for all forms of electronic information: sound, video, and print. Computers are forcing a massive restructuring of older media services and, at the same time, creating a new set of competing services. Traditional lines between one medium and another erode when they share a common digital base. Fax machines are newspapers. Compact discs are books. Satellites are television transmitters. The old distinctions are smudged as computers transform traditional products and add new ones. Technology has always determined the shape and scope of the mass media. It will continue to do so in the coming years as the media industries adjust to new operational and product opportunities.

At first, the new information technologies served mainly the needs of big business and big government, the institutions that could pay for (and, in effect, subsidize) the electronic expansion of the American information structure.[2] This is changing. We are now witnessing a rapid consumerization of these advanced information resources. The mass media will be a primary beneficiary of this change as communications networks expand to supply electronic services to homes and other consumer locations.[3]

THE COMING AGE OF TELECOMPUTING

This shift to consumer services is paced by the technological merging of two familiar machines: computers and television sets. Computers are becoming more like television sets, and television sets are being computerized. The result is a new kind of electronic hybrid, the telecomputer. The telecomputer may eventually replace old-fashioned TV receivers, as well as personal computers, videocassette recorders, game machines, digital record players, and the other electronic gadgets that clutter up American homes.[4] Television sets will be transformed from passive receivers of distant pictures into multimedia interactive instruments, capable of handling all types of video, print, and sound services. These services will be delivered to homes and other locations by both wire and wireless networks, each with a capacity of hundreds of interactive video channels and thousands of two-way data links. For the first time, a full range of media, both old and new, will be available electronically to consumers.

What will this new technology-driven pattern look like? We can see its broad outlines with some clarity for perhaps a decade into the future. Beyond that, the vision blurs. Predicting the impact of new technologies is a risky business. Even the astute managers at IBM, that bastion of sophisticated technologies, sometimes get it wrong. In the late 1940s, they predicted the worldwide market potential of their newfangled mainframe computers at about a dozen machines. More recently, in 1981, when IBM marketed its first personal computer, company executives projected that overall sales would be about a quarter million machines. Since then, over 200 million small computers, built by IBM and its competitors, have been sold in the United States and abroad.[5]

IBM's corporate blind spots in measuring the market for its products put the firm in good company. Alexander Graham Bell saw only a narrow usefulness for his telephone invention. He thought its primary value was as a transmitter of musical concerts and other entertainment into homes. It was the relatively unknown Theodore Vail, an early president of Bell's telephone company, who recognized the possibilities for a national telephone network connecting people. Vail understood, as Bell did not, the wider social and economic implications of telephone technology. The critical decisions in the adoption of any technology, in fact, are made overwhelmingly on political and economic grounds.[6]

This is a point to keep in mind as we survey the range of technologies available for expanded mass media services in the coming decade. Many promising technologies will fall by the wayside because they do not fit a clear economic or social need. In the competitive scramble to exploit new techniques, there will be both corporate winners and corporate losers. None of the players involved knows for certain the size and shape of the market for new services.

Their doubts are reinforced by a record of recent failures to sell the new electronic services. In most cases these projects ran up against a stone wall of consumer resistance to the glitzy new products, no matter what advantages they promised. Despite that experience, most major media firms are committing large amounts of money and other resources to advanced services. Increasingly, these companies are caught up in tough decisions on how to manage the new opportunities. Whatever their private hesitations about the prospects for success, they know that they cannot afford to be left behind in an increasingly competitive, technology-intensive marketplace.

Two basic technologies are forcing these decisions: advanced computers and high-capacity telecommunications circuits. Together they are creating an information structure that is reshaping American society and, by extension, the rest of the world. Michael Dertouzos, chief of the Massachusetts Institute of Technology (MIT) Laboratory for Computer Sciences, predicts awesome results from the growing integration of computers and communications:

> This relentless compounding of capabilities has transformed a faint promise of synergy into an immense and real potential. . . . These two giants, computers and networks, can be fused to form an infrastructure even more promising than the individual technologies.[7]

Mass media are a small part of the social and economic institutions being shaped by this change. Banks and other financial organizations, for example, are almost totally dependent on the new computer/communications links. The media sector is just beginning to catch up. Increasingly, it sees its future role as that of an electronic supplier of information and entertainment products.[8]

THE CHIP REVOLUTION

The key to these new services is a fingernail-sized device shared by computers and communications machines—the semiconductor chip, the building block of the information age. Most electronic advances in recent decades are based on improvements in chip technology. A new generation of more efficient chips has emerged every two years on average since the first silicon semiconductor devices were developed in the 1960s. Theologians once pondered the question of how many angels could dance on the head of a pin. Semiconductor researchers now ask how many transistors can fit on a silicon flake. The first commercial microprocessors developed by Intel, the biggest U.S. chipmaker, in the early 1970s contained 2,740 transistors. In the late 1990s, Intel's Pentium II chip held 7.7 million transistors. In 1998, a University of Maryland research team reported that it was working on an advanced chip that might contain as many as 700 million transistors.[9]

Advanced chip technology has already shrunk computers from room-sized boxes to handheld devices. A recent technology—the flash-memory chip—will result in even smaller computers. Unlike earlier chips, flash-memory chips retain information when the computer is turned off. This makes it unnecessary to use bulky disk-drive storage systems in lightweight devices such as laptops and other small computers. Intel manufactures a two-ounce flash card that can hold as much data as a PC hard drive, literally placing enormous amounts of media and other information resources into the hands of consumers.

Chip-based technologies are transforming the media industries in two ways: in the computerization of information production and in the distribution of media products over high-capacity communications circuits. Although these functions will eventually converge in a single information utility, they are still distinct enough to be looked at separately. In this chapter, we will survey the technologies that are changing the way media services are produced. In Chapter 3, we will examine the role of high-tech communications channels in distributing these services.

COMPUTERS: ENGINES OF THE NEW MEDIA

First, let's look at computers in their many forms. Until recently, media organizations lagged in supplying computer-based products to consumers, since home computers and related equipment were not available on a mass scale. This has changed in recent years with the dramatic increase in computer sales, as manufacturers lowered retail prices below a thousand dollars—the longstanding magic figure for creating a truly mass market. With this drop in price, the number of computers per thousand persons in the United States soared to over 400.

In earlier years, the media industries regarded computers primarily as tools to improve their internal operations. This began with routine administrative chores such as payrolls, customer billing, and inventories. By the 1980s, however, computers were being put to use extensively in media production. Newspapers took the lead by introducing word processing terminals in newsrooms, replacing typewriters. Stories could be written and edited more quickly, then sent electronically to production facilities as part of a continuous computer-driven process. Newsroom computing became more sophisticated, with electronic mail and Internet data retrieval added to conventional word-processing capabilities.

Another change has been the increasing use of portable computers. Reporters carry them along to news events, punching in their stories as they happen, then transmitting them directly via telephone lines to their editors. An early example of laptop journalism took place during the 1991 Persian Gulf war. Print reporters in the war zone made use of an ingenious small suitcase, known as Mascot Nomad. It contained a minicomputer, an omnidirectional aerial, and a telex printer. The aerial permitted direct transmission to a communications satellite that relayed reports to news organizations around the world. Meanwhile, television journalists covering the war sent live video reports to their home offices from small, portable earth terminals via a satellite stationed above the Indian Ocean.[10]

Editorial computerization has been expanded with the introduction of desktop publishing, the editing and making up of newspapers and other publications on small computers. Text, photos, and graphics are assembled electronically in a variety of page layouts, then transmitted for final printing. Desktop publishing is now routinely used by newspaper, magazine, and book publishers. It is a particular boon to small publishers because it cuts costs and, at the same time, results in a more attractive product.

PUBLISHING ON DESKTOPS

A newer high-tech variation on desktop publishing is video composing. Used extensively in the television and film industries, this technique goes beyond ordinary desktop manipulation of print and graphics by incorporating sound and video. Just as a print reporter can rearrange sentences and paragraphs on a word processor, a video composer can assemble sight, sound, and print materials in any combination, creating different versions (including a choice of hundreds of colors) and storing them on a compact disc before selecting the best combination for the finished film or videotape product. Video composing, also known as nonlinear editing, may eventually replace videotaping in television and film studios. In the late 1990s, a number of companies began marketing tapeless recording machines capable of storing animation, graphics, and video for news, entertainment, and other programming.

Meanwhile, print publishers have turned to computers to store information both for internal editorial uses and for new consumer sales opportunities. Newspapers and magazines have, over the years, accumulated vast amounts of data which can be marketed in new ways. Traditionally, this information was stored in file cabinets, with a high probability that much of it would be misplaced or forgotten. A generation ago, microfilm technology brought a measure of efficiency to such information storage, but it tended to be an awkward means of retrieving information.

Microfilm archives have since been replaced by videotext, stored in computers or on compact discs. In the process, a new and potentially profitable revenue source, videotext publishing, is opening up for the newspaper and magazine industries. The pioneer in exploiting this resource is the New York Times, whose managers decided in the late 1960s to store the contents of the newspaper in a computer and to market it as videotext to computer sites.

In the 1980s, a number of news organizations followed the New York Times's lead in marketing information electronically. An early and successful entrant was

Dow Jones, publisher of the *Wall Street Journal* and other financial publications. The Dow Jones News/Retrieval Service offered sixty online financial and business data services. McGraw-Hill made most of its magazines and newsletters available in electronic formats. Another major videotext provider is Reuters, the old-line British news agency. It has developed its computerized financial data videotext services to the point where its news operations account for less than 10 percent of the firm's revenues. As we shall see, many of these early online services, including the *New York Times*, have in recent years shifted their operations to the Internet's World Wide Web.

Supplying business firms and other organizations with online data, on or off the Internet, has become a thriving part of the publishing business. These operations are expanding rapidly, with a broader base among ordinary consumers. This trend represents both a competitive threat and a product opportunity for print publishers. The potential extent of the shift to consumer-based networks is illustrated by the activities of the largest publisher in the world, the U.S. government. Traditionally, the government distributed a large variety of printed publications, from its best-selling baby care manual to NASA's maps of Mars, through the U.S. Government Printing Office (GPO). By the early 1990s, however, only 35 percent of government publications were still available in print through the GPO; the rest could be accessed only electronically through 1,200 dial-up videotext services.[11]

Prompted by these changes in the information market, newspapers and other publishing firms have taken a fresh look at consumer electronic services. They want to avoid the mistakes of the early 1980s, when a number of American media groups made premature forays into electronic publishing. Time Inc., the Knight-Ridder newspaper chain, the *Los Angeles Times-Mirror*, and CBS, among others, invested millions of dollars in computerized data services. In each case, they were unsuccessful, bedeviled by inadequate technology, weak products, and massive consumer indifference.[12]

The new entrants want to repeat the initial success enjoyed by a number of recent European ventures into large-scale consumer videotext services. The most extensive of these ventures is Minitel, managed by France Telecom, the French national phone system. Minitel technology consists of a small computer monitor attached to home telephones. The Minitel service was originally intended only to supply phone directory information, replacing printed directories. Minitel later expanded into a full-scale videotext service, with over 35 million subscribers in homes, businesses, and other locations. Subscribers have access to data banks run by over 17,000 information services, ranging from daily horoscopes to weather reports.[13] More recently, Minitel has added the Internet's World Wide Web to its menu of services.[14]

COMPETING FOR THE PC DATA MARKET

The first American service to offer a full menu of consumer-oriented data was Prodigy, developed by IBM and Sears Roebuck in the 1980s. Its offerings included home shopping, travel guides, restaurant ratings, an encyclopedia, games, news, stock prices, weather reports, bill-paying services, and an electronic-mail network.[15] Prodigy soon faced heavy competition from rival services, particularly America Online which overtook Prodigy in the competitive race for subscribers.[16] Each scrambled to outdo the other with innovative information formats, "chat rooms," and glitzy graphics. However, the rapid growth of these online services in recent years has been due largely to their improved ability to provide easier access to the Internet and its World Wide Web resources.

AOL and other consumer data services face new competition from networks with strong corporate sponsorship. The Microsoft Network (MSN) went on line in 1995 as an integral part of Windows software. It is a formidable player in the business given its corporate backing and its links with the MSNBC cable news network. The other big player in consumer online services is AT&T, with a customer base of over 50 million homes. Its 1998 merger with Telecommunications Inc., the second-largest U.S. cable network, positioned AT&T to become a major provider of online consumer services, including the Internet, in the coming years. Neither MSN nor AT&T was able to dislodge AOL as the dominant supplier of consumer online information in the late 1990s. In 1998, AOL passed the 10 million mark in subscribers, with MSN in second place at 2.3 million and AT&T with less than 1 million.

Until recently, online networks did not represent a serious economic threat to newspapers, television, and other old media. Online services were seen as supplements to, not replacements for, traditional media. Moreover, as already noted, early attempts by media companies to operate consumer electronic services were largely unsuccessful. However, their views on electronic services have changed radically in recent years as the Internet and other technologies have expanded their offerings and their audiences. We will now take a look at the technologies that promise to have a major impact on the U.S. media industries in the early years of the new century.

COMPACT DISCS: FROM MUSIC TO MULTIMEDIA

We begin with a familiar technology found in most American homes—the compact disc. Originally introduced as a digital replacement for vinyl long-playing records, the CD's capabilities have been vastly expanded in the past decade. A new generation of discs can store huge amounts of print data, as well as graphics and video programming. The entire contents of the *Encyclopaedia Britannica* can be put on a single disc, using CD-ROM technology. One commercially available CD includes a directory of 9 million U.S. business firms. A flourishing industry for putting printed materials on CDs already exists. One of its customers is the U.S. Navy, which has transferred to a handful of CDs all of the information from the twenty-six *tons* of technical documents previously required for each of its cruisers.[17] CD technology also makes it easier to store photographs, charts, and other images. About 10,000 images can be stored on a single disc the size of a compact music disc.

The information-storage capacities of CDs and similar devices are expanding dramatically. A prototype, developed at the University of California's Irvine campus, has the potential for storing 6.5 trillion bits of information, the contents of a million books. This is roughly 2,000 times more data than can be stored in one of today's commercial computers.[18] In another breakthrough, Matsushita, Japan's largest consumer electronics company, is developing a device that will have a storage capacity of more than 1,000 times that of magnetic or optical discs.[19] Matsushita's technology will be able to store the contents of a present-day compact disc on a space as small as a period on this page. A competitor to disc storage, already in production, is a laser-based tape system whose storage capacity represents a quantum leap over present-day magnetic tapes. A twelve-inch laser-tape reel can store the same amount of data as 170 CDs or 5,000 magnetic-tape cartridges.

These advanced devices are still largely in the research and development stage. Meanwhile, digital discs are an increasingly ubiquitous part of the way information is stored and retrieved. Increasingly, videotext discs are being marketed as a mass-consumer product, as the prices of both the discs and the machines that play them drop. Almost all new PCs have built-in CD capabilities for interactive games and other uses. The most popular of the interactive games, *Myst*, has sold over five million copies. Meanwhile, the range of other uses of digital discs has expanded rapidly. Microsoft Corp.'s "library" includes a full range of reference works such as *American Heritage Library* and *Bartlett's Quotations*. Oxford University Press offers its twelve-volume *Oxford English Dictionary* on a single disc. The complete works of Shakespeare are available on a single disc priced under $25. Overall, CD products are booming. The authoritative *CD-ROM Periodical Index* lists over 30,000 periodicals and books issued by 2,000 organizations.

In addition to CD players built into desktop computers, manufacturers are marketing portable CD player devices. The earliest and most successful of these machines was Sony's Data Discman, a handheld device that provides printed text as well as CD-quality music, still pictures, and speech. Data Discman's software library includes, among other features, eleven dictionaries, language lessons, travel guides, quiz games, and the Bible. More recently, Sony has developed a "subminiature disc," about half the size of a conventional disc, that can hold the equivalent of 32,000 pages of double-spaced typed pages.[20] In the late 1990s, the first generation of "notebook" computers with CD-ROM drives made their appearance, adding a new dimension to CD portability.[21]

THE MEDIA'S STAKE IN DISC TECHNOLOGY

The greater promise for the media industries, however, lies in a more advanced disc format that can supply a full range of sound, video, and print information on a single disc. This is the multimedia DVD (for digital video disc), which is a major technological upgrade over older compact discs. DVDs can mix and match any combination of voice, video, or data information with superior visuals and sound. They also have greater storage capacity. A DVD can play a full-length Hollywood film with a pin-sharp picture and six-channel sound.[22]

The first uses of DVDs have been as upgraded replacements for conventional music discs. DVDs offers a six-channel "surround sound" format that is technically superior to the two-channel capabilities of older CDs. Moreover, an audio DVD has seven times the playing capacity of a conventional disc. DVDs were slow to gain consumer acceptance in the 1990s primarily because they required a more expensive player, but consumer resistance has diminished as prices have dropped.[23]

Although music companies are the first beneficiaries of DVD technology, other media sectors also stand to profit from it. The Hollywood film studios are shifting their videotape products to DVD formats. Book publishers are marketing disc editions of traditional books, complete with video and audio segments. Newspaper and magazine publishers have begun to repackage their printed products, with accompanying audio and visual material, on discs.

Multimedia disc technology will become a stronger challenger (and product opportunity) for the traditional media in the coming years. More print, video, and voice services are already available on discs as stand-alone storage devices, replacing traditional media outlets.[24] Newer technologies allow the discs to be connected online to information and entertainment networks. Forrester Research, the media consultancy, estimates that over 53 million households will have computers equipped with DVD drives by 2002, a fivefold increase over 1999.

America Online has been a leader in developing DVD technology, with the expectation that its subscribers will change the way they think about using compact discs. Deborah Baker, AOL's director of multimedia services, points out:

> Traditional CD-ROMs are designed to give the individual an exciting or fun experience through interaction with the computer. Through integration with America Online, the user can also interact with other people. It adds a whole new dimension to multimedia by allowing people to send mail, chat or enter an auditorium for a special event.[25]

TELECOMPUTER POWER

These multimedia developments have won an expanding audience of computer users. However, a different kind of multimedia delivery is needed to bring a full range of information and entertainment services to a mass audience. For the media industries, this prospect is the main hope for expanding their consumer markets in the next decade.

What will the new machines look like? Until now, multimedia technology has evolved largely as a high-tech extension of conventional computers. The next generation of computers will, of course, contain many multimedia applications for business and professional uses. However, multimedia machines for home entertainment and information purposes will probably look not like computers but more closely resemble television receivers, albeit with capabilities well beyond today's sets. The consumer market for advanced media services will probably not emerge fully until video, sound, and print technologies are integrated in a single household machine.

The result will be the telecomputer, which will supply multimedia services to homes via high-capacity cable or satellite channels. In addition to these links from outside the home, telecomputers will be equipped with interactive CD capabilities. Consumer telecomputers (or "smart TV," as they are sometimes called) can be the master link, supplying both conventional and new media services to mass audiences at home and in other locations.[26] Telecomputers will come in different shapes and forms. One possibility is to hang them on a wall: Xerox Corporation has developed a wall-display panel no thicker than a pad of paper that displays multimedia computer functions. Japanese electronic manufacturers have taken the lead in manufacturing similar panels for the new generation of telecomputers.[27]

When will the telecomputers be available? MIT's Media Lab, among other research units, has been working on various prototypes since the early 1980s. In the early 1990s, the lab's associate director, Andrew Lippman, declared that telecomputing's time had come:

> Forget television sets. In three years, there won't be any. Instead there will be computers with high-quality display screens. Inside, there will be digital instructions allowing them to receive ABC, HBO, BBC and anything we can dream up.[28]

He was wrong. The three-year deadline came and went without the predicted demise of old-fashioned TV sets. Like so many digital-age enthusiasts, Lippman had underestimated the economic and social barriers to adoption of unfamiliar new technologies. No one in the media industry seriously questions, however, that telecomputers and other consumer multimedia resources will be increasingly common in the early years of the new century. Marketing surveys have shown, however, that consumers will probably not rush to exchange their old TV sets for the expensive new models. As a result, the television industry—both broadcasters and equipment suppliers—has taken a generally cautious approach in investing in the advanced technologies needed to bring interactive resources into American homes.

These doubts do not extend, however, to the computer industry. Its leaders see multimedia in all its forms as their chance to replicate the successes they have had with small computers. Microsoft Corporation's Bill Gates, the wunderkind of the computer industry, is even more expansive: "Multimedia will be bigger than everything we do today."[29]

THE TRANSITION TO DIGITAL VIDEO

A number of problems had to be mastered before advanced telecomputers become an affordable mass-consumption product. One of these is the technology of digital compression, the squeezing of data into a more compact form for electronic storage and transmission. The data can be in video, audio, or print form or any combination of the three. Video displays, in particular, call for enormous compression power, involving millions of calculations every second.

As we have seen, chip technology has advanced rapidly to meet the storage needs of advanced multimedia devices. The remaining problem is to upgrade the networks that will link telecomputers to information and entertainment resources outside the home. This requires replacing most of the present equipment in telephone, broadcasting, and other telecommunications systems—an expensive and time-consuming process. Many of these systems still transmit analog signals, a nineteenth-century technology that gave us telephones and broadcasting but that is increasingly obsolete in the computer era. Analog signals can handle only one application at a time, say, a music recording, a TV show, or a phone call. They copy the shape, timing, and type of signal they record, in effect tying the receiver (phone, TV set, etc.) to the transmitter in lockstep fashion.

The digital signals needed for telecomputers and other high-tech machines are more flexible. Based on binary digits, these signals make no distinction between video, sound, and print transmissions. They can handle them all in a single stream, originating, storing, editing, transmitting, and receiving messages at increasingly faster speeds.[30] Eventually, all the world's telephone, broadcasting, and data networks will be digitized. The changeover has critical implications for telecomputers and for the mass media—both old and new—that will supply information and entertainment programming to them.

SPEEDING UP THE DIGITAL TIMETABLE

Until very recently, digital television was regarded as a long-term prospect, given the enormous computational requirements involved in video images. This timetable has changed as a result of technological breakthroughs. Digital television receivers for household use are already on the market as the forerunners of a new generation of multimedia telecomputers.[31] Digitization will transform television in much the same way that digitized CD technology has changed the musical recording world. Present-day TV sets will become relics. The new sets will not only display a much better television picture but also serve as an all-purpose computing device, offering a wide range of information and entertainment services piped into homes from outside suppliers or from interactive CD resources built into the set.

The telecomputer will be a central feature of what industry enthusiasts call "the smart house," in which computerization becomes an essential part of domestic life. Researchers at MIT's Media Laboratory have embarked on a project, called Things That Think, that utilizes tiny computers, scattered ubiquitously throughout the house, to receive and carry out a range of instructions. Media Lab experimenters have already wired a room so that a person can walk in and say, "Show me a movie," and a computer embedded in the wall will instruct lights to dim and a videotape to begin. More complex applications are on the agenda, for example, a refrigerator that can sense when the milk has run out and will automatically order more from the market. Perhaps the most interesting aspect of the Things That Think project is that over thirty U.S. corporations have invested in it, each in the hope that the Media Laboratory's far-out experiments may lead to practical ideas that can be turned into marketing prospects.[32]

Media companies are only beginning to identify the opportunities (and pitfalls) in adjusting to consumer markets based on telecomputing in the home.

What was once a media executive's pipe dream is now a production and marketing challenge.

HIGH-DEFINITION TELEVISON

The timetable for meeting this challenge was advanced during the 1990s through a series of political and economic decisions that sped up the prospects for telecomputing's key technology—high-definition television (HDTV). It is superior video, a digital system that will eventually replace sets that now operate on an analog standard adopted a half century ago. The HDTV screen contains twice the lines of the old standard, enhanced by stereo sound.

For years, high-definition television was regarded as simply an upgrade of conventional television broadcasting signals, using the same analog format. This prospect changed dramatically when the Federal Communications Commission decided in the early 1990s that it would give preference to an HDTV system based on digital, not analog, technology. It was a bold move, considering that digital TV was still a laboratory experiment at the time. Moreover, there was the risk that Japanese electronics firms would introduce their version of a high-definition system based on analog standards, capturing the market before a U.S. digital system could be developed.

The implications of the FCC's decision went far beyond the idea of simply improving the quality of conventional over-the-air broadcasting. It meant that television sets could supply a full range of voice, video, and data to home viewers. In effect, the TV industry's options were expanded to becoming a full-fledged provider of digitized multimedia services well beyond traditional television offerings.

This prospect alarmed the computer industry, which saw itself in the lead in providing consumer multimedia services. Moreover, the original FCC standards for HDTV heavily favored over-the-air broadcasters. A bare-knuckled fight between the broadcasting and computer lobbies in Washington took place before a mutually satisfying compromise was reached. At the same time, the broadcasters extracted an agreement from Congress and the FCC that permitted them to use the new HDTV technology for data and voice services as well as over-the-air broadcasting. This decision gave them the technical platform to enter into the digital multimedia business, competing against the telecommunications and computer industries for consumer business.[33]

HDTV will be an integral part of telecomputer technology. Despite HDTV's attractions, however, media firms face barriers in developing and marketing high-definition multimedia products. One hurdle is their limited experience with multimedia techniques; another is the size of the investment needed to develop advanced products, whose appeal to consumers is still untested. No one, in or outside the media industries, knows for certain how HDTV resources will be delivered to consumers. Technically, they can be transmitted by computers, cable TV systems, satellites, or over-the-air broadcasts. Another likely candidate is

HDTV videocassettes. Toshiba, the Japanese electronics company, has already demonstrated a prototype of an HDTV videorecorder.[34]

HDTV services will probably not become widespread until around 2005. Television stations have to be re-equipped at great cost to handle the new technology. Overall, the industry has lagged in meeting FCC deadlines for phasing in HDTV services. Despite this foot-dragging, network affiliates in the top ten U.S. cities began HDTV telecasts in the middle of 1999.

Another problem is consumer resistance to the high price of HDTV sets. The first sets on the market for the 1998 Christmas season were priced at over $5,000. Although prices are dropping sharply as HDTV services spread, most industry observers do not expect wide consumer acceptance until these prices fall below $1,000. Meanwhile, both the set manufacturers and television networkers are preparing to market HDTV not simply as a superior form of old-fashioned TV but as an all-around multimedia telecomputer providing a full range of voice, video, and data services.[35]

UPGRADING THE INTERNET

The other technology that will drive the media industries in future years is, of course, the Internet. Until recently, media access to the network has been limited largely to providing print data along with some graphics. Now the Internet is rapidly becoming part of the digitized multimedia pattern, changing the ways that the old media companies create and market their products. For the first time, they face the prospect of competition from companies not normally associated with the media sector.

One such group of competitors is the telephone industry. In recent years, the Internet's capabilities have been extended to phone calls. The sound quality in early Internet phone systems was poor, somewhat akin to talking down a rain barrel. The technology has since been improved to the point where it matches that of conventional phone service.

Despite these problems, Internet telephony is expanding rapidly. One of the incentives has been economic: Internet phone calls can be made anywhere in the world for the price of a local call. This has led to a scramble among phone companies to deal with what could be a major threat to their revenues. At one level, they are asking the Federal Communications Commission to tighten regulations on Internet telephone calls. At another level, they are preparing for the day when Internet telephony will be a regular, hopefully profitable part of their own operations. AT&T already offers an Internet-based phone service, and other phone companies have followed suit.[36]

Internet telephony may seem a bit removed from the problems that media companies have in developing multimedia services on the network. However, Internet telephony opens up the prospect that the phone companies can use these circuits to offer other services. This could include access to information and entertainment resources, competing with media companies. This may not happen soon, but it has to be factored into the long-range strategies of these companies as they move on to the Internet.

Meanwhile, other media firms are exploiting the Internet's new multimedia capabilities. One is old-fashioned radio programs. Radio transmissions are possible on the Internet because of advances in audio-on-demand software. Until recently, sound files on the Internet had to be fully downloaded before they were played, which made live broadcasting impossible. Newer technology allows radio stations to transmit data from the station's computer to users' PCs. Receiver software then converts the data to audio that plays through the PC's soundcard. Hundreds of U.S. radio stations now transmit over the Internet twenty-four hours a day.[37]

Internet video is more complex, but it involves the same basic technology. Because of the bigger bandwidth requirements, online video is limited for the present to a small screen in one corner of a Web page. The resultant image is poor, comparable (as one observer put it) to a demented postage stamp come jerkily to life. Nevertheless, Internet video is a growth sector. It began in 1996 when MTV, the pop music network, launched an around-the-clock cable TV channel that offered simultaneous viewing on PCs and Web pages containing related data. This and similar developments led to the production of "cybersoaps," digital versions of TV soap operas. One early cyberserial, *Techno 3*, was a takeoff on the 1970's series, *Charlie's Angels*, in which three beautiful and intelligent female investigators are controlled by a cyberterrorist.

The old-line media companies are not immediately threatened by these Internet developments. It will be a long time, for instance, before the Internet can deliver the kind of quality HDTV broadcasting can supply. Nevertheless, Internet audio and video services are expanding. By 1999, a Dallas-based company, Broadcast.com, was "streaming" live transmissions on the Web from 385 radio stations and 40 television outlets. Its prospects have attracted the attention of the investment community. Despite the fact that the company had never made a profit, Wall Street records were set in July 1998 when the price of its stock jumped 250 percent the day after it was put on the market.[38]

CABLE SYSTEMS: THE NEW VIDEO FRONTIER

Other media companies are assessing the long-term impact of these new Internet services, and they are moving ahead in developing their own multimedia Internet products. Their initial targets of choice were the opportunities made available by Web sites developed by cable TV services. These sites reached millions of U.S. households, with the technical capability of delivering a wide range of multimedia products. A high percentage of cable TV networks are owned by large conglomerates who also control multimedia production assets.

A leader in exploiting the Internet's multimedia capabilities has been Time Warner's Cable News Network. CNN's Web site had been a print-and-graphics service, similar to those operated by MSNBC, ABCnews, and USA Today. It is the most heavily visited news and information page on the Web, in large part due to its around-the-clock operations. In 1997, CNN's managers decided to shift to a full multimedia format, a project they completed the following year.

Their decision was based on CNN's competitive advantage in handling more news video than any other TV or cable news organization. "CNN is a TV company, first and foremost," says Jeff Garrard, executive director of CNN Interactive. "We think that as people with good computers and connections come online, they should be able to access video as easily as they access text."[39]

The result was Videoselect, the CNN service that supplies a steady stream of video and audio programming on the network's Web site. The service began in 1998 by offering stand-alone video versions of up to twenty news stories a day. In addition, CNN's print Web page provided shorter video clips, including the capability of offering six live feeds simultaneously. Another new offering, Videovault, allows Web viewers the option of retrieving older stories from CNN's extensive digital-video archives.

With Videoselect, CNN pioneered what is eventually going to be a ubiquitous feature on the Internet—multimedia voice, video, and print offerings. MSNBC and CNN's other competitors scrambled to offer similar products. Meanwhile, America Online began introducing video-based features in a move to strengthen its position as the main gateway to the Internet for the nation's households.[40]

Despite their hesitations about moving into an expensive, and largely untested, field, media firms know that their future will be determined by DVD, HDTV, the Internet, and similar advanced technologies. Telecomputers and other multimedia outlets will compete for the time, attention, and dollars now being spent on conventional media equipment and services. At one level, this will mean lost business for the old-line media, but at another, it will open new opportunities to supply information and entertainment in attractive, profitable new formats.

VIRTUAL REALITY: TRAVELS IN CYBERSPACE

Other technological prospects promise to intrude into the media industry's strategies. One is virtual reality (VR) programming, a newcomer that may be added to the multimedia mix. VR is a new kind of human-computer interface, offering a fantasy world in which games and other information resources are made available to home consumers. Also known as cyberspace (a term borrowed from William Gibson's 1984 novel *Neuromancer*), VR allows the user to create and experience fantasy situations that are generated by computers filled with interactive software. Its one-of-a-kind effects are limited only by the imagination of the individual user. Instead of keyboards, users give instructions by voice commands, head movements, finger pointing, and other gestures.[41]

The ultimate goal of VR engineers is to simulate an environment in which one can walk around and manipulate objects at will. Current technology is based on data gloves, which project a user's hand into a three-dimensional, computer-generated environment. Another technique uses data goggles with stereoscopic viewscreens, worn like a helmet, to take the wearer into a virtual-fantasy world.[42]

VR is more than a science fiction game. It is also a fast-growing subdivision of the U.S. media industry. It has its own newsletters and journals, trade shows, and a penchant for describing itself as the virtual reality profession. One VR enthusiast, Dr. Sandra Key Heisel, describes VR's emergence as "the most profound gestalt shift of the twentieth century." She and other practitioners see important applications for their devices in the education and training fields. Bill Travers, a British conservationist, suggests that VR techniques might create a different kind of zoo in the next century, one without real animals that would use VR to bring people to animal images. Travers also envisions live satellite linkups to all parts of the world, with experts talking directly to zoo visitors from an African rain forest or the Gobi Desert.[43]

The National Aeronautics and Space Administration (NASA) uses VR techniques in its Virtual Planetary Exploration project at Ames Research Center in California. NASA has created, in computer imagery, a three-dimensional terrain of Mars and other planets based on the thousands of still photographs sent back by satellites. A trillion bytes of data from satellite photographs were used to create a "virtual Venus" landscape, which is the closest any Earthling will get to a planet where the surface temperature is 460° C.[44]

PUTTING VIRTUAL REALITY TO WORK

VR is already being tested extensively in business applications. One early experiment involves Wall Street stocks. Using VR equipment, a stockbroker wanders through a surreal computer-generated landscape made up of colored squares. The squares change color as the market changes: Blue squares might signify rising stocks, red ones losers. Traders see immediately how a stock is performing relative to others. Such information, available much more quickly than by studying lists of prices, could mean the difference between turning a profit or sustaining a loss in today's fast-paced financial markets.[45] VR may eventually have an impact on consumer markets, upgrading current home shopping networks into a cyberspace experience in which shoppers "walk" through a computer-generated mall, enter as many stores as they wish, and select merchandise without ever having to leave their own homes. To make a selection, the shopper could point to a product and take hold of it cybernetically. To buy a product, he or she would need only to drop it into a virtual-image shopping bag. A prototype for such a system, "In the Bag," has been developed as a joint project of the University of California, San Diego, and the San Diego Supercomputer Center.

Whether VR will become a media force or remain just another interesting technological toy is not yet clear. As an information tool, it could add new dimensions to our understanding of the world.[46] As an entertainment device, it could be the Super-Nintendo toy that puts other computer gaming in the shade.

Virtual reality aside, we are moving into an environment in which computer-based information machines are changing the ways we produce and store information. After years of tentative experiments with these new techniques, the mass media industries are adapting them to present services and seriously examining their potential for new products.

In Chapter 3, we look at the changes taking place in the communications channels that will distribute these services.

NOTES

1. The social impacts of an increasingly computerized society are discussed in Kevin Robins and Frank Webster, "Cybernetic Capitalism: Information, Technology, Everyday Life," in *The Political Economy of Information*. Edited by Vincent Mosco and Janet Wasco, Madison: University of Wisconsin Press, 1988, pp. 44–75.
2. For general descriptions of this transformation, see "The Death of Distance: A Survey of Telecommunications," a special supplement of *The Economist* (London), 30 September 1995; and "Crossroads on the Information Highway," a publication of the Institute for Information Studies and the Aspen Institute Program on Communications and Society, Washington DC, 1995.
3. The implications of telecomputer technology are discussed in "Retina Projection, Tactile Fields and Other Toys," *Broadcasting*, 9 December 1991, pp. 66–67.
4. "The Computer Age: Still a Work in Progress," *New York Times*, 11 September 1991, p. E-3.
5. The point is documented, with interesting examples, in Carolyn Marvin, *When Old Technologies Were New*, New York: Oxford University Press, 1988.
6. Marvin, ibid.
7. Michael Dertouzos, "Communications, Computers and Networks," *Scientific American* 265, no. 3 (September 1991): 63.
8. "Two Industries Unite to Pave the Way for High-Speed Internet Access," *New York Times*, 4 January 1999, p. C-18.
9. "When Tiny Progress Is a Huge Deal," *Washington Post*, 10 July 1998, p. F-1.
10. "Getting Video Home from the Persian Gulf," *Broadcasting*, 3 September 1990, p. 23.
11. Bob Dixon, "Recent Developments in Network-Produced Information," *Cast Calendar*, Center for Advanced Study in Telecommunication, Ohio State University, June 1991, p. 7.
12. For an analysis of early U.S. attempts to develop videotext networks, see Gary Stix, "What Zapped the Electronic Newspaper," *Columbia Journalism Review* 26, no. 1, May–June 1987, pp. 45–48.
13. Minitel and other European videotext ventures are surveyed in "The Dynamics of Videotext Development in Britain, France and Germany: A Cross-National Comparison," *European Journal of Communications* 6, no. 2, June 1991, pp. 187–212.
14. "IBM Picked to Bring World Wide Web to France's Minitel Users," *Wall Street Journal*, 6 October 1998, p. B-11.
15. "Can Prodigy Be All Things to 15 Million PC Owners?" *New York Times*, 2 June 1991, p. F-4.
16. "CompuServe Is Next to Regroup," *Interactive Week*, 10 July 1995, p. 36.
17. "CDs Store the Data, But Sifting's a Chore," *New York Times*, 4 August 1991, p. F-9.
18. "Imagine Storing Proust in Just a Crumb of Cake," *New York Times*, 1 September 1991, p. 43.
19. "Matsushita, in Lab Test, Reduced Disk to a Dot," *New York Times*, 19 September 1994, p. C-2.

20. "Disks for Tiny Computers," *New York Times*, 5 April 1992, p. F-7.
21. "Boomer Babies: First Generation Multimedia Notebooks," *New Media*, August 1995, pp. 81–83.
22. "Making the Move to DVD," *New Media*, August 1998, p. 20.
23. "Slipped Disc," *Economist* (London), 3 January 1998, p. 60. See also: "CD-ROM; what went wrong?" *New Media*, August 1998, p. 33.
24. "DVD Strives to Be a Player," *Washington Post*, 8 July 1997, p. C-1.
25. "Hybrid CD-ROMs: New Tools For the Multimedia Consumer," *Multimedia Online*, June 1995, p. 64.
26. George Gilder, *Life after Television*. Knoxville, Tenn.: Whittle Direct Books, 1991, p. 23.
27. "NEC Joins Race for Flat TV Set," *New York Times*, 7 July 1995, p. 43.
28. Quoted in "Now or Never," *Forbes*, 14 October 1991, p. 188.
29. "It's a PC. It's a TV—It's Multi-Media," *Business Week*, 9 October 1989, p. 153.
30. For a description of the transition from analog to digital technology, see "When Analog Meets Digital on a Single Chip," *New York Times*, 13 October 1991, p. F-11.
31. "The Digitization of TV Continues," *Broadcasting*, 28 October 1991, pp. 34–43.
32. "Here a Computer, There a Computer," *Scientific American*, September 1995, pp. 11–12.
33. "A Clear Advantage With a Hazy Outlook," *Washington Post*, 10 January 1998, p. F-2.
34. "All-New HDTV at NAB," *Broadcasting*, 13 April 1992, p. 43.
35. "PC Industry Calls For a Truce in TV Wars," *New York Times*, 6 July 1997, p. D-2. See also: "HDTV: Not Worth Losing C-SPAN," *Washington Post*, 23 July 1998, p. A-19.
36. "Internet Telephony: Growing Up," *Economist* (London), 2 May 1998, p. 56.
37. "A Couple in Sync, Airing Programs on the Internet," *Washington Post*, 10 May 1998, p. 6.
38. "Loopy.Com?" *Economist* (London), 25 July 1998, p. 61.
39. "Recasting CNN Interactive," *New Media*, August 1998, p. 58.
40. "Making AOL a Media Company," *Wired*, November 1997, p. 233.
41. Virtual reality is developing a special literature of its own. For an authoritative view of the subject for laypersons, see Howard Rheingold, *Virtual Reality*. New York: Summit Books, 1991. For a media-oriented account of the subject, see Richard B. Cutler, "Calling Up Cyberspace: On the Threshold of Telecommunications Research," Center for Research on Communications Technology and Society, University of Texas at Austin, July 1991. See also "Virtual Reality: Is It an Art Yet?" *New York Times*, 5 July 1992, p. H-1.
42. "Video Immersion: Programming Virtual Worlds," *Broadcasting*, 9 December 1991, pp. 64–72.
43. "London Zoo Is Falling Down," *Washington Post*, 2 September 1991, p. D-1.
44. "Planet of the Mind's Eye," *Economist* (London), 9 November 1991, pp. 99–100.
45. "Virtual Reality," *Washington Post*, 16 September 1992, p. H-1.
46. For a useful discussion of VR's potential, see "Virtual Reality: A Communications Perspective," a collection of seven articles in *Journal of Communication* 42, no. 4 , Autumn 1992: 5–172.

New Media Technologies: The Networks

Despite the many improvements in media technology, the industry still delivers most of its products in old-fashioned ways. Newspapers are tossed onto front porches. Magazines make their uncertain way through the postal system. Hollywood films are shipped in reel cans. Until recently, the only significant breach in these horse-and-buggy practices was the use of communications satellites for product delivery by radio, television, and cable TV networks.

In the late 1990s, however, the older media caught up with the high-tech telecommunications revolution. One goad was that their distribution methods were expensive and often unreliable. Even more important was the need to compete more effectively with the new generation of computer-based information services. Advanced telecommunications facilities are a critical element in the media industries' plans to upgrade their operations from product production to final delivery to consumers.

"Telecommunications has made information into a weightless commodity," says former London *Economist* editor Norman Macrae, surveying the role of communications technology in the modern world.[1] Increasingly, information travels at the speed of light as digitized binary digits—symbolic 1s and 0s that can represent any combination of voice, video, or print information. A fiber-optic cable can deliver a signal across the United States in thirty milliseconds.

Computers and the networks that connect them share a common electronic module: the semiconductor chip. As a result, they are converging technologically into a single machine: an integrated information utility that can deliver both old and new services electronically to mass audiences.[2] The advanced communications networks that have been built in the United States over the past two decades in order to serve business and government needs are now being consumerized, reaching down to homes and other locations.

MEDIA AND TELECOMMUNICATIONS

American media industries face complex decisions regarding adaptation of their operations to this new structure. As recently as twenty years ago, such decisions were relatively simple because the options were fewer. U.S. public telecommunications were almost synonymous with one company: AT&T. Since 1934, AT&T had enjoyed a near monopoly on national communications services, granted by the federal government in exchange for a promise to provide universal phone service, a promise that the company fulfilled. By the 1980s, as computer usage spread, it was apparent that a system dominated by a single telecommunications company could not fully serve national needs. In Chapter 4, we look at the events that led to both more open competition in the telecommunications structure and the breakup of AT&T in 1984.[3] This competitive environment has had a significant effect on the media industries, particularly in widening their distribution choices.

The new telecommunications structure is essentially an expanded, higher-performance extension of the old telephone network. Americans dial into the telephone network a billion and a half times a day. Telephones are more ubiquitous than ever, as exemplified by the explosive growth of mobile telephone services. Originally intended for use in automobiles, mobile phones are now found in shirt pockets and handbags as well. The Motorola Corporation sells an eight-ounce portable phone that can make connections with any of the world's 800 million phones.[4] Newer models, developed by AT&T and other firms, combine telephone and computer capabilities in a small, handheld unit.

The phone system's primary use is still what the engineers call POTS: Plain Old Telephone Service—that is, two people talking. Increasingly, however, the system provides other services, such as computer-data links, fax messages, and videoconferencing. Phones are now routinely equipped with sophisticated semiconductor-chip technology that makes them, in effect, limited computer terminals.[5] Phone-based communications services such as voice mail, 800 numbers, and voice-response services are already a multibillion-dollar industry. More important, telephone circuits are a critical link in providing Internet services. These innovations have an impact on the old media as phone services compete with those traditionally supplied by newspapers, magazines, newsletters, and radio.

One phone service, toll-free 800 numbers, is a threat to the advertising base of newspapers, magazines, and broadcasting stations. From small beginnings twenty years ago, 800 numbers have become an essential marketing tool, generating over $135 billion in goods and services annually in the late 1990s. The opportunity to order goods and services through free phone calls is attracting more and more consumers and at the same time cutting into traditional media advertising revenues. Toll-free calling has expanded so rapidly that the telephone industry had used up most of the 7.6 million numbers assigned to the service, forcing the FCC to authorize two new exchanges—888 and 878—for toll-free calls.[6]

FAX MACHINES: NEW MEDIA TOOL

Another telephone-based technology affecting media operations is the facsimile machine. Fax is both an important operational tool within the media industry and a newly competitive service. It is a thirty-year-old technology that has blossomed in recent years because of the introduction of low-cost, chip-filled machines with more sophisticated capabilities. Originally used to transmit documents from one business office to another, the fax machine has been consumerized,[7] making it the fastest-growing service in the new telemedia environment. Although fax is still used primarily for direct messages between individuals, it is rapidly becoming a distribution device for many kinds of information products.

"Junk fax" advertising—uninvited and generally unwanted—is a familiar example. More useful is the proliferation of information services that offer fax-on-demand information as a public service or for a fee. One typical commercial service, FaxFacts, supplies technical support, marketing information, and installation instructions from industrial companies to their customers. FaxTicker allows callers to access information on a portfolio of fifteen stocks by using their personal identification number.[8] The National Cancer Institute in Washington offers callers to its CancerFax lines a list of cancers and their symptoms.

The success of these information services has encouraged traditional media operators to experiment with fax delivery in order to reach old customers and attract new ones. The biggest users to date have been newsletter publishers, whose stock in trade is their ability to deliver specialized information to customers as quickly as possible. Fax delivery is fast replacing post office delivery as the communications channel of choice for newsletters. A variation of these services is "broadcast fax," a technique whereby messages can be sent simultaneously to thousands of fax machines across the country. Broadcast fax first came into public prominence in national election campaigns as candidates used the service to get their partisan messages quickly to newspapers, broadcasting stations, and other media outlets.[9]

Beginning in the 1980s, newspapers began testing fax delivery of their products. The nation's oldest daily newspaper, Connecticut's *Hartford Courant*, set up FaxPaper, a 1,500-word summary of stories appearing in its next day's regular edition, available to paying subscribers. "Rather than recycling information, in a sense we are precycling it," said the *Courant*'s publisher, Michael Davies.[10] Other news organizations followed up on the *Courant*'s experiment. The *Honolulu Star-Bulletin* issued a daily Japanese-language summary called "Facts Hawaii," faxed to Japanese-owned businesses in the state.[11] The *New York Times* established a daily TimesFax news service for readers in places where the daily *Times* was not readily available, including hotels overseas and cruise ships.

Newspaper fax services have grown slowly in recent years. Most experiments in delivering faxed information to the general public have not been financially successful, and those that have been successful are the ones that identified a relatively small niche market and then provided faxed information for a fee in response to specific requests. This technique, known as fax-on-demand, has been used by the *Detroit Free Press* and other newspapers around the country.[12]

ELECTRONIC NEWSPAPERS

More recently, newspapers have tested the use of notebook computers as a replacement for paper editions. One experimental model, a hand-held computer, displays a sharp, 8½-by-11-inch newspaper-style page, including color capabilities, on a thin, flat panel. The contents of electronic newspapers can be downloaded to subscribers by cable TV networks, direct-broadcasting satellites, or high-capacity telephone circuits. The subscriber makes a selection from a "front page" menu of news and features by tapping the display with an electronic pen to pick stories or sections for viewing. Eventually, electronic newspapers will have interactive capabilities. The reader could, for instance, tap an advertisement on the computer screen to order goods or services from the advertiser.

Hand-held electronic newspapers are still in the early stages of development. For the present, most electronic delivery of news is by means of the Internet and other online networks. By the late 1990s, thousands of newspapers and magazines were supplying summaries or full-text versions of their contents on America Online and other information providers.

Online news services are only one example of the advanced information delivery techniques being developed by telephone companies and other electronic networkers. This development is made possible by recent improvements in transmission technology involving both the circuits that carry the traffic and the switches that control them. The critical improvement has been the transition from analog to digital transmission, an extension of the changes taking place in computer technology (described in Chapter 2). The world's communications networks are being rapidly digitized, permitting a compatible standard for linking digital-based computers, telephones, and other electronic machines with one another. Uncounted trillions of symbolic binary digits flow through communications networks, each a coded part of a message that may involve a phone call, a credit card transaction, a TV program, or the contents of a newspaper.

Today's advanced communications circuits are generally one of two types: wireless microwave or wire cable. Microwave circuits travel through the atmosphere or (in the case of satellites) in outer space. Thanks to improved digital switches, their capacities have increased exponentially in recent decades. A communications satellite is, in effect, a microwave switch in space, capable of handling tens of thousands of telephone and data circuits, plus many video transmissions.[13]

FIBER OPTICS: MEDIA ON LIGHT WAVES

The most dramatic change in telecommunications circuits, however, involves fiber-optic cables. Fiber circuits transmit information in optical form (i.e., in light waves) along a silicon wire as thin as a human hair. Fiber wires have immense information-carrying capabilities. A single fiber cable can transmit tens of thousands of phone calls or dozens of television programs simultaneously. These cables have other useful attributes. Unlike conventional copper wires, they are unaffected by heat, moisture, or corrosion. Their light source—lasers—may be no larger than a grain of salt and may emit continuously for a hundred years.

Fiber-optic networks have a special place in the changing pattern of American mass media industries. National fiber-optic networks have existed since the early 1980s and are heavily used by the media industries for internal operations. Fiber networks are also replacing copper wire links internationally. One such network, stretching from Western Europe to Japan, went into service in 1998 with a capacity for transmitting 600,000 phone calls simultaneously. Another network, scheduled to be operative in the early years of the new century, will include nearly 100,000 miles of high-capacity fiber cables, linking seventy-four countries on all continents.[14]

The next step is to extend the network into homes and other mass-market locations, creating new opportunities for the delivery of advanced information and entertainment services to consumers. Although there are competitive technologies such as cable television and satellites, it is probable that fiber-optic cable will be used to deliver most of these media services in the coming years. Building a full-scale fiber-optic network is a massive and expensive construction project, requiring the rewiring and upgrading of large parts of the national telecommunications structure.

This involves a major economic gamble, both by the communications companies that are rebuilding the network and the media companies who will be important users of the new facilities. Estimates of the cost of installing fiber networks to serve American households run as high as $1 trillion.[15] Despite confident assurances from fiber-to-the-home enthusiasts, many experts question whether homes need the enormous circuit capacities that fiber cables can provide. Experimental fiber-optic networks offering a wide range of media services were authorized by the Federal Communications Commission more than a decade ago.

Results from these early tests were mixed. Surveys showed that most consumers think they get enough information and entertainment from their present media services—television, newspapers, and the like. They are generally reluctant to pay for access to more channels, particularly since it is often unclear to them just what the added channels will deliver.[16] Meanwhile, billions of dollars, as well as the future shape of the American media industry, will be at stake as consumers vote with their pocketbooks on the superabundance of information and entertainment that could become available in their living rooms.

Full-scale installation of fiber-optic networks to homes may be delayed, or even short-circuited, by another technology that is more immediately available. It involves the upgrading of cable television networks that use coaxial cable, the standard means of piping programs into homes for the past forty years. "Coax" has considerably less transmission capability than fiber-optic circuitry. However, its capacity can be upgraded to hundreds of channels through digital compression, a computer-driven process that squeezes more transmission capacity into existing circuits.

Digitally compressed coaxial cables are being installed by many cable system operators to expand their conventional video channels and to add new services, including digitally based interactive video, stereo music, and videotext.[17] Tele-Communications Inc., the country's largest cable system owner, has been a leader in building a digital network that will ultimately provide its customers with hundreds of channels of information and entertainment programming. The firm's 1998 merger with AT&T, a leader in installing fiber circuits, will make their combined operations a formidable competitor in supplying a full range of communication services to American homes. AT&T expanded this prospect in 1999 when it made a deal with Time Warner Inc. to provide telephone and Internet services to the 20 million homes subscribing to Time Warner's local cable systems.

The telephone and cable TV industries are competing with each other to determine which will be the primary deliverer of advanced information and entertainment services directly to homes. Both industries also face competition from entrepreneurs who want to use communications satellites to deliver these services. Each of the three groups claims superior competence to do the job. These claims form the basis for one of the most intense debates in American business history, which is currently being waged in corporate boardrooms, in the courts, and in the halls of Congress.[18]

ASSEMBLING THE NEW NETWORKS

The media industries have also been drawn into this debate over delivery systems. Broadcasters, publishers, and filmmakers see their future dependent on decisions about how and when the new high-capacity consumer networks will be built. Their concerns are well founded. Fiber-optic and advanced coaxial cable circuits will move them a giant step toward creation of the national information utility, a sophisticated network for a wide range of voice, video, and print products transmitted on a common channel to homes and other consumer locations. It is likely that the utility itself will be a hybrid mix of technologies: fiber optics, satellites, and cable TV. This will allow the telephone companies and their rivals to compete on more or less equal terms, using different networks, for the consumer information market.[19]

This network of networks will displace many of the separate circuits that now provide consumer telephone, cable TV, broadcast television, radio, and computer services. Ultimately, all information and entertainment services could be brought into homes on one common digitized channel.

This all-purpose channel will be, in the engineer's phrase, an "information pipe."[20] The question of how to set a common global technical standard for this pipe has been under debate for twenty years, mostly by obscure technical committees at the International Telecommunications Union, a United Nations agency in Geneva. By the early 1990s, the broad outlines of a common standard had been codified in international agreements identifying the kinds of computer-based software needed to operate digital networks. The new standards allow access to any kind of information—print, video, or sound—through all telecommunications networks, many of which are now technically incompatible with one another.[21]

These standard-setting agreements may appear arcane to a layperson, but they are the necessary foundation for building a universal information utility. In particular, they bear directly on media-industry decisions about adapting high-tech telecommunications to their operations. For example, as noted in Chapter 2, the broadcasting and film industries have an important stake in HDTV services transmitted on a common standard. The print industries—newspapers, magazines, and books—will be equally involved in promoting standardized delivery of advanced electronic information services.

SETTING TECHNICAL STANDARDS

This standardization will encourage new kinds of services in media markets. One of these is electronic home shopping services, a fast-growing phenomenon on the Internet and other interactive channels. Marketing goods and services in this manner provides an option for consumers that is having a direct competitive effect on newspaper, magazine, and broadcast advertising, the primary revenue source for these media.

In summary, the universal information utility puts the media industries into competition with the telephone companies and other network providers. The phone companies, in particular, have expanded their consumer information services, including the Internet, to justify the expense of building and operating expensive new facilities.

Traditionally, they had been shut out of these activities by government regulation, except for such services as weather and time-of-day information, Dial-a-Prayer, and Dial-a-Joke. This barrier was breached in 1991, after intense legal maneuvering, which led to cancellation of most information-provider restrictions by the federal courts.[22] Most of the remaining restrictions were eliminated in the Telecommunications Act of 1996, the congressional legislation that, in effect, allows phone company, cable TV, and satellite firms to compete against each other in information as well as in transmission services. As we shall see throughout this survey, these communications carriers are actively expanding into the consumer information markets, competing against newspapers, television broadcasting, and other old-line media groups.

CHOOSING NEW TECHNOLOGIES

Meanwhile, the media companies are looking at the new technological prospects, deciding which are best suited for marketing advanced digital services to households and other locations. The cable TV industry is upgrading its networks in several ways. One is to increase the capacity of their present coaxial cables by compressing the amount of digital bits that can be sent down the cable. Other companies are building a mix of these compressed coaxial facilities and fiber-optic cables that (unlike their present cables) allows them to provide a wide range of interactive voice, video, and data services.

An important part of this conversion process is adding high-speed modems, similar to those in computers, to household cable boxes. Cable modems can download services as much as a hundred times faster than the modems found in ordinary personal computers. Although there were only about 100,000 cable-modem installations in the United States in 1998, the major cable companies were marketing high-speed cable modems intensively as part of their strategy for capturing a large share of the advanced interactive-services market.[23] At the same time, information networkers such as Microsoft's WebTV, AOL, and the telephone companies were moving into the market, counting on a rapid expansion of advanced-modem-equipped households in the next few years.[24] The telephone companies have their own technical strategy for meeting this cable competition. It centers around software known as asymmetric digital subscriber line—ADSL, for short. Like the cable industry's modems, ADSL can provide a full range of high-speed digitized voice, video and data services. It has the important marketing advantage of being able to provide these services over the phone system, the country's largest communications network. As a result, there is intense competition in the phone business over who will supply the new services. AT&T and the local Bell companies are being challenged by industry upstarts with names like Starpower, Qwest, and ICG Communications. The newcomers are relying on advanced fiber-optic networks to outpace the older companies. Each of Qwest's fiber-optic cables can handle half a million phone conversations simultaneously—twelve times more than a traditional phone network.[25]

ADSL may play an important role in supplying 185 million U.S. telephone outlets with full multimedia capabilities. The prospect is too tempting for the telephone companies to fall behind its competitors for multimedia customers, despite the high conversion costs involved.[26] By 1999, ADSL field trials had been conducted in all parts of the country, with the prospect that the service would be available to most phone company customers early in the new century. "We really want to drive this to be a mass-market service," says Jeff Walduter, Bell Atlantic's technology director. "We want it to be as common as Touch-tone or caller ID."[27]

MEDIA WITHOUT WIRES

ADSL and most other high-capacity circuits that deliver interactive services into homes will use wire technology, either fiber-optic or coaxial cable. The alternative is advanced wireless systems, which transmit signals over the airwaves. The most familiar of these are mobile telephone networks. Although used primarily for voice telephony, advanced mobile phone instruments can also receive and transmit data information. Other uses of wireless technology include transmitting media services to homes via "wireless cable" on the ground and broadcasting satellites in space. Both promise to be active competitors in the delivery of media services to homes.[28]

Wireless cable is a consumer-oriented version of the microwave networks that crisscross the country, carrying telephone and data traffic. It arrived on the scene twenty years ago in cities and suburban areas that did not have conventional cable TV systems and used high-frequency microwave signals to transmit television programming to small dishes on houses and apartment buildings. Current systems, known as local multipoint distribution service (LMDS), are an expanded version of these early systems, upgraded to include a greater range of services.

LMDS wireless systems have several advantages over other delivery services. They can supply program services for the estimated 10 to 15 million homes in small towns and rural areas that are still beyond the reach of cable TV systems. Also, wireless systems are relatively cheaper to install than cable or phone networks because they transmit through the air directly to households from antenna towers and therefore bypass the expense of digging up streets to install wire cables. As a result, wireless cable systems are now being installed extensively in urban areas. Moreover, wireless systems can deliver the same menu of advanced multimedia services, including the Internet, as the upgraded wire systems.[29]

For these reasons, wireless networks have become a competitive force to be reckoned with by telephone companies, cable TV networks, and other suppliers of multimedia entertainment and information services. By 1999, LMDS multimedia services were being marketed by start-up companies in New York City and other cities across the country. More recently, Time Warner and other large media firms have moved into LMDS operations.

THE SATELLITE OPTION

The other microwave technology challenging broadcasting and cable delivery of advanced media services to homes is communications satellites. Satellites have been used by media organizations for news and entertainment transmissions since the first "birds" were sent into orbit in the mid-1960s. Media-related traffic expanded as satellites became more sophisticated and as transmission costs dropped. By the early 1990s, network television and cable TV firms were the largest customers of the almost two dozen satellites serving the U.S. market.[30]

Satellite transmission has also become an important tool for the internal operations of U.S. television stations. A National Association of Broadcasters survey estimates that local stations have an average of four satellite earth stations on their premises. One of these earth stations is usually dedicated to receiving national network programs. The others are used for local or regional services, including news "remotes," events covered by station reporters operating from satellite news-gathering vehicles.[31] Satellite news gathering gained greater technical flexibility after 1995 when a mobile satellite system, capable of providing remote coverage from any point in North America, began operations.[32]

Satellite technology has allowed U.S. television and cable operators to expand their operations abroad. The pioneer was the Cable News Network, whose programs are available live around the clock in over a hundred countries abroad. As we shall see in later chapters, all of the large television and cable networks have extensive program operations abroad, using satellite delivery of their news and entertainment products. In the cable field, for instance, HBO, ESPN, and MTV are familiar to hundreds of millions of viewers abroad.

A new dimension will be added to this kind of global media coverage in the early years of the new century. An advanced mobile satellite system, dubbed

Teledesic, will become operational, using nearly 300 satellites to provide a range of new communications services. It will be one of several American-sponsored satellite systems offering mobile telephone service between any two points on earth—a dramatic extension of ground-based cellular services. However, Teledesic will go one step further by offering video and audio services to audiences worldwide. This could open up a profitable new distribution outlet for American media enterprises.[33]

Radio stations have also benefited from advances in satellite technology. A profitable satellite delivery service is being exploited by FM radio stations that use part of their frequency assignment (known as a subcarrier) to deliver paging messages, stock quotations, and other consumer information. These messages are sent to the FM station by satellite, then retransmitted to local subscribers by telephone lines for a fee.[34]

Satellites also figure in one of radio broadcasting's latest technological advances, digital audio broadcasting, which provides a level of digital sound quality that is a distinct improvement over current FM transmissions. Satellites already deliver a significant volume of such programming, particularly music, to local radio stations. A number of satellite entrepreneurs have announced plans to deliver high-quality music programs directly to home receivers, bypassing FM stations altogether.

Meanwhile, a new generation of satellites is demonstrating its ability to compete in delivering multimedia services, including the Internet, from space to homes. The technology is direct broadcasting satellites (DBS), the fastest-growing sector of the satellite industry at the turn of the century. DBS has one unique advantage over cable systems, telephone networks, wireless systems, and its other earthbound competitors: Each of its satellites, floating 22,000 miles in space, has the capability of sending a signal to every home in the country.

This had been a technological possibility for over twenty years, ever since the development of satellites that could transmit a video signal to small earth terminals. Its introduction as a direct-to-home media service was repeatedly postponed, however, primarily because no one, including the managers of some of the nation's most prestigious media firms, was successful in putting together a financial and marketing package to exploit the technology. In the early 1980s, a dozen national DBS networks were proposed in response to a Federal Communications Commission decision to issue satellite broadcasting licenses. All of these projects failed due to a combination of inadequate technology, weak financing, and poor marketing strategies.

DIRECT BROADCASTING FROM SPACE

In the late 1990s, a new generation of advanced broadcasting satellites set the stage for a DBS comeback. Originally, DBS technology was seen as a means for reaching the 15 million American homes in rural areas not adequately served by conventional television and cable systems.[35] This is still a potentially important market, as indicated by the millions of earth stations already dotting the rural landscape.

The new DBS entrepreneurs saw a wider market involving broadcast transmissions to urban and suburban homes. Three national DBS systems—DirecTV, Primestar, and USSB—were inaugurated in 1995.[36] Programs are delivered to very small terminals, most less than two feet in diameter. Instead of the familiar round dishes, many of the new terminals are square-shaped. Known as squarials, they can be attached unobtrusively to roofs or to the sides of houses and apartment buildings.

By 1999, DBS operators had signed up over 10 million households. This was a small proportion of the national media audience, but it is expanding steadily in ways that represent a distinct threat to the cable TV industry in particular. In part, this expansion is driven by technological changes that make it possible for DBS companies to offer Internet services. By one 1998 estimate, 70 percent of new DBS satellite resources had been adapted to permit Internet access.[37]

The success of DBS networks in the next few years will depend, in part, on the parallel expansion of high-definition television (discussed in Chapter 2). HDTV can be transmitted to homes in several ways, including fiber-optic telephone lines, advanced cable TV circuits, standard broadcast channels, and by microwave on the ground or from space satellites. The new DBS networks are based on the economic premise that satellites can capture a significant share of the HDTV delivery market. Satellites have some significant advantages over other technologies in this market. Not only can they be configured to provide the extra power and spectrum bandwidth needed for HDTV, but as previously noted, they can send a signal directly to every home in the country. The successful introduction of HDTV multimedia services in the next few years will center on the question of how the market will be split among satellites, cable systems, and broadcasting stations.[38] Because satellites have some built-in advantages in supplying HDTV service, national DBS networks will be very competitive in the marketing battle to attract HDTV viewers.

Direct satellite broadcasting has been primarily the concern of the broadcast television and cable TV industries, but it has also attracted Hollywood's attention. The film industry expects to be the major supplier of the HDTV entertainment programs that are broadcast from satellites as well as by terrestrial broadcast television and cable TV. Hollywood studios are also looking at ways they can use satellites to deliver films from a central point to theaters and other locations for direct projection. Such a distribution system would eliminate projection booths as well as unionized projectionists. It would also do away with the need for hundreds of copies of films in cans and would eliminate shipping costs.

In summary, the American mass media industry is being offered a range of new technological choices for the delivery of its products. No one technology will dominate. Each has its special attributes that will make it attractive to individual consumers. Whatever the ultimate mix of technologies, the old-line media sectors will provide the largest share of the video, sound, and print products that move through the advanced networks. The leading edge of these new services will be interactive products, giving consumers a wider choice of how, when, and what information and entertainment resource will be delivered to their homes.

PREDICTING TECHNOLOGICAL CHANGE

How will the media industries restructure themselves and their products in the face of direct broadcasting satellites, HDTV, and other technological prospects? There is no simple answer. History demonstrates the unintended effects, both positive and negative, that accompany any major technological innovations in the media. A classic example can be found in historian Elizabeth Eisenstein's study of the introduction of the printing press in the fifteenth century. She notes that the early presses were intended primarily to copy treasured, old volumes, mostly religious writings. Soon, however, printers found lucrative markets for other types of publications; those additional products, covering a wide range of subjects, spurred the Renaissance and the Reformation.[39]

A generation ago, Canadian communications scholar Marshall McLuhan suggested that the dominant medium technology in any age is a powerful force in shaping the social structure by its imposition of a particular mental regimen that enables people to process the information encoded in the technology. In other words, McLuhan argued, media technology teaches us how to think.[40] Another scholar, Carolyn Marvin, advances the view that the impact of each new technology depends less on the innovative aspects of the technology itself than on the convergence of economic and social forces favoring its adoption.[41]

Predicting technological outcomes is more difficult today than ever before, as *Scientific American*'s editor in chief, John Rennie, points out:

> "The future is not what it used to be," wrote the poet Paul Valery decades ago, and it would not be hard to share his disappointment today. As children, many of us were assured that we would one day live in a world of technological marvels. And so we do—but, by and large, not the ones foretold. Films, television, books and World's Fairs promised that the twilight of the 20th century and the dawn of the 21st would be an era of helpful robot servants, flying jet cars, moon colonies, paper clothes, disease-free lives and, oh, yes, the 20-hour work week. What went wrong? . . . The truth is that as technologies pile on technologies at an uneven pace, it becomes impossible to predict what patterns will emerge.[42]

These observations are relevant to our study of the electronic future of the media industries. There is, in the economist's phrase, a "diffusion lag" that has more to do with administrative, economic, and social factors than with the capabilities of the new technologies. The videocassette boom in the 1980s was a prime example of the kind of bonanza that can occur when technology, economics, and consumer preferences converge. A small handful of media technologies will share similarly happy fates in the coming years. Many others will be laid to rest in the same technological graveyard as Sony Betamax, Atari computer games, and 3-D movies—technologies that failed to meet their promise in recent decades.

LOW-POWERED TV: USEFUL BUT UNWANTED

One example of a useful but largely unsuccessful media technology is low-powered television (LPTV). Hailed as a breakthrough in the 1980s, LPTV uses special broadcast frequencies that permit low-cost television stations to operate within a limited range of ten to fifteen miles. The idea was to allocate these short-range video channels to minority groups and public service organizations for local programming purposes. Technically, thousands of such stations could operate throughout the United States; in fact, only a few hundred are operating, and most of them are struggling to survive. Their problems stem primarily from the fact that such specialized programming cannot compete with the glitzy program offerings of commercial broadcasting and cable TV for the time and attention of most people.[43]

LPTV is a minor example of both the failure of a useful technology and the difficulty of modifying people's media habits. There is psychic resistance to giving up such media standbys as the daily newspaper, couch potato television, and the weekend trip to the movies complete with a cardboard tub of popcorn. Nevertheless, the electronic transformation of U.S. media will continue. Popular tastes and comfortable habits will change. In a postindustrial society, people will simply need more information to function in their jobs and in their private lives. The dimensions of the so-called information age are already discernible. Over 60 percent of the workforce is employed in information-related activities, including the mass media. All these activities share one characteristic: They depend on the diffusion of information and telecommunications resources. The mass media are increasingly a part of this evolving electronic national information utility. The distinctions that formerly separated one mass medium from another are blurring as all media become more dependent on shared, computer-driven delivery systems.

NEW MEDIA AND THE AMERICAN ECONOMY

This transformation toward a universal information utility is more than a matter of restructuring the media industries. The long-term health of the U.S. economy, as well as our political and social future, depends on how information resources are integrated into this utility. For the present, the United States is the global leader in setting the pace and direction of such a resource. The development of similar resources by European and Japanese industries is a significant element in their efforts to match the U.S. economy.[44]

America leads in electronics, but we cannot take too much comfort from this. There are signs of slippage, particularly in the failure to clear many of the political and economic hurdles that stand in the way of maintaining a strong position in the telecommunications and information sectors.[45] Economically, there are doubts about the U.S. industry's ability to provide the goods and services for the new consumer-based information structure. Thirty years ago, when consumer electronic products such as TV sets and radios were largely a U.S. monopoly, the answer would have been clear. The director of MIT's computer lab, Michael Dertouzos, points out that over 90 percent of all consumer electronics worldwide were produced in the United States in the early 1960s. That U.S. share has dropped to 5 percent. The largest share now is supplied by Japan and other East Asian countries.[46]

This decline in U.S.-produced consumer electronics was not accidental. We need only look at the pattern of change over the past three decades in the television receiver industry. Thirty years ago, the United States was the world's largest producer of TV sets. Within a few years, a series of corporate decisions resulted in effectively closing down most production lines in this country. In 1995, the last domestic producer of TV receivers, the Zenith Corporation, transferred its facilities to Mexico. Retailers have become totally dependent on imports (many of them bearing U.S. labels) from Asia and Latin America.

This was industrial suicide, according to Professor Dertouzos. With U.S. producers opting out, Japanese firms soon dominated global consumer markets. By the early 1990s, 70 percent of Sony's orders came from outside Japan.[47] More important, that production and marketing lead gave Japan the economic clout and technological skill to pursue advanced research in television and in other consumer electronics areas. Japan and other East Asian countries have enjoyed a strong lead in the race to supply the consumer products needed to take advantage of new technologies in the media industries. Research in HDTV equipment, for example, was pioneered largely by Japanese companies and encouraged by their government. As a result, those firms may have the edge in marketing HDTV equipment around the world. Japanese industry is making similar research gains in developing such advanced media machines as laser-based videocassettes and digital audio equipment.

Not surprisingly, the ability of U.S. companies to cope with Japanese and other foreign competition in this area has become a political issue. One side argues for economic protectionism, calling for a retreat to an electronic Fortress America. This, however, is a self-defeating strategy. A better case can be made for recognizing the critical importance of the electronics sector and for developing an aggressive strategy to surmount foreign competition with more technologically advanced products.[48] The outcome will have a critical impact on the future of U.S. media.

REVIVING AMERICAN COMPETIVENESS

There are, however, encouraging signs that the American consumer electronics sector is rebounding at home and abroad. The United States leads the world overall in semiconductor chips, the engine driving all of the sector's production. The media industries are the special beneficiaries of the advanced microchips and software that make possible its new range of multimedia products.

There are still pitfalls, however, on the road to rebuilding U.S. leadership in consumer electronics. Industry observers recall that one of the most successful products in recent decades—videocassette recorders—was invented in California by the Ampex Corporation in 1961. After that, however, Hitachi, Sony, Sharp, and a half dozen other Japanese companies outdeveloped, outproduced, and outmarketed Ampex and other American firms. The moral is that it could happen again with the new wave of advanced multimedia products.[49]

The media industries have a critical stake in how the U.S. economy deals with these changes. The transition to a new mass-communications pattern involves more than technological innovation. The new media technologies have to be fitted into the larger realities of an evolving postindustrial society.

In Chapter 4, we take a closer look at the ways in which political forces are affecting that transition.

NOTES

1. Norman Macrae, "The Next Ages of Man," *Economist* (London), special section, 24 December 1988, p. 10.
2. For discussions of the information utility concept, see "Communications, Computers and Networks," special issue of *Scientific American*, September 1991; Michael Dertouzos, "Building the Information Marketplace," *Technology Review*, 30 January 1991; Robert L. Stevenson, *Global Communications in the Twenty-First Century*. New York: Longman Publishers, 1993; and "The Death of Distance: A Survey of Telecommunications," *Economist* (London), 30 September 1995.
3. Robert W. Crandall, *After the Breakup: U.S. Telecommunications in a More Competitive Era*. Washington, DC: Brookings Institution, 1991.
4. "Motorola Plans Sale of a New Small Phone," *New York Times*, 7 August 1991, p. D-4.
5. "Phones Getting Smarter with Built-in Computer," *New York Times*, 17 April 1991, p. D-1.
6. "Popularity Takes Toll on 800 Numbers," *Washington Post*, 5 July 1995, p. A-1.
7. "Extra! Extra! Hot off the Faxes," *Business Week*, 23 December 1991, p. 84-E.
8. "Fax-on-Demand," *Infotext*, July 1991, pp. 38–48.
9. "Syscom Campaigns for the Right to Help Candidates Communicate," *Washington Post* business supplement, 2 November 1992, p. 5.
10. "First Way to Get News That's Hot off the Fax," *New York Times*, 3 July 1989, p. D-10.
11. "Gannett Plans Japanese Issues," *New York Times*, 4 November 1991, p. D-8.
12. "Papers Finding New Ways to Make Faxes a Business," *New York Times*, 6 July 1992, p. D-6.
13. For a useful survey of the prospects for wireless technology, see "From Wires to Waves," *Forbes*, 5 June 1995, pp. 125–141.
14. "20,000 Gigabits Under the Sea," *Business 2.0*, September 1998, p. 100.
15. Leland Johnson, *Common Carrier Video Delivery by Telephone Companies*, report R-4166-MF-RL Santa Monica, CA: Rand Corporation, 1992.
16. Consumer confusion over choices of advanced information services is documented in *Fiber Optics to the Home: What Does the Public Want and Need?* Donald McGannon Communication Research Center, Fordham University, May 1989.
17. "What Cable Could Be in 2000: 500 Channels," *Broadcasting*, 1 April 1991, pp. 27–28.
18. For a useful survey of the parties in the debate, see "The Information Arena," a special supplement to *Congressional Quarterly*, 14 May 1994, pp. 7–44.
19. Leland Johnson and David Reed, *Residential Broadband Services by Telephone Companies? Technology, Economics and Public Policy*, report no. R-3906-MF/RL (Santa Monica, CA: Rand Corporation, June 1990).
20. Stephen Weinstein and Paul Shumate, "Beyond the Telephone: New Ways to Communicate," *The Futurist* 23, no. 6. November–December 1989, pp. 12–16.
21. "Filling the Need for Speed," *Business Week*, 28 December 1998, pp. 50–52.
22. "Bells Win Right to Offer Information Services," *Communications Week*, 14 October 1991, p. 5.
23. "Cable Modems Really Rock," *Business Week*, 16 February 1998, p. 120E6.
24. "Faster Access Finally Gets Real," *Interactive Week*, 10 August 1998, p. 32.
25. "Building the Future-proof Telco," *Wired*, May 1998, p. 126.
26. "Bells Bearing Down on ADSL," *Interactive Week*, 12 October 1998, p. 30.

27. "Digital Subscriber Line Service: Ban the Splitter," *Tele.com*, August 1998, p. 44.
28. For a discussion of these changes, see G. A. Keyworth and Bruce Abell, *Competitiveness and Telecommunications: America's Economic Future—the House-to-House Digital Fiber-Optic Network* (Indianapolis: Hudson Institute, 1990).
29. "Integrated Wireless Service May Be Coming Soon to a Windowsill Near You," *New York Times*, 6 July 1997, p. D-3.
30. For an overview of communications satellite development in the 1990s, see "Satellite Technology: Decades of Development Pay Off," *Via Satellite*, July 1995, pp. 32–39.
31. Marcia DeSonne, *Spectrum of New Broadcast/Media Technologies*. National Association of Broadcasters, Washington, DC, March 1990, p. 23.
32. "Satellite Newsgathering," *Via Satellite*, July 1995, pp. 41–43.
33. For a useful survey of the direct-broadcasting satellite field, see "1998 Global Satellite Survey," a special issue of *Via Satellite*, July 1998.
34. DeSonne, *Spectrum*, 21.
35. Early attempts to develop DBS services are described in David Owen, "Satellite Television," *Atlantic Monthly*, June 1985, pp. 45–62.
36. "Two More Players Enter the DBS Derby," *Broadcasting & Cable*, 28 August 1995, p. 30. See also "U.S. DBS: The Competition Heats Up," *Via Satellite*, September 1995, pp. 28–34.
37. "Satellite Regulators Need to Move Cautiously On Internet Services," *Satellite News*, 3 August 1998, p. 1.
38. Leland Johnson and Deborah Castleman, "Direct Broadcast Satellites: A Competitive Alternative to Cable Television," report no. R-4047-MF/RL (Santa Monica, CA: Rand Corporation, 1991).
39. Elizabeth Eisenstein, *The Printing Press as an Agent of Change*. New York: Cambridge University Press, 1980.
40. Marshall McLuhan was a prolific writer on media subjects. His media views are summarized in *Understanding Media*. New York: New American Library, 1964. For information on the evolution of research on the effects of technology on the media, see "Mass Media Effects," in *International Encyclopaedia of Communications*, vol. 2. New York: Oxford University Press, 1989, p. 495.
41. Carolyn Marvin, *When Old Technologies Were New*. New York: Oxford University Press, 1988.
42. "The Uncertainties of Technological Innovation," *Scientific American*, September 1995, pp. 57–58.
43. DeSonne, *Spectrum*, 23.
44. These prospects are discussed in U.S. Department of Commerce, *U.S. Global Trade Outlook*, Washington DC, March 1995, pp. 121–128.
45. For a useful survey of the political and economic factors affecting telecommunications and media developments in the new global economy, see Daniel Yergin and Joseph Stanislaw, *The Commanding Heights: the Battle Between Government and the Marketplace That Is Remaking the Modern World*. New York: Simon & Schuster, 1998.
46. "Fast Forward—a Survey of Consumer Electronics," *Economist* (London), 13 April 1991, p. 18.
47. Ibid., p. 17.
48. These alternatives are discussed in U.S. Department of Commerce, National Telecommunications and Information Administration, *Telecommunications in the Age of Information*, Washington, DC, August 1991.
49. "High-tech Karma," *U.S. News & World Report*, 21 August 1995, pp. 44–46.

New Media: The Political Dimension

"America is the country which is inventing the future." These words were written a generation ago by French sociologist Michel Crozier. American influence may have diminished since in some areas, but Crozier's observation still applies in the sectors we are examining here: the old and new media in mass communications. Most of the new technologies that are setting the pace for global media changes have come out of American laboratories and are being applied here first. These innovations are not happening in a vacuum. They are nurtured by a political and cultural environment that encourages them.

It is useful therefore to look at the political and social factors that are shaping the transition from old to new media patterns in postindustrial America. The event that has had the most influence in stimulating new media developments in the past twenty years took place outside the media sector. It began with the lifting of many regulatory restraints on the U.S. telephone industry, starting with the 1984 breakup of the AT&T monopoly. The competitive telecommunications structure that has emerged since then has given the media industry a powerful incentive to develop new electronic services and modify older ones. This transition is still in its early stages; the coming decade will see its full flowering, with more far-reaching changes than in any other period in the history of U.S. mass media. The United States has become the test case for a new media environment that is taking us beyond old industrial era patterns into a postindustrial society.

This trend was first documented twenty-five years ago by Harvard sociologist Daniel Bell in a seminal book, *The Coming of Post-Industrial Society.*[1] Professor Bell forecast an America in which the production, storage, and distribution of information would be the dominant social and economic activity. His ideological thesis was given economic underpinning by two other academics, Fritz Machlup and Marc Porat, who were the first to document the growth of information-based activities in the U.S. economy.[2] Most recent research has confirmed their findings, although not without challenges to some of their conclusions.[3]

NEW MEDIA IN THE AMERICAN ECONOMY

The future of American media is directly tied to this evolving postindustrial pattern and its emphasis on information activities. It is a pattern with many strands—economic, ideological, demographic, and political. As the dominant force in mass communications, the media play a dual role, both influencing these developments and being influenced by them.

The most identifiable force acting on the media is the economy. The United States is the largest and most successful free-trade area in the world, involving a quarter-billion people. A critical part of this economic commonwealth consists of a massive information and communications infrastructure, the resource that binds the commonwealth together and makes it work. No other society is more dependent on these resources in its day-to-day activities. Americans average over a billion and a half phone calls each day: six for every man, woman, and child in the country. The economy would be immobilized if there were a serious national disruption of telephone and computer networks. The media industries are increasingly vulnerable, given their greater dependence on electronic resources to produce and distribute their products.

Beyond economics, the mass media in the new information-based environment are sustained by a national ideology. It is embodied in the First Amendment and the cat's cradle of laws, regulations, and practices that the amendment has fostered over the course of two centuries. The decision of the writers of the Constitution that government should not license or otherwise control the press was revolutionary in an era when such controls were taken for granted. Today it is still a unique proposition in most parts of the world. Despite setbacks, the First Amendment is a remarkable force, now expanded to include all forms of public information resources from television to computerized data banks. Its power is complemented and energized by another American belief—that of salvation through technology. The idea that technology and democratic ideals can combine to form a new kind of society has been a continuing theme from the time of Ben Franklin and his kite to the high-tech laboratories of today.[4]

Such is the tradition within which the mass media are adjusting to their new role in postindustrial America. They must adapt old ways of doing business—and even their identities—to the realities of a stunning array of technological prospects. New media technologies have always been disruptive, from the Gutenberg printing press to present-day electronics.[5] There is, however, a difference in the current transition. Previously, media innovations developed slowly, separated by many years, allowing time to adjust new techniques to existing social realities. In contrast, we are now witnessing the simultaneous convergence of a wide range of media technologies. The time allotted for sorting out their political and economic implications has been dramatically shortened.

This change has complicated the traditional pattern in which the existing media organizations try to slow down the introduction of threatening new technology. They do this to protect their entrenched interests, usually through a combination of political and economic pressures. In the early days of radio broadcasting, for instance, newspapers refused to run program schedules in the hope of discouraging listenership. When television was new, the major Hollywood studios would not sell films to the networks. In these and similar instances, the boycotts ended only after the economic interests of the contending parties—the challengers and the defenders—were satisfactorily accommodated. This pattern of resistance and eventual accommodation is being repeated in the current wave of new media technologies. The outcome will shape the future pattern of the U.S. mass media industries. It is useful to examine the interplay of the economic and political elements that will influence the tone and direction of both the old and the new media in the coming decade.

The media are part of a $500 billion communications sector (see Table 4.1) in which nearly all information and entertainment products compete in the marketplace. Commercialism has been the hallmark of the U.S. media industries almost from the beginning. In the early days of the republic, newspapers were often subsidized directly by political parties or other factions. That practice faded with the rise of the penny press and other publishing ventures that depended on mass-circulation revenues rather than on direct patronage and subsidies.[6]

TABLE 4.1   Advertising, End-User, and Specialty Media Spending

Year	Advertiser Spending	Consumer Spending	Institutional End-User Spending	Specialty Media Spending	Total
1992	$ 96,523	$ 76,704	$ 57,648	$ 67,546	$298,421
1993	100,926	82,237	61,041	73,008	317,213
1994	109,937	87,670	64,560	78,427	340,593
1995	117,213	92,910	69,127	85,041	364,291
1996	126,859	99,893	75,286	88,997	391,036
1997	136,889	106,279	81,206	98,703	423,077
1998	149,045	114,664	87,669	107,290	458,668
1999	161,040	122,581	95,046	115,130	493,797
2000	177,760	131,881	102,993	124,390	537,025
2001	189,490	141,379	110,871	132,050	573,790
2002	204,300	150,497	119,094	139,850	613,741

SOURCES: Veronis, Suhler & Associates, Wilkofsky Gruen Associates

BARRIERS TO NEW TECHNOLOGIES

In the last century, the introduction of the new electricity-based technologies created tensions between the old and new media that are still with us. As media historian Erik Barnouw points out:

> Euphoric predictions greeted the advent of Morse's telegraph and the communication wonders that followed it—telephone, wireless, radio, television and the others. Each was seen to have a special significance for a democratic society: each seemed to promise wider dissemination of information and ideas. It can be argued that this has happened, as predicted. But other results, in a contrary direction, were not so readily foreseen. Each new medium offered new possibilities for the centralization of influence and control, and introduced monopoly possibilities.[7]

The managers of the new technologies did, in fact, attempt to establish monopolies in ways that threatened the existing media. The Western Union telegraph company, a monopoly in its early years, withdrew its services from newspapers that criticized its policies.[8] Decades later, the American Telephone and Telegraph Co. (now AT&T) attempted to take over commercial radio broadcasting until it was forced by the federal government to abandon the effort. Similar actions were taken by the government in the late 1930s to modify the control that the big radio networks exercised over the programming aired on local stations.

THE COMMUNICATIONS ACT OF 1934

These early federal government efforts to manage the introduction of new media technologies had, on balance, a beneficial effect. They led to the passage of the first national law to deal with the electronic technologies, the Communications Act of 1934. For over sixty years the 1934 act defined the basic ground rules for U.S. telecommunications and for the electronic media, until it was replaced in 1996 by new legislation. Given the relatively primitive technology of the era, the 1934 act dealt only with telephone and telegraph systems and radio broadcasting.

Nevertheless, the act served to establish a social consensus among government, industry, and public interest groups on the role of communications and information resources in U.S. life. Most important, it mandated the goal of universal telephone service—a bold objective considering how few telephones there were at the time. It also created the Federal Communications Commission to regulate the telecommunications industry and radio. The commission's regulatory powers were later expanded to include newer technologies: television, cable TV, satellite broadcasting, and the like.

The 1934 Communications Act ushered in a period of relative stability for the electronic media that lasted more than thirty years. This was a period of expansion and general prosperity for the media industries. FCC regulation of broadcasting was generally benign and focused largely on protecting the industry from outside competition.[9]

It was the heyday of the traditional mass media—newspapers, radio, film, and (after World War II) television. By the 1960s, however, rumblings of change had begun. Radio declined as a nationally networked medium, retreating before the mass appeal of television. Cable TV expanded from its origins as a small-town relayer of broadcast television and began to develop its own programming resources. Its status as a major medium was confirmed in the mid-1970s when cable programmers began using satellites to distribute an expanded schedule of sports and entertainment products simultaneously across the country, similar to the broadcasting network pattern.

THE BIG BUSINESS OF MEDIA

Another less visible development had important consequences for the media industries in those years: It was the new perception of the media as big business. In the late 1990s, communications, in aggregate, was the seventh-largest industry in the American economy. If measured by compound annual growth standards, it ranked second. With some exceptions, the annual growth rate in individual media sectors during the 1990s rose steadily, in many cases doubling over a five-year period.[10]

The U.S. financial community came to view the media as something more than a collection of separate, unrelated enterprises. It also recognized that the industry's assets, by Wall Street standards, were generally undervalued. This sparked an interest in mergers, buyouts, and other proposals for consolidating media operations into larger and potentially more lucrative combinations. The result has been major changes in the ownership and operational patterns of many old-line media businesses. These firms first became hot properties in the great bull market of the 1980s. Companies changed hands, often at inflated prices, which led to heavy debt loads. Many media organizations were adversely affected, even wiped out, during the persistent economic recession of the early 1990s.

Another consequence of the new investment interest in mass communications was the emergence of a new breed of media managers. As a group, these entrepreneurs were intent on gaining control over a range of media services they could market in ways that would provide profitable synergies among their products. The result was a spate of takeovers and consolidations by "information packagers." The merger of Time Inc. and Warner Communications in 1989 formed the world's largest multimedia conglomerate. It was a position Time Warner held until the August 1995 merger of Capital Cities–ABC and the Walt Disney organization and then recaptured when the firm acquired Ted Turner's multimedia assets a few weeks later.

Along with other information packagers such as Rupert Murdoch of News Corporation, Sumner Redstone of Viacom, and Telecommunication Inc.'s John Malone, Time Warner expanded the information packaging concept to international markets.[11] Multimedia packaging took on a new dimension in 1998 when

AT&T acquired Telecommunications Inc. (TCI), the country's second-largest cable system. For the first time, one major company had resources to deliver a full range of media services to most American homes.[12]

DEREGULATING COMMUNICATIONS

The reorganization of the U.S. telecommunications sector over the past twenty years reflects new social and economic realities, a transformation brought about largely by federal government decisions designed to make the sector more competitive by removing or modifying regulatory restraints on its operation. These moves ended the virtual monopoly over national communications networks that had been granted to AT&T in the Communications Act of 1934.

The deregulatory process began in 1968 when the FCC ruled against AT&T claims that only equipment made by the firm's manufacturing subsidiary, Western Electric, could be used in its network. (The company's imperious attitude was reflected in its characterization of non–Western Electric equipment as "foreign devices.") A year later, MCI, then a struggling young telephone firm, was given permission by the FCC to operate the first interstate long-distance network in competition with AT&T. Over the next dozen years, the AT&T monopoly was gradually cut back in a series of decisions by the FCC and the courts. Finally, in 1982, AT&T agreed to divest itself of its local telephone operations in order to settle a long-standing U.S. Justice Department antitrust case against the company. As part of the settlement, the company was given permission to compete in other kinds of communications and information businesses previously denied to it.[13]

The media industries have benefited immensely from these changes in the national communications network, particularly because they speeded up the introduction of advanced new services. The old monopolist, AT&T, is still the major player in U.S. telecommunications, competing with thousands of firms, each offering new services or improving on old ones. AT&T added to the diversity in 1995 by splitting itself up into three companies. The result of these changes is that a new mix of technologies, entrepreneurs, and audiences is reshaping U.S. mass communications.[14]

By the end of the 1990s, the media industries were in a state of splendid disarray as a result of these changes. Old-line firms were positioning themselves, with some hesitation, for life and profitability in the new environment. This involved formidable obstacles, beginning with the high cost of modernizing media facilities.

Media industries also faced demographic challenges as the postwar baby boomers—the media targets of the 1980s—settled into two-paycheck families with responsibilities that left less time for such activities as reading and TV viewing.[15] Another demographic reality, critical to the industry's long-term strategy, is that over two-thirds of U.S. population growth in the next fifteen years will be accounted for by minority groups: African Americans, Hispanics, and Asians.

The strongest trend within these groups is rapid growth within the Hispanic community, a segment largely ignored by mass media organizations until recently.[16]

THE FIRST AMENDMENT IN A NEW AGE

The federal government's decision to deregulate the national communications structure has had, as noted earlier, a major economic impact on the mass media. This decision also subtly changed the political balance between government and media, particularly in the sensitive area of media freedoms. The First Amendment's prohibitions against political interference with media remain a formidable barrier against direct government intervention. There is no guarantee, however, against more indirect kinds of interference.

The First Amendment appears to be an absolute prohibition: "Congress shall make no law . . . abridging the freedom of speech, or of the press." This is more easily understood in its original eighteenth-century context than in today's more complex communications environment. The media industries still want First Amendment protection of their freedom from government intrusion, but at the same time they press for government-mandated advantages at all levels. They have sought and won lower postal rates, favorable radio spectrum allocations, exemptions from wage-and-hour laws for newspaper deliverers, and antitrust relief for newspapers, among other concessions. Special privileges for the media, granted by government, are a long-standing tradition and are almost always justified by a somewhat tenuous appeal to the First Amendment.

On the other hand, federal, state, and local governments have their own agendas in dealing with the media. This often reflects a sensitivity to the media's self-appointed role as watchdog over public policies and actions.[17] Occasionally, that sensitivity erupts into active political pressure on the media. One notorious example was the Nixon administration's attempt in the early 1970s to intimidate the television industry with regulatory threats because of the industry's alleged opposition to the administration's policies. The campaign was led by Vice President Spiro Agnew, who attacked the New York networks as "a concentration of power over American public opinion unknown in history." More recent official attempts to put pressure on the media have usually been more subtle.[18]

The government will continue to play an active role in media affairs—as lawmaker, regulator, and supplier of public services. Such government involvement is inevitable as American society becomes more dependent on information resources, including the media, to survive and thrive in a postindustrial era. A study sponsored by Harvard University's Institute of Politics describes the development as the transition to an "electronic commonwealth." The study sees the new communications technologies as a critical factor in determining whether democratic government in the United States can adapt to the complexities of a postindustrial society.[19]

The political issues involved in the transition go well beyond protecting First Amendment rights of expression, however important that may be. Federal and state governments regulate public telecommunications systems and other areas of the economy that affect the media. Washington bureaucracies also finance, directly or indirectly, the development of many of the new information technologies on which the media depend. Government at all levels sets standards affecting the media in such areas as environmental controls, tax regulations, workplace safety rules, and data privacy protection. New electronic services have placed increasing pressures on the radio spectrum, a natural resource that is managed by the federal government and is critical to broadcasting and other media operations.

The media industries have also become an important element in U.S. trade policy in recent years. Information and entertainment products and services represent one of the largest net export earners in U.S. international trade. This advantage will probably be maintained in the coming years, although it may diminish as the stake of foreign companies in U.S. media operations increases. The most publicized and controversial example of this was the takeover of several large Hollywood studios by Japanese firms in the late 1980s.[20] More recently, Bertlesmann, a German publisher largely unknown to Americans, has acquired a major stake in the U.S. book publishing industry, including its 1998 acquisition of Random House.[21]

POLICY CHOICES IN THE INFORMATION AGE

The government's involvement in media-related issues, both direct and indirect, is becoming more pervasive. There are fundamental public policy issues involved in the decisions now being made about the shape and direction of information resources, including the mass media. The litmus test for judging these government policies on media issues is whether they help or hinder the prospects for greater access to the information we need to thrive, individually and collectively, in a more complex democratic society. In the United States, this test usually occurs in the marketplace, which sets a monetary value on information whether it is the price of a daily newspaper or data on a compact disc.

The marketplace will continue to drive the development of media resources in the new digital environment. There are no longer any serious barriers to the creation of a full-scale information utility in which the mass media will play an important role. The technologies needed for the venture are tested and available. We are now crossing the economic divide as well. This is evident from the extraordinary expansion of competitive new information resources in recent years. The major unresolved issues now are political and social, involving public decisions on the form and purpose of the new information structure.[22]

These political decisions are not simple, constrained as they must be by First Amendment limits on government involvement. They go against the powerful impetus to let the marketplace decide, based on past American success in generating the most extensive information resources any society has yet developed. The marketplace is, however, powered by its own internal dynamics, dealing with particular outcomes based largely on bottom-line standards governing economic growth.

Is reliance on market economics enough to ensure the information resources we need for a postindustrial democracy? The basic issue is power, particularly power to control information. That issue takes on greater urgency these days, given the tendency of many new technologies to foster centralization and manipulation of a wider range of information resources whether by government or by private entities. This fact argues against our present inclination to assign most decisions in the communications and information fields to the marketplace. Former AT&T board chairman John DeButts defined the issue when he said, "It is not technology that will shape the future of telecommunications in this country. Nor is it the market. It is policy."[23]

BALANCING GOVERNMENT'S ROLE

Which policy is the issue—hands-off by government or more involvement? The First Amendment is an important standard, but it is not a blueprint for building an advanced information structure. It was never meant to be one. As communications scholar Ithiel de Sola Pool has pointed out, the writers of the Constitution did not take an absolutist approach to government's role in information. Their constitutional injunctions were somewhat contradictory, but their goals were quite consistent. In one clause the government was told to keep its legislative hands off speech and press, while in two other clauses it was told to promote the conveyance of knowledge by means of copyright laws and the postal service. Both injunctions have the same objective: assuring open access to information by all citizens.[24]

Professor Pool's point is important to remember as we dig deeper into decisions about the future form and direction of information resources, including the mass media. Ensuring a workable outcome is not a zero-sum game, a legalistic choice between rights and wrongs. It calls for a broadened policy debate that includes both the public and private sectors. The purpose of the debate should be to arrive at a national consensus beyond particularistic interests. The critical question is how we can build on the legacy of two centuries of information freedoms in ways that ensure a communications structure suited to the needs of a democratic postindustrial society.

The mass media are an important part of this consensus, both as active participants defending their own interests and as public recorders and analyzers of the debate. The media industries find themselves on familiar ground in this debate, given their continuing and often confrontational relations with political authorities on issues involving First Amendment freedoms.

The government has seldom resorted to the kind of cynical, direct efforts at intimidation and control exhibited by the Nixon administration in its attack on the television broadcasters in the 1970s. Media relations with government are not always confrontational. More often, media firms have sought the government's help and protection against other media. A good example is the attempt by over-the-air broadcasters in the early 1990s to curb, through congressional legislation, what they regarded as unfair competition by the cable television and telephone industries in providing advanced information services.

It was a classic case of the government being asked to serve as referee in settling competing claims between an older medium and newer ones. In such cases, both sides loftily claim First Amendment rights even when their proposals, directly or indirectly, call for imposing controls on the media operations of their opponents.[25]

Appeals for government intervention are likely to become more strident as new forms of high-tech information products challenge powerful existing media. The trend will be complicated, as it is now, by the fact that there is no central agency, no "Department of Communications," in the federal government with overall policy or regulatory authority in this area. Decision making is scattered among a dozen major Washington agencies, the Congress, state and local agencies, and, ultimately, the courts. The resultant confusion can be salutary in that it helps diffuse political power in this sensitive area.[26]

This fragmentation of responsibilities was compounded in the 1990s by the lack of up-to-date legislative guidelines defining the government's relationship to the electronic media at a time when technology and economics were eroding all the old rules. The 1934 Communications Act laid down a useful foundation for national communications policy, but its frame of reference was the technology and economics of a simpler time. The congressional framers of the 1934 legislation could not have anticipated the massive changes that took place in media and telecommunications, such as television, cable systems, satellites, and data networks.

An attempt was made in the 1970s to bring the 1934 legislation up to date. The effort stalled after hundreds of hours of congressional committee hearings over a period of five years. The communications structure had become so complex that a consensus could not be reached among all the public and private interests, including the media industries that have a stake in setting new directions in national communications policy. As a result, the 1934 law was modified piecemeal over the years, primarily to establish some ground rules for integrating new technologies into the communications structure.

THE TELECOMMUNICATIONS ACT OF 1996

It was not until the early 1990s that another attempt was made to bring the 1934 legislation up to date in ways that reflected technological and economic realities in a new information-age environment. This push to rewrite the old law was given momentum by the Clinton administration's "information highway" initiative, which focused public attention on the need for advanced communications resources in an increasingly information-dependent society.

The guiding spirit for the information highway initiative was Vice President Al Gore, who, in his years as a senator from Tennessee, had sponsored the first legislation that gave serious attention to information-age issues. The Clinton–Gore initiative was politically popular, drawing bipartisan support. Republicans in Congress scrambled to get on the information-highway bandwagon, motivated in part by surveys showing that registered Republicans were the heaviest subscribers to online services. When he was Speaker of the House, Newt Gingrich, a self-styled conservative futurist, challenged Vice President Gore as Washington's leading cheerleader for cyberspace programs.[27]

There were other pressures for Congress to act on new legislation, particularly from the business community. Communications companies, including the media, wanted relief from government restrictions that, they argued, limited their ability to compete for business opportunities in areas opened up by new technologies. Although the federal government had removed a number of regulatory barriers in the 1970s and 1980s, many companies in the telephone, cable TV, and broadcasting sectors were still restricted from operating outside their traditional business, even though electronic technologies were converging into a single digital standard.

The drafting of a comprehensive new law took four years, from 1992 to 1996. The result was the Telecommunications Act of 1996. The legislation reflects a series of compromises and accommodations among the major industries affected by its provisions. The long-distance phone companies (AT&T, MCI, and Sprint) lobbied hard to limit the ability of the regional Bell companies (the "Baby Bells") to compete in their markets. The broadcasting and cable TV industries in turn tried to limit phone company plans to develop their own information and entertainment services.

The telecommunications and media industries spent tens of millions of dollars in advertising and direct lobbying to influence the legislation. One senator, Larry Pressler, a Republican from South Dakota, received almost a half-million dollars, mostly from corporate political action committees, in one six-month period in 1995. Scores of other representatives and senators from both parties were the beneficiaries of similar corporate largesse.[28]

The result was a flawed law. At one level, it serves a useful purpose in defining the ground rules for a more competitive environment within the telecommunications and media industries. At another level, the new communications act is filled with special-interest provisions, benefiting particular corporations, that will have the effect of stifling competition.[29] Little attention was paid by Congress to public interest groups who lobbied for a strong commitment in the law to universal access to advanced communications facilities for ordinary citizens.[30]

BEYOND THE TELECOMMUNICATIONS ACT

The new legislation set the stage for some of the most far-reaching changes in the history of American media. By dropping most of the regulatory restrictions on the telecommunications industry, the Baby Bells, cable TV operators, and long-distance companies were permitted to invade each other's turf. The 1996 communications act also relaxed restrictions on the broadcasting industry, particularly those that limited the number and types of local stations individual companies could own. For the media industries in general, the legislation expanded the number of consumer outlets for products and services, particularly as phone companies and cable networks move into a new stage of competition for consumer information and entertainment services.[31]

Nevertheless, the new legislation fell considerably short of being a comprehensive plan for creating a universal information utility available to all citizens. One provision of the 1996 law called for supplying Internet links to all U.S. schools and libraries. By 1998, the Schools and Libraries Corp., a public group set up to manage the project, had received over $2 billion in requests to provide such links. The project was stalled, however, by telecommunications industry complaints that the project was too costly. It was an egregious example of how corporate interests could take precedence over broader social considerations in carrying out the law's provisions.[32]

If the rhetoric of corporate executives during congressional hearings was to be believed, the bill's passage would have triggered a massive rush to multimedia competition in the communications industries. This did not happen. The fact is that most of the industry liked the old regulatory rules which were designed over the years to protect, not limit, their operations. These firms had prospered in a world in which regulation was more important than competition. The new legislation raised for them the specter of agile new companies, upsetting old ways of doing business. These upstarts wanted to replace copper wire with fiber, replace normal telephony with the Internet, and capture customers with aggressive marketing. It was an uncomfortable prospect for the old-line firms, and they tried to hold off its consequences.

Instead of competing with one another, they adopted a two-track strategy to resist the new competitive rules. At one level, they went to court to block competition to their existing operations. In particular, the local Bell telephone companies argued in defense of their right to compete in long-distance services while challenging the plans of long-distance firms like AT&T and MCI to provide local services, as envisioned in the congressional legislation. These legal maneuverings continued at the turn of the century.

Second, many of the big communications companies tried to fend off competition by merging or forming alliances among themselves to consolidate their service regions. By 1999, the number of Bell regional phone companies had been reduced from seven to four through such mergers. As Eli Noam, a Columbia University communications specialist notes, "They have ended the notion of territoriality within business segments. Managers used to eat the other guy for breakfast; now they are inviting him over *for* breakfast."[33]

The 1996 legislation assumed that the industry would move quickly toward multimedia operations, taking advantage of the new digital technologies. Instead, the new spate of mergers and acquisitions was based largely on preserving the old single-media pattern. The takeover frenzy reached its height in 1997 and 1998. In the space of ten months, mergers and alliance-building deals worth $250 billion were concluded in the U.S. communications industry.[34]

The corporate justification for these moves was, in essence, that bigger is better and that consolidation of resources will result eventually in better service to consumers. In fact, most of the mergers since 1996 have been based on somewhat less altruistic motives, such as boosting stock prices and cutting costs to raise profits. Consumer complaints to the FCC about telephone and other services soared 25 percent in 1997.[35]

THE RISE OF INTERNET POLITICS

Meanwhile, Congress and government agencies at both the federal and local levels have been addressing problems related to the extraordinary expansion of the Internet.[36] The key issue has been the easy availability of access to pornographic Web sites by children. In 1996, Congress passed a Communications Decency Act, restricting access to vaguely defined, indecent material on the Internet. The law was struck down by the Supreme Court in 1997 on First Amendment grounds. More recently, Congress has debated a law mandating technology that allows parents to block out what they consider to be objectionable Web sites.[37]

Another issue, which affects the media industries more directly, is how to tax Internet services. As tax-free electronic commerce expands into a multibillion-dollar business, the loss of revenues is being felt by the nation's 30,000 taxing jurisdictions, from the U.S. Treasury to small-town tax collectors. The National Governor's Association has been particularly aggressive in calling for national regulations for collecting electronic-commerce taxes. The Clinton administration and business groups have generally advocated postponing a decision, using the argument that it would be wrong to burden Internet trade with tax regulations early in its development. In 1998, a compromise moratorium was reached that postponed any Internet tax legislation for several years.[38]

Political decisions on these Internet-related subjects will have an impact on how fast and how far new digital services will be introduced. The basic technology is available, and the entrepreneurial urge to exploit its potential is strong, particularly among the new start-up companies. However, as the recent spate of industry mergers shows, the major levers of power are still in the hands of a relatively small number of corporations that have the resources to dictate the pace and direction of communications growth. They will continue to make deals among themselves to accommodate their own economic interests.

The mass media industries have a big stake in how this pattern works out in the next few years. We will look at its current and potential developments as it affects individual media sectors—broadcasting, cable TV, publishing, and film—in the chapters that follow. Two basic questions have to be resolved before a full-service advanced network can become a reality: Who will build the new utility? How can it be organized to ensure equitable access by consumers? These issues are, of course, related. For the present, the question of access has been overshadowed in the fierce competition for rights to build the network.

BUILDING THE INFORMATION UTILITY

The chief contenders to build the information utility are the cable television and telephone industries. There is also a third competitor in the wings: the direct-broadcast satellite industry. This latter group is made up of companies building satellite networks that transmit advanced information and entertainment services directly into small earth stations mounted on houses and apartment buildings. As noted in Chapter 3, DBS networks have an advantage over telephone and cable TV systems in that they can transmit a signal directly into every U.S. home. Beaming programs from 22,000 miles away in space, the satellites have a "footprint"— their coverage area—that includes the entire country, as well as parts of Canada and Mexico.

DBS services were slow in entering the market, mostly because of delays in developing a successful economic formula for making them work. The technology has been available for over twenty years, but full-service DBS networks did not become fully operational in the United States until the mid-1990s. Currently, there are three operational DBS systems serving U.S. households. Within a few years, they will have competition from a new generation of advanced satellites providing a mix of voice, video, and data services. Among the companies planning such services in the late 1990s were Microsoft, Boeing, Lockheed Martin, Motorola, and General Electric.[39]

The DBS networks will be part of the evolving information utility, but it is doubtful that they will overtake the lead currently enjoyed by telephone and cable TV networks in the race to provide advanced multimedia services to U.S. homes.[40] Industry analysts estimate that over 10 million households will have subscribed to DBS programming by the turn of the century.

The telephone and cable TV industries bring special strengths to building the new information infrastructure. Over 11,000 cable systems directly serve two-thirds of U.S. homes; cable lines pass by another 30 percent of homes that are not cable subscribers. Most cable systems already provide sixty or more channels of information and entertainment programming. That capacity is being doubled or tripled, using the same cables, through the digital compression techniques described in Chapter 2. Many cable systems are currently being upgraded so that they can provide any form of interactive video, sound, or print services.

Telephone companies have equally impressive qualifications, including more than a century of experience in wiring the 95 percent of U.S. households that subscribe to their services. The companies also have a long history of supplying specialized information services, ranging from weather reports to Dial-a-Prayer. Their laboratories have pioneered most of the technologies needed for a high-capacity consumer information utility. The Bell Laboratories, developed by AT&T and now part of Lucent Technologies, were responsible for the basic research that led to transistors, communications satellites, and fiber-optic cables, among other technologies. AT&T and other phone companies have installed millions of miles of fiber cables throughout the country, gradually replacing much of the 200 million miles of copper wire in the national phone system. The phone companies also have the financial resources to undertake what will be the largest single construction project ever built by any U.S. industry. As a result, consumer information channels and services will be a primary area of U.S. economic growth well into the new century as each sector of the telecommunications industry—telephony, cable TV and satellites—builds its version of an advanced information highway.

THE MEDIA'S STAKE IN THE INFORMATION UTILITY

The media industries are directly involved in these changes, both as users of newly expanded communications facilities and as active participants in developing advanced information services. Although the telephone and cable TV industries are the leading contenders, the mass media and other information producers cannot be dismissed as future challengers. Media firms in television, films, and publishing are beginning to assess the long-term impact of a high-capacity, integrated information network, as we shall see in later chapters when we discuss individual media sectors. Even more intriguing is the entry of new media entrepreneurs, particularly consumer database providers such as America Online and Microsoft's MSN. They are now positioning themselves to compete with the older media in video and audio services.

Despite the promise of long-term financial rewards from the new network, Wall Street and other financial centers have often been wary about funding new information utility projects. Their reluctance stems from a familiar management dilemma in dealing with expensive new facilities: Which should come first—market demand or a fully functioning system? The conventional answer is market demand. However, the communications industries face the fact that consumer demand for the kinds of new or expanded information services has generally been weak. Moreover, the potential market is demographically skewed. Industry analysts estimate that, at the end of the 1990s, 1 percent of U.S. multimedia customers accounted for 30 percent of the business.[41]

These marketing realities worry mass media firms as they try to measure the potential demand for new information and entertainment product. It is small comfort to them to suggest that, eventually, consumers will want the new services. The immediate question facing the industry is whether to spend large sums of money now to develop high-tech products for a market that may take a long time to mature.[42]

TIMETABLE FOR THE ADVANCED NETWORK

A full-scale consumer information utility will probably not begin to emerge until well into the first decade of the new century. Even when the legal and political issues are sorted out, the problem of assembling the capital investment needed for the project will be formidable. Two hundred billion dollars is an optimistic estimate for completing a fiber-optic network reaching into most U.S. homes; a more realistic estimate, according to many experts, is a half-trillion dollars.

How will the new network evolve? The 1996 Telecommunications Act set general ground rules under which communications companies would compete in assembling the network. It did not, however, lay out any definitive plan on what the system should look like, or when it should be completed.

A reasonable prediction is that the multimedia consumer network will be built in two phases: a limited grid early in the new century and a full-service information utility by the year 2010. The interim network will be made up of competitive networks—telephone, cable, and satellite broadcasting—each seeking a stake in an expanded electronic information and entertainment market. This arrangement of networks would establish a base for the evolution of a more advanced information utility later, which would widen the range of services as demand grows.

How will this full-scale utility evolve? Will it evolve at all? Might not consumers be satisfied with the limited expansion of services promised in the next few years? These are practical questions that must wait for marketplace answers. The answers will determine the shape and direction of the mass media industries well into the next century.[43]

The leading technology of choice for the full network will probably be fiber-optic cable, barring another major (and unanticipated) technological breakthrough in information delivery. Fiber cable services to the home will require a massive expansion of the fiber networks that currently serve mainly business and government needs. The economics and technical capabilities of this advanced system are proven. The question now is how and when to extend the network efficiently to over 100 million households, schools, and other consumer locations.[44]

Which industry will eventually gain the upper hand in providing a full-service network? Separate fiber-optic links to homes by the phone and cable TV companies would be an unnecessarily expensive, and wasteful, solution. Simple efficiency argues for a single high-capacity wire, which suggests that the telephone industry may become the dominant provider of fiber cable for homes. The phone companies generally have more technical experience with fiber systems. Moreover, they have greater financial resources, with annual revenues five times those of the cable TV industry. Another possibility is that the fiber-optic utility will be developed jointly by cable TV and telephone companies, each providing different services that share a single line. This option has already been tested in several U.S. cities.[45] Such a partnership could hasten construction of the network, particularly if the phone companies are given financial incentives (in the form of accelerated depreciation of their investment) to build their part of the grid.[46]

THE FIRST AMENDMENT IN A MULTIMEDIA WORLD

The eventual resolution of the issue may turn on an important constitutional principle. For the first time, we are dealing with what may be called a multimedia First Amendment issue: information rights in a technological system in which all kinds of communications resources will be squeezed into a two-way information pipe (e.g., fiber cable) for delivery to U.S. living rooms and other consumer locations. This involves a significant extension of First Amendment principles, well beyond the guarantees to information access developed over the past two centuries. The modern reformulation of the First Amendment is known as the Associated Press principle after a 1943 antitrust action brought by the U.S. Justice Department against the Associated Press (AP) news agency. In deciding against AP, the court asserted that the First Amendment's underlying premise is to foster "the widest possible dissemination of information from diverse and antagonistic sources." In his opinion in the AP case, Judge Learned Hand said:

This principle presupposes that right conclusions are more likely to be gathered out of a multitude of tongues, than any kind of authoritative selection. To many, this is, and always will be, folly; but we have staked our all on it.[47]

The new information utility makes possible an unprecedented expansion of Judge Hand's multitude of tongues: thousands of channels of information in voice, video, and print formats. The First Amendment purpose is to guarantee full access to the utility by both the providers and the users of its information. There are, however, few direct precedents for determining the information utility's role in maintaining First Amendment rights in the coming years.[48]

For the immediate future, that role will be defined by political decisions on how the new utility is to be organized. As noted earlier, the utility will be a network of networks in its early years, involving telephone, cable, and satellite circuits. Such diversity gives useful assurance of competitive information channels. However, it does not in itself guarantee First Amendment rights. To protect these rights, the utility will have to be organized as some form of common carrier, the regulators' term for a system that provides nondiscriminatory access for all users. The classic example, of course, is the telephone network, open to all who pay their phone bill at the end of the month.

In summary, some variation of the common carrier telephone system will be the best model for ensuring First Amendment freedoms in any future information utility. This fact seems to strengthen the case for strong phone company participation in building and operating the new utility. Both the phone and cable TV companies will still be monitored regarding the information and entertainment services they can own or lease. The result will be an imperfect formula for ensuring a wide variety of information resources available to consumers. Economist Leland Johnson argues that any limitations placed on the telephone and cable TV industries should be roughly comparable in the interests of providing competitive symmetry and encouraging diversity of services.[49]

The eventual pattern of a full-scale information utility is difficult to predict. It will emerge from a series of political compromises that satisfy the interests of the industries involved. Government intervention in the process will always be problematical, but it will be necessary. The London *Economist* notes:

As the transmission of information is increasingly digitized, the boundaries between the telephone, the television and the computer are blurring. Put the three together and all sorts of unpredictable new products and services start to evolve from the fun of television, the brain and memory of the computer, and the two-or-more-way human contact of the telephone. How fast this new world arrives will depend on governments.[50]

The ultimate test of the new information utility will be its power to strengthen First Amendment freedoms. Will the media and other information providers be free to supply a full range of competitive information resources? Is there reasonable and affordable access by all Americans to these services? This latter consideration will be critical. Americans are accustomed to cheap (or even free) access to consumer information services, from public libraries to inexpensive newspapers. The new electronic services, involving expensive equipment, may jeopardize that tradition. We may be moving toward what communications researcher Vincent Mosco calls the "pay-per society," involving the new (and usually escalating) costs to consumers for access to electronic information and entertainment.[51] This could isolate large segments of already underprivileged Americans from the benefits of the new technologies.

In Chapters 5 through 8, we examine this and other issues that are emerging in the electronic transformation of the American media.

NOTES

1. Daniel Bell, *The Coming of Post-Industrial Society*. New York: Basic Books, 1973.
2. Fritz Machlup, *The Production and Distribution of Knowledge in the United States*. Princeton, NJ: Princeton University Press, 1962; Marc Porat, *The Information Economy*, 9 vols., Office of Telecommunications special publication 77–12, U.S. Department of Commerce, Washington, DC, 1977.
3. See Stephen S. Cohen and John Zysman, *Manufacturing Matters: The Myth of the Post-Industrial Economy*. New York: Basic Books, 1987. Also James Beniger, *The Control Revolution*. Cambridge, MA: Harvard University Press, 1986; Michael Traber, *The Myth of the Information Revolution: Social and Ethical Implications of Communications Technology*. Newbury Park, CA: Sage, 1988; and Michael R. Rubin and Mary T. Huber, *The Knowledge Industry in the United States, 1960–1980*. Princeton, NJ: Princeton University Press, 1986.
4. The idea of salvation through technology is analyzed in Leo Marx, *The Machine in the Garden*. New York: Oxford University Press, 1964.
5. This pattern is documented in Carolyn Marvin, *When Old Technologies Were New*. New York: Oxford University Press, 1988.
6. Richard D. Brown, *Knowledge Is Power: The Diffusion of Information in Early America, 1700–1865*. New York: Oxford University Press, 1989.
7. Erik Barnouw, "Historical Survey of Communication Breakthroughs," in *The Communications Revolution in Politics*. Edited by Gerald Benjamin. Proceedings of the Academy of Political Science 34, no. 4 (1982): 13.
8. Alvin F. Harlow, *Old Wires and New Waves*. New York: Appleton-Century, 1936, p. 337.
9. The FCC's performance is documented in Stanley Besen, *Misregulating Television: Network Dominance and the FCC*. Chicago: University of Chicago Press, 1984.
10. Veronis, Suhler & Associates, *Communications Industry Forecast: Industry Spending Projections 1998–2002*, 12th annual ed., New York, October 1998, p. 38.
11. The rise of the new international information packagers is documented in Greg MacDonald, *The Emergence of Multi-Media Conglomerates*, working paper 70, Multimedia Enterprises Program (Geneva, Switzerland: International Labor Organization, 1990). See also Anthony Smith, *The Age of the Behemoths: The Globalization of Mass Media Firms*, Twentieth Century Fund paper. New York: Priority Press, 1991.
12. "AT&T Buys TCI, Looks to One-Stop Future," *Washington Post*, 25 June 1998, p. 1.
13. The AT&T divestiture and its implications are discussed in Robert W. Crandall, *After the Breakup: U.S. Telecommunications in a More Competitive Era*. Washington, DC: Brookings Institution, 1991, and George H. Bolling, *AT&T—Aftermath of Antitrust*. Washington, DC: National Defense University Press, 1983. For critiques of the decision to divest AT&T of its local phone operations, see Alan Stone, *Wrong Number:*

The Breakup of AT&T. Boston: Basic Books, 1989, and Vincent Mosco, "The Mythology of Telecommunications Deregulation," *Journal of Communication* 40, no. 1 (Winter 1990): pp. 36–49.

14. For a useful summary of the changes, see Jeffrey B. Abramson, Christopher Arterton, and Garry R. Orren, *The Electronic Commonwealth: The Impact of New Media Technologies on Democratic Politics*. New York: Basic Books, 1988, pp. 32–65.

15. Jib Fowles, "The Upheavals in the Media," *New York Times*, 6 January 1991, p. D-13.

16. "Hispanic Youth Outnumber Blacks," *Washington Post*, 15 July 1998, p. A-2.

17. The subtleties of government-media relationships have been extensively explored. See, for example, Gerald Benjamin, *The Communications Revolution in Politics*, Proceedings of the Academy of Political Science 34, no. 4 (1982); Montague Kern, *Thirty-Second Politics: Political Advertising in the Eighties*. New York: Praeger, 1989; W. Lance Bennett, *The Governing Crisis: Media, Money and Marketing in American Elections*. New York: St. Martin's, 1992; and Jarol B. Manheim, *All the People, All the Time*. Armonk, NY: M. E. Sharpe, 1991.

18. Morton Mintz and Jerry S. Cohen, *America Inc.: Who Owns and Operates the United States*. New York: Dell, 1972, pp. 156–157.

19. Abramson, Arterton, and Orren, *The Electronic Commonwealth*, pp. 274–280.

20. Trade in information services, including the media, has become such an important issue for the United States that it lobbied, successfully, to include such trade for the first time in the most recent round of trade liberalization negotiations conducted under the General Agreement on Tariffs and Trade, which were completed in 1993. The regulations that were agreed to in the negotiations are administered by a new international body, the World Trade Organization.

21. "Springtime for Bertlesmann," *New Yorker*, 27 April 1998, p. 104.

22. For a discussion of these issues, see Andrew C. Barrett, "Shifting Foundations: The Regulation of Telecommunications in an Era of Change," *Federal Communications Law Journal* 46, no. 1 (December 1993): pp. 1–35.

23. John DeButts, "Policy, Not Technology, Will Shape the Future of Communications," *Communications News*, June 1975, p. 47.

24. Ithiel de Sola Pool, *The Technologies of Freedom*. Cambridge, MA: Harvard University Press, 1984, p. 18. See also T. Carter, M. Franklin, and J. Wright, *The First Amendment and the Fifth Estate: Regulation of Electronic Mass Media*, 2d ed. Mineola NY: Foundation Press, 1988.

25. For a useful summary of public policy issues affecting the mass media and other communications industries, see U.S. Congress, Office of Telecommunications Policy, *Critical Connections*, publication no. OTA-CIT-407, Washington DC, 1990.

26. There have been a number of attempts to centralize government control over information policy, notably during the First and Second World Wars. More recently, the Nixon administration set up a White House Office of Telecommunications Policy in 1969, designed to advise the president on communications matters. It quickly became politicized, playing a major role in administration attacks on the media. It was abolished by the Carter administration in 1977 and replaced by a more research-oriented agency, the National Telecommunications and Information Administration in the Department of Commerce.

27. "Will America Log On to the Internewt?" *Business Week*, 5 December 1994.

28. "Pressler Top Corporate Fundraiser," *Broadcasting & Cable*, 21 August 1995, p. 39.

29. "Role Out the Telepork Barrel," *Business Week*, 21 August 1995, p. 36.

30. For a detailed description of the politics of the Telecommunications Act, see Wilson P. Dizard, *Meganet: How the Global Communications Network Will Connect Everyone on Earth*. Boulder CO: Westview Press, 1997, pp. 122–142.

31. "The Information Superhighway: Trolls at the Tollgate," *Federal Communications Law Journal.* vol. 50, no.1, December 1997, pp. 53–65.
32. "Business Notes," *Washington Post,* 5 May 1998, p. D-2. See also "FCC Hears from Schools, Libraries," *Communications Industries Report,* July 1998, p. 21.
33. "Too Close for Comfort, *Washington Post,* 7 January 1996, p. H-1.
34. "So the Elephants Danced," *Economist* (London), 1 August 1998, p. 20.
35. *Trends in Telephone Service.* Industry Analysis Division, Common Carrier Bureau, Federal Communications Commission, Washington DC, July 1998, p. 10.
36. "Internet Is New Pet Issue in Congress," *New York Times,* 28 June 1998, p. 16.
37. "Tyranny in the Infrastructure," *Wired,* July 1997, p. 96. See also "A New Battle Shapes Up Over Internet Smut," *Washington Post,* Washington Business supplement, 10 August 1998, p. 23.
38. "Washington vs. the Web," *TechCapital,* May/June 1998, p. 70. See also "Senate Panel Would Reduce Tax Moratorium on Internet," *New York Times,* 3 August 1998, p. D-5.
39. "Broadband Services," *Satellite Markets,* Summer 1998, p. 14.
40. For a survey of satellite prospects for delivering multimedia services, see Nancy E. Salvati, "Satellites in the Multimedia Skyway," *Satellite Communications,* February 1995, pp. 24–26.
41. "Phone Firms May be Unable to Make Good Corporate Connections in Megamergers," *Washington Post,* 4 August 1998, p. C-3.
42. "Interactive TV: The Leap Looks a Long Way Off," *Washington Post,* 2 July 1995, p. H-1.
43. For a discussion of the policy issues involved, see "Strategic Alliances and Telecommunications Policy," Communications and Society Program, The Aspen Institute, Washington DC, 1995.
44. "The Telecom Big Top," *Washington Post,* 24 May 1998, p. H-1.
45. "The Condo Approach to Telco Entry," *Broadcasting,* 3 February 1992, pp. 26–28.
46. This case is made forcefully in Henry Geller, "Fiber Optics: An Opportunity for a New Policy?" Annenberg Washington Program, Washington, DC, November 1991, pp. 31–39.
47. *United States v. Associated Press,* 52 F. Supp. 362, 372 (S.D.N.Y. 1943).
48. Fred H. Cate, "A Law Antecedent and Paramount," *Federal Communications Law Journal* 47, no. 2, December 1994, pp. 205–211.
49. Leland L. Johnson, *Common Carrier Video Deliver by Telephone Companies,* report R-4166 MF/RL Santa Monica, CA.: Rand Corporation, 1992.
50. "The Revolution Begins, At Last," *Economist* (London), 30 September 1995, p. 15.
51. Vincent Mosco, "Information in the Pay-per Society," in *The Political Economy of Information.* Edited by Vincent Mosco and Janet Wasco. Madison: University of Wisconsin Press, 1988, pp. 3–26.

Broadcast Television: Decline or Renewal?

Nowhere is the impact of the new media on the old more visible than in television broadcasting. Over-the-air television is under siege these days, as its audiences (and its revenues) are being depleted by cable television, home videocassette recorders, and the Internet. The pressure will accelerate as newer technologies such as direct satellite broadcasting and fiber-optic delivery of information and entertainment services compete for consumer attention.

Television is, nevertheless, still the most powerful and pervasive mass medium in the United States. No other can match the hold it has on the tens of millions of viewers who spend hours daily in front of the tube. "Television is our common cultural ground," said media critic Charles Paul Freund. "It is the only thing most Americans know and experience more or less together, and whatever is next on the list is small beer compared to it."[1]

Television has evoked strong reactions, pro and con, from its earliest days. In the 1950s, radio satirist Fred Allen saw it creating a race of people "with eyes as big as grapefruits and no brains, no brains at all." Architect Frank Lloyd Wright called it "chewing gum for the eyes." Historian Daniel J. Boorstin noted, "We can no longer say, with Oscar Wilde, that life imitates art, for now life imitates television."[2] According to communications researcher George Gerbner, "If you can write a nation's stories, you needn't worry about who makes its laws. Today, television tells most of the stories to most of the people most of the time."[3]

The most famous critique of the medium came from former FCC chairman Newton Minow in a 1961 speech to broadcasting executives. He characterized television as "a procession of game shows, violence . . . sadism, murder, western bad men, western good men, private eyes, gangsters, more violence and cartoons." Television was, he concluded, a "vast wasteland," a phrase that has since become the standard epithet for the medium.[4]

These assessments give a rough measure of television's impact on American life. Each of them contains some degree of truth. Too often, the television industry has squandered its social and cultural potential. On the other hand, television has also recorded and shaped such critical events as the civil rights movement, the Kennedy assassination, Watergate, the Vietnam and Persian Gulf wars, and the collapse of Soviet communism. For fifty years, current history has been defined for Americans largely through television images.

CHANGING TELEVISION PATTERNS

In short, broadcast television continues to exert a powerful influence despite the challenges posed by the new technologies. With almost 3,000 outlets of all kinds reaching into American homes, broadcast television is second only to radio as the most available mass medium. The decline in its viewing audience is leveling off from the precipitous drop of recent years. At the end of the 1990s, TV-viewing households increased in number to about 100 million, up 10 million from the late 1980s. The industry overall is still very much alive despite the falloff in prime-time viewing (see Table 5.1).

Broadcast television is, however, an industry in long-term decline. The erosion in network viewing is irreversible. Former FCC chairman Alfred Sikes has summed up the industry's position thus: "The transmission medium that has been dominant is now secondary. . . . Broadcasting has been eclipsed by cable."[5]

A debate over the causes of television's decline is already in full swing. In an influential 1991 book, *Three Blind Mice*, investigative reporter Ken Auletta focused on corporate mismanagement and greed.[6] Other industry watchers have argued that the audience decline was inevitable due to the aging of the postwar baby boomers, the broadcasters' most sought-after viewer segment in the past thirty years. Economists cite rising program costs at a time of decreasing audiences. Other analysts point to the early 1970s as the beginning of TV's decline. It was then that cable TV changed from being a system retransmitting local television stations into a national entertainment service, with dozens of new entertainment channels.

The problem was magnified by the simultaneous spread of remote-control devices ("zappers"), which allowed viewers to graze through program offerings, creating havoc among program-listening surveys.[7] Viewer loyalty to individual programs has dropped sharply. A study of viewer habits by the J. Walter Thompson advertising agency found that over 70 percent of viewers watched only one or two of their favorite shows in a month.[8]

TABLE 5.1   Network Prime-Time Television Viewing

Year	Network Prime-Time Rating*	Network Primet-Time Audience Share	U.S. TV Households Reached (Millions)	Total U.S. TV Households (Millions)
1977	52.3	92%	39.0	74.5
1978	52.7	89	40.2	76.3
1979	51.7	88	40.2	77.8
1980	50.1	85	40.0	79.9
1981	48.7	82	39.7	81.5
1982	46.1	78	38.4	83.3
1983	46.0	76	38.5	83.8
1984	44.1	74	37.4	84.9
1985	44.3	74	38.0	85.7
1986	43.5	73	37.8	86.8
1987	41.0	70	35.8	87.4
1988	39.1	68	34.6	88.6
1989	38.8	67	35.1	90.4
1990	38.2	64	35.2	92.1
1991	37.3	64	34.7	93.1
1992	38.1	65	34.4	92.1[†]
1993	38.2	65	35.6	93.1
1994	38.3	64	36.1	94.2
1995	35.4	60	33.8	95.4
1996	34.4	60	33.0	95.9
1997	32.7	56	31.7	97.0
1998	31.4	54	30.8	98.0
1999	30.0	51	29.7	99.1
2000	29.0	50	29.1	100.2
2001	28.5	49	28.9	101.4
2002	28.0	48	28.7	102.5

SOURCES: Veronis, Suhler & Associates, Wilkofsky Gruen Associates, Nielsen Media Research

*For calendar year, January–December; includes Fox beginning in 1987, UPN and WB beginning in 1995

[†]Revised downward based on 1990 census

Note: Figures for 1995–2002 include UPN and WB.

CHALLENGES TO THE BIG THREE NETWORKS

Each of these factors contributed to television's woes in recent years. The industry's critics tend to simplify a complex situation by focusing on the Big Three networks, thus slighting other important players such as independent local stations, public broadcasting, Hispanic networks, and religious broadcasters. Spanish-language stations are particularly formidable competitors in a dozen major markets. During the February 1998 "ratings sweep," one Hispanic station, Miami's WLTV, rated first in audience viewing, well ahead of the city's six English-language stations.[9]

The old-line networks also face increasing competition from newer national networks. The earliest of these was Fox Broadcasting, started in the late 1980s with the formidable financial and programming resources of Rupert Murdoch's News Corp. empire behind it. Fox Broadcasting is one of three divisions in the Fox Group, a company created in 1998 to handle Murdoch's major media interests outside the newspaper field. The broadcasting division also includes twenty-two television stations plus interests in five cable TV networks. The other two divisions manage the 20th Century Fox film studios and News Corps' sports acquisitions, including the Los Angeles Dodgers.[10]

Fox Broadcasting has not been immune to the audience erosion shared by the Big Three networks. In the 1997–1998 season, it averaged a 7.1 rating overall and a 12 percent share of household viewers. Overall network viewing was down 8 percent from the previous season.[11] At the same time, Fox scored a major success by coming in second among the networks in attracting viewers in the 18–49 age range, the demographic group most sought after by advertisers. It did this with fast-paced programs such as *The Simpsons*, *Ally McBeal* and *The X-Files*, leading the *New York Times* to declare in 1998 that Fox was "the hottest network in prime-time television."[12]

Two other national networks went on the air in the mid-1990s. Each was sponsored by a major Hollywood studio: WB Television, owned by Time Warner Inc.'s Warner Brothers, and UPN, bankrolled by Viacom Inc.'s Paramount Pictures. In both cases, the studios pursued a strategy of creating captive, brand-name distribution outlets for programs they produce and buy, just as Fox Broadcasting has done for the Murdoch organization.[13]

More recently, a sixth network has challenged all of the present incumbents. It is USA Network. the brainchild of Barry Diller, who brought to the project a reputation as the boy-wonder head of ABC programs at the age of twenty-six and as chief of the Paramount movie studio at thirty-two. USA Network consists of a group of local TV stations, plus the Home Shopping Network and some production facilities. Diller's strategy is to produce programs in a dozen cities around the country for his network, basically ignoring the long-standing practice of relying on big Hollywood facilities. He estimates that he can do this for a quarter of the costs involved in film-studio production, while still attracting viewers from the older networks.[14]

The Big Three networks are still, however, the most important single factor in U.S. television. A majority of local stations are beholden to them for their most popular programs. ABC, NBC, and CBS provide stability for the whole system by supplying large audiences for big-spending national advertisers. Prime-time viewing of their programs may have dropped below 60 percent, but it is still greater at most times than viewership of the three new Hollywood-sponsored networks and of individual cable TV channels.

More than any other medium, broadcast television depends on national advertising. The networks have thrived on rating formulas that put them in competition with each other for programming that attracts audiences the big advertisers want to reach. As independent program producer Norman Lear once observed:

> Commercial television's moral north star, from which nearly all bearings are set, is quite simply: "How do I win Tuesday night at eight o'clock?" That is the name of the game, the only thing that matters.[15]

This has been a spectacularly successful formula for over forty years, but it is in trouble. The networks' share of television advertising revenue is still high, but it is leveling off as advertisers turn to local network affiliates, cable TV, and the Internet to reach the audiences they want. Ad sales for the Big Three 1998–1999 prime-time shows were flat, marking the second time in recent years that this barometer of the Big Three's economic health had failed to rise.[16] This has happened despite the fact that NBC, ABC and CBS have increased their prime-time advertising slots in recent years from nine to eleven minutes.

Meanwhile, the advertising industry is going through its own shake-up, shifting its dollars from television and other mass media to campaigns that target consumers more directly, such as supermarket coupons, telephone marketing, and mail-order catalogues.

In summary, the Big Three networks have experienced a domino-style falling off of audiences, advertising revenues, and overall influence. One result was that they began losing control over their affiliated stations, the ones committed to taking network programs. Most network managers, out of myopia, inertia, or self-delusion, failed to see the changes coming. It was a case of corporate whistling past the graveyard. As early as 1987, total audience viewing of programs broadcast by network affiliates had dropped below 60 percent during some weeks, well under the happy projections made by the networks at the time.[17]

Network managers tended to dismiss such figures as temporary aberrations that would self-correct in the next cycle of program ratings. They persisted in regarding their business as a closed competition among the Big Three networks, an attitude that masked the steady viewer shift to cable networks and home videocassettes. Warnings from executive-suite Cassandras went unheeded. But the Cassandras were right. Media historians may someday identify more precisely the moment when the forces leading to an irreversible downturn in network fortunes came together. Such a moment may have occurred in October 1991 when comedian Bill Cosby, star of the highest-rated program of the 1980s, decided to desert the networks and market his new show, *You Bet Your Life*, directly to local stations. As it turned out, the show was not a success and was canceled in 1993.[18]

THE NEW NETWORK CONGLOMERATES

The most important event that changed the status of network broadcasting, however, took place in the mid-1980s. It was the simultaneous takeover of the Big Three networks by outside corporate interests. This shift in ownership transformed the shape and direction of the networks, with particular implications for their role in the new media environment.[19] The initial wave of takeovers all took place within a year, in 1984 and 1985. Each was unique in terms of who took over and why.

ABC was bought by Capital Cities Communications ("Cap Cities"), the largest nonnetwork owner of television stations in the country. Cap Cities was the only one of the new network owners that brought a range of direct media experience to its acquisition. In addition to its ABC television holdings, Cap Cities owned nine AM and eight FM stations, a videocassette production company, and interests in cable programming services. The ABC acquisition included the ESPN sports network, the oldest and largest in the cable industry.

NBC became a division of General Electric as part of a takeover of RCA, the electronics firm that owned NBC. The CBS takeover came about through the acquisition of a controlling interest in its stock by Laurence Tisch, head of Loews Corporation, a conglomerate previously best known for its chain of hotels and control of Lorillard, the tobacco company. Unlike Cap Cities, the new owners of NBC and CBS did not have any significant holdings in other electronic media beyond their over-the-air TV operations.

The three firms involved in these takeovers represented a curious mix of corporate cultures. Their operating styles were different, but they shared a belief that network television was a profitable business that would strengthen their overall balance sheets. They were right. In the mid-1980s, ABC, CBS, and NBC were all big moneymakers, both in their network operations and in the small group of local stations that each owned.

Those local stations, whose individual profits ran as high as 40 percent of their revenues, were of particular interest to the takeover groups. At the time, the FCC limited network ownership to seven stations apiece. For years, the networks had lobbied for a loosening of this restriction. In the pro-business, deregulatory spirit of the Reagan era, the commission relaxed the rule to permit ownership of up to a dozen stations. That decision opened possibilities for greater profits for the networks. What the networks had not adequately foreseen was that the new potential for profit would also make them a more attractive investment and therefore more vulnerable to corporate takeover.

Although network profits were high in the first years of the takeovers, the new owners found themselves dealing with the dilemma of rising costs at a time when their audience base was being eroded by the expansion of cable television channels and home videocassette players. NBC was particularly hard hit. In 1988, it was the top network, enjoying sixty-nine straight weeks as the Nielson audience survey winner. At the end of that year, it had posted $500 million in profits. Three years later, the company's profits had disappeared, and it had sustained the largest viewer decline among the networks.

New management at all three networks reacted to harsh fiscal realities with tough cost-cutting programs. ABC laid off 2,000 employees soon after the Cap Cities takeover. NBC's personnel dropped from 8,000 to 5,700 in five years. Cutbacks at CBS were equally severe. The old management teams were decimated; the executives who remained were made grimly aware of the new importance of bottom-line economics. GE sent NBC managers to its in-house Management Development Institute, where the curriculum included three days of survival training on an isolated Maine island.[20]

The personnel cuts saved money but did not directly address the networks' primary problem, which was the combination of viewer decline and rising program costs. That combination changed the rules for network television. Gone were the days of simple three-way competition among the three networks for audiences, advertising dollars, and profits. Now they faced uncomfortable outside competition, including the successful fourth network, Fox Broadcasting.

THE CHALLENGE OF CABLE TV

The more immediate challenge to the Big Three, however, came from cable television. The networks were at a structural disadvantage in their attempts to match cable's appeal. They had only one channel with which to reach the home audiences that advertisers wanted. They were, in effect, delivering a single mass audience, a large segment of which was of no interest to many individual advertisers. Local cable systems, with fifty or sixty channels, could better target the audiences these advertisers wanted to attract. It is, as one industry observer has noted, the difference between precision bombing and carpet bombing.

Moreover, network program costs rose as advertising revenues fell. This was especially true of the more popular programs networks had to offer in order to keep what was left of their competitive prime-time edge. A classic example was *Seinfeld*, the long-running saga of footloose, young New Yorkers. The show was a critical element in NBC's efforts to stanch audience losses during the 1990s. *Seinfeld's* costs escalated wildly. In addition to mounting production expenses, Jerry Seinfeld and his three co-stars were each earning a million dollars per episode by 1997.

This escalation was offset by NBC's ability to charge up to a million dollars a minute for ads on the program, a bonanza that ended when the series closed down in 1998. *Seinfeld* is expected to earn a billion dollars in syndication. This money, however, will not flow to NBC but to Sony, the program's distributor, and to its production company, Castle Rock, which is a Time-Warner unit.[21] Meanwhile, NBC saw its audience levels fall by as much as 15 percent during the 1998–1999 season, a drop attributed by industry observers largely to the closing down of the *Seinfeld* series.[22]

As the Big Three's economic fortunes continued to decline, they began to look like an endangered species, or at least one that needed a new identity. Increasingly, there was speculation that they were "in play," the Wall Street term for companies ripe for takeover. These rumors were particularly insistent about NBC and CBS, both of which reportedly had been put on the block at various times by their owners. The speculation centered on who the new buyers would be. Most rumors center around the film industry, which clearly has an interest in maintaining the viability of the networks, since they are major buyers of Hollywood's products.[23]

Meanwhile, the pressures for change intensified. Cable TV's growing audiences and its ability to produce its own programs posed a larger threat to the New York networks. The Internet was attracting a significant audience of young men and women—the prime target for most network advertisers. The Big Three also faced the prospect of competition from a new source: the big, cash-rich telecommunications companies that successfully lobbied to end government restrictions on providing information and entertainment services. As we saw in Chapter 4, the final barriers to their entry into the business were lifted in 1996 when congressional legislation gave the phone companies and other networkers broad authority to compete against both over-the-air broadcasting and cable TV.

The legislation also gave the New York networks several important breaks that made them more attractive targets for takeover. It expanded their right to own more local TV and radio stations, a traditionally lucrative enterprise for them. At about the same time, the FCC lifted decades-old restrictions that had barred the networks from owning their own prime-time entertainment programs. The result was to give the networks a promising new revenue source—their own prime-time entertainment shows. Equally important, they could enter the lucrative business of syndicating these shows after their initial network run. The stage was set for major change.

MERGER MANIA IN 1995: DISNEY BUYS ABC

It began during one week in August 1995. On a Tuesday, the Walt Disney Company bought out Capital Cities–ABC in a $19.3 billion deal that created the largest media company on earth. Two days later, Westinghouse made a $5.4 billion offer to take over CBS. The two deals were different in a number of ways, but they both were based on the concept of synergy, combining multimedia production and distribution resources under one corporate roof. The word was repeated like a mantra in the complex negotiations that resulted in the biggest shake-up in broadcasting history.[24]

The Disney–Cap Cities merger dominated the week's business news if only because the sheer size of the deal commanded attention. The new company brought together operations across the mass media landscape. They included Walt Disney Pictures and two other movie production units; 11 TV stations, 228 TV affiliates, and 21 radio stations; 4 major cable channels (ESPN, Lifetime, Arts & Entertainment, and the Disney Channel), newspapers in 13 states, as well as 2 publishing companies, Fairchild and Chilton. Disney also brought to the merger fifty years' experience in marketing media products through its theme parks and in the licensing of Disney-logo products such as toys, games, Mickey Mouse watches, and T-shirts.

The ESPN sports channel played a featured role in the negotiations leading up to the Disney–Cap Cities merger. It was a prime example of the kind of product the merged companies hoped to market on a global basis. Sports broadcasting has universal appeal, transcending language, geography, and other barriers. At the time of the merger, ESPN was available in most American households with cable and was distributed to 70 million additional cable households in 130 countries abroad. It was ABC's largest single profit center on a percentage basis. The merger with Disney was propelled by the fact that the most exportable forms of entertainment are sports and children's programming, in which ABC and Disney were, respectively, the acknowledged leaders.[25]

THE WESTINGHOUSE–CBS DEAL

The Westinghouse–CBS deal was smaller than the Disney–Cap Cities merger, but it was cut from the same pattern, combining production and distribution facilities under one corporate roof. The major difference between the two transactions was that Westinghouse–CBS was primarily a broadcasting alliance, without the multimedia resources of the Disney–Cap Cities merger. CBS had been in the music record and publishing sectors in the 1980s, but the company had sold these assets in a misguided effort to consolidate its financial position.

Nevertheless, the combined Westinghouse–CBS broadcasting capabilities are formidable. Although Westinghouse was best known for producing refrigerators and other appliances, it also owned Group W, a well-regarded and profitable nonnetwork broadcasting group. These assets, together with the CBS stations, made Westinghouse the country's biggest broadcaster, with 15 wholly owned TV stations and 39 radio stations. This gave the company direct access to about a third of all U.S. households, in addition to the programming it supplied to 200 CBS affiliates. It also expanded its radio broadcasting base, acquiring 79 radio stations in 1996 for $4.9 billion. The company also began selling off its industrial assets, and it dropped the venerable Westinghouse name. It is now CBS Corp.[26]

Less than two months after the ABC and CBS mergers in 1995, Time Warner made an equally bold move when it bid for Ted Turner's far-flung media operations including CNN, entertainment cable channels, and film operations. The $8 billion merger strengthened Time Warner's position as the largest multimedia company in the world. Although Time Warner does not compete directly against the big New York networks (except for CNN), it is a formidable threat to their aspirations to expand into multimedia operations over and above their traditional network activities.

The 1995 takeovers of ABC and CBS, together with the Time Warner–Turner merger, were generally interpreted as strengthening the broadcasting industry, enabling it to operate more effectively in a synergistic multimedia environment. There are, however, many who questioned this strategy. Some media observers see the big megamedia combinations as a threat to information diversity. They point out that the mergers reduced the number of competitive outlets and put control in the hands of fewer corporate organizations.[27]

Other observers question the basic assumptions that drove the mergers. The synergy argument is particularly suspect in the media sector, where predicting which products will and will not sell has always been notoriously risky. "You can make a network carry your stuff if you own a network, but you can't make anyone watch it," New York media consultant Al Gottesman points out. In television, most new prime-time programs, launched with great hype each year, fail. Four out of five Hollywood films don't turn a profit. The week that saw the change in ownership at CBS and ABC also witnessed the opening of what was one of the most expensive failures in media history, a $200 million Hollywood film, *Waterworld*. As Rajindra Sisodia of George Mason University's business school noted at the time of the Disney–Cap Cities merger:

> All of the ballyhooed synergies being talked about in this merger could as well be accomplished through nonexclusive strategic alliances between the companies. For example, if it indeed does make sense to package the Disney Channel and ESPN together to penetrate overseas markets, as analysts are suggesting, the same outcome could be achieved without a merger. Companies would remain free to seek appropriate alliances in various markets.[28]

In the aftermath of the 1995 mergers, the three New York networks were still, collectively, the keystone of U.S. TV broadcasting. As of the late 1990s, they continued to earn large gross revenues from advertising, but in 1997 only NBC earned a profit. Their future remains hostage to long-range trends that seem to be irreversible: smaller audiences, higher costs, and lower revenues.

How do the networks deal with this new economic environment? One network watcher suggests that the continuing financial squeeze is "forcing network executives into a schizophrenic dance of mixed messages."[29] They are working out new management patterns that build on their still formidable ability to produce and distribute programming that attracts tens of millions of people every day.[30]

NETWORK-AFFILIATE TENSIONS

These plans for reinventing themselves are necessarily long range in nature, constrained by the squeeze on financial resources. At the same time, they face more immediate difficulties. Not the least of these problems is keeping their networks intact. ABC, CBS, and NBC each have over 200 affiliated local stations that contract to transmit their national programming. The affiliates are, in fact, a basic element in the networks' programming and advertising strategies. As media journalist Les Brown points out, "Keeping these affiliates happy was always the vital concern of the Big Three because a U.S. network can only be as great as the sum of its parts."[31]

The affiliates (some of which are owned by the networks) are very profitable operations. Not only do they rake in the lion's share of the advertising revenues earned by all local stations, but they also receive direct compensation from New York for carrying network programs.[32]

By the mid-1990s, network-affiliate relations were on rocky ground. The networks clearly need the affiliates, but the question is whether the affiliates need the networks in quite the same way. The overall decline in network audiences has obviously hurt the local stations. More and more, the affiliates see that they can make more money (via advertising they control) with popular syndicated programs such as the *Oprah Winfrey* show and *Wheel of Fortune*, rather than sharing ad revenues from network programs.

The local affiliates are also reconsidering their reliance on network news programs. Local news is usually their biggest money spinner, often accounting for a third of station revenues and an even higher share of profits. Increasingly, the affiliates are moving toward nonnetwork regional and national news coverage through cooperative agreements with independent news organizations. Many local stations now have agreements to broadcast CNN programming, lessening their dependence on network news from New York.

The New York networks were hit by a wave of affiliate defections to Fox Broadcasting in the mid-1990s. Although most local stations have not cut themselves off from their network affiliations, the relationship is weakening. As part of their cost-cutting, ABC, CBS, and NBC have reduced the compensation they pay to local affiliates for running network shows. They have also cut back the number of network programs local stations are required to carry in response to affiliate demands for control of prime-time programming and the advertising revenues that go with it.[33] In their struggle to attract audiences for their evening programs, the networks have been forced into high-stakes competition for high-rated programs. This competition reached a climax of sorts in 1993 when CBS lured talk show host David Letterman from NBC, reportedly offering him an annual salary of $14 million.

The networks' difficulties with their affiliates are part of the much larger problem in their primary business: national programming that appeals to big audiences. The Big Three networks operate virtually around the clock, from the morning wake-up shows to the late-night talk programs. The rules for success have always been vague, and they are more so these days. Introducing new programs can be financially perilous. A show's fate is usually sealed, for better or worse, within a month after it is introduced. Most new shows are eventually canceled, resulting in heavy losses.

NEW PROGRAMMING STRATEGIES

Programming problems have complicated the networks' effort to meet the growing competition from cable systems, telephone companies, and the Internet. Although partial relaxation of government regulations now permits the networks to produce more of their own entertainment programs, they have not come up with a programming pattern strong enough to recoup their audience losses. In the search for solutions, the industry's operating cliché has been "quality television," a phrase that has proved difficult to translate into successful programs. The problem was defined succinctly by Warren Littlefield, an NBC executive:

> You have to be clear about what your goals are. We're in a rebuilding era, and we have to invest in new product. It's hard to predict what the audience will like. But we figured if we were at the crap table, why not gamble on high-quality shows?[34]

The industry's strategy for higher-quality programs had mixed results. There have been attempts by the networks to invest more money in shows that rise above the usual lowest-common-denominator standard. More often than not these programs failed to attract the larger audiences needed to justify their higher costs.

Meanwhile, local stations rely increasingly on low-cost syndicated programs to bolster their revenues. When King World Productions, owners of *Wheel of Fortune* and *Jeopardy*, negotiated an extra thirty seconds of advertising time, the change added an estimated $30 million in annual revenues from the two shows. In addition, the networks and the local stations are turning to sleazier shows in an effort to turn a bigger profit. These syndicated programs, known euphemistically as tabloid TV, include *A Current Affair*, *Inside Edition*, and *Jerry Springer*. They are big moneymakers as well as—by any standard—mindless and exploitative.

Meanwhile, the networks have had trouble holding onto audiences in three other traditionally successful program areas: soap operas, news, and sports. The afternoon soap operas have suffered audience declines, primarily because the largest segment of their audience, women, are now out of the house and into the workforce.

News program viewing has also been declining for over a decade. By the early 1990s, network newscasts were attracting only 54 percent of viewers, a loss of nearly one out of every three viewers over the previous ten years.[35] More recently, a 1998 survey by the Pew Research Center for the People and the Press found that the share of Americans who watch the evening news shows was only 15 percent, half the figure of five years earlier. Young people in particular are turning to Internet news sources, the survey found.[36]

Another factor contributing to audience losses for network news is competition from CNN, created by Ted Turner and now owned by Time Warner. At a time when the networks were cutting back their news budgets in the 1990s, CNN expanded its operations. Its worldwide staff of 1,500 gives it a news-gathering advantage, compared with the 1,000 or so employees who were left at each of the networks after their big budget cuts. CNN's around-the-clock coverage has adversely affected network news viewing, particularly when important news is breaking. CNN also has challenged the networks by negotiating agreements with network affiliates and other local stations to feed and receive news footage that duplicates, and often improves on, the networks' news offerings. CNN's television affiliate supplies news services to over 250 local stations nationwide.

THE DECLINE OF NETWORK SPORTS

The networks have also taken a big hit in sports programming, once a certified moneymaker. Their longtime control of baseball and football broadcasting has been eroded by competition from cable TV sports channels. Another factor that cuts into profits has been the astronomical rise in prices demanded by sports organizations for broadcast rights. CBS paid $1.6 billion in 1988 for a four-year contract for major league baseball programs. One industry analyst estimated that, given the depressed advertising market since then, CBS may have overpaid by as much as $400 million.[37] CBS lost its strongest sports attraction, Sunday afternoon NFL football, in 1994 when Rupert Murdoch's Fox Broadcasting outbid it with an offer of $1.6 billion to telecast the games until 1998.

CBS re-entered the competition for big-money sports programming in 1998 when it paid a half-billion dollars for the right to televise a package of NFL games until 2006. Meanwhile, NBC and ABC continue to have problems in their sports programming. NBC took a major step toward reviving its sports image in 1995 when it successfully bid the record sum of $1.27 billion for the television rights to both the summer and winter Olympics in 2002. NBC later trumped itself in the sports bidding game when it paid $2.3 billion for broadcast and cable distribution rights to a package comprising the summer Olympics in 2004 and the summer and winter Games in 2006.

Despite these deals, the long-range threat for the networks has been the shift of major sports events to cable systems. ESPN and other sports cable channels have already cut heavily into the networks' traditional lead in sports broadcasting. Increasingly, cable sports are shifting to a pay-per-view formula (PPV), charging for each event. At first, the networks had an ally in the U.S. Congress, whose members are mindful of the fact that sports-loving voters resist the idea of paying for what they now get free. In 1991, a congressional committee extracted a promise from the National Football League that it would not seek PPV arrangements for several years.[38] It was a rear-guard action. No one, not even congressional leaders, doubts that PPV will eventually be the norm in broadcasting major sports events. Billions of dollars will accrue to the baseball and football leagues as they expand into PPV deals.

The NFL took a significant step in this direction during the mid-1990s when it inaugurated NFL Sunday Ticket, a satellite-based seasonal subscription package that gave fans access to all 183 Sunday games. The original package cost home subscribers $139; commercial subscribers (primarily bar and restaurant owners) paid up to $399, depending on the size of their establishment.[39] At the same time, owners of major league baseball teams shifted to the new mix of cable and television programming when they signed a five-year, $1.7 billion contract for coverage of their games. The media companies involved in the deal included NBC, Fox Broadcasting, the TCI cable group, and ESPN, the leading sports cable channel, now owned by Disney.

Another sports development that has an impact on the future of broadcast television is the changing pattern of ownership among major sports franchises. The Disney Company, owner of the ABC network, also owns ice hockey's Mighty Ducks, together with a large financial interest in baseball's Anaheim Angels. Rupert Murdoch's News Corp. bought the Los Angeles Dodgers. By 1999, News Corp. had become a partial investor in all but four of the nation's twenty-three regional sports networks.

Faced with the prospect of losing audiences and revenues from programs that were once gilt-edged winners, television networks are adapting their traditional broadcasting operations to a changing media environment. They have several options for applying their production and marketing know-how to new projects. They can further expand into international operations through investment, co-production deals, and other arrangements with foreign broadcasters, or they can move aggressively into other domestic media fields, particularly cable TV and the Internet, through mergers, buyouts, and production arrangements. These options became more attractive with the passage of the Telecommunications Act of 1996, which effectively eliminated most of the regulatory barriers that had limited such moves.

TELEVISION'S GLOBAL REACH

Another option open to the networks is to expand their overseas operations. This is a return to a strategy they had adopted in the 1960s. At that time, the Big Three networks focused on program sales. It was an era when foreign stations were forced to draw heavily on U.S. shows to fill their schedules. This became a profitable business for the networks and other program producers. It also established a trend that has made American programs an important part of overseas television schedules. One survey indicated that, by the early 1980s, U.S. programs accounted for 77 percent of program offerings in Latin America, 70 percent in Canada, and 44 percent in Western Europe.[40]

This led to a political backlash in many countries against the sheer volume of American programming on local television. It manifested itself as attacks on "American cultural imperialism," which resulted in efforts within the United Nations to place international restrictions on television exports. Although the UN effort failed, many individual countries did impose quotas on American program imports and prohibited or limited foreign investment in their television systems.

American television's overseas impact has been enhanced in recent years by the introduction of direct broadcasting satellite (DBS) networks in Europe, Asia, and Latin America. One network, Star TV, owned by Rupert Murdoch's News Corp., broadcasts directly into homes and into cable systems in over thirty Asian countries, stretching from the Western Pacific to the Persian Gulf. Star's success has prompted entrepreneurs to set up several rival networks in Asia. Meanwhile, two U.S. satellite companies—Hughes and PanAmSat—compete in providing satellite programming within Latin America. Collectively, these DBS operations have helped boost U.S. overseas television sales to over $3 billion annually.

THE *BAYWATCH* PHENOMENON

The most popular American TV program overseas in the 1990s was *Baywatch*, a series about California beach lifeguards and their bikini-clad girlfriends. (In the industry, the program is known as *Babewatch*.) The series enjoyed a wider audience worldwide than any other entertainment show in history. It has been seen in 144 countries and been dubbed in 15 languages. *Baywatch* had only modest success in the American market initially, and it was canceled by NBC after its first season. The show's producers decided to make additional episodes for syndication domestically and abroad. Their decision has earned them hundreds of millions of dollars since then.[41]

The television industry's overseas prospects are similar to those now faced by other U.S. businesses in increasingly competitive global markets. The demand for more programming has soared recently, spurred by satellite broadcasting along with the increase in the number of privately operated television stations abroad. (Until recently, most overseas stations were controlled by governments.) These new stations tend to favor U.S. programs and advertisements featuring globally available products. Tony the Tiger, the Kellogg Company's Frosted Flakes salesman, makes his television pitch in more than twenty countries and in just about as many languages; Procter & Gamble advertises Ivory soap and Pampers diapers in fifty-four countries.

LOOKING FOR NEW MARKETS

U.S. program exporters are also looking for new sales opportunities in previously closed markets such as Russia and Eastern Europe. One of the most popular programs on Polish television in the 1990s was a dubbed version of the *Oprah Winfrey* show. In the former Soviet Union, tens of millions of viewers got their first glimpse of American prime-time shows, from *Murphy Brown* to *Perfect Strangers*, in 1992. The shows, dubbed in Russian, were part of a festival of U.S. programs organized by U.S. exporters eager to crack the Russian market. U.S. programs are also seen regularly on television stations in China. They include older prime-time serials such as *Night Court*, *Falcon Crest*, and *Hunter*, all dubbed in Mandarin.[42]

Exports will continue to be an important revenue source for the networks and other program producers. The networks are also stepping up their direct investments in overseas projects. Cap Cities–ABC took the lead with an investment of over $100 million in European operations in the early 1990s. The company has held minority stakes in a number of French, Spanish, and German production firms as well as a half-interest in the satellite-based European Sports Network. These investments have provided Disney, Cap Cities' successor, with a variety of local bases in Europe from which to explore further business relationships in the rapidly developing program production market there. Disney has also expanded distribution of its ABC *World News Tonight*, *Nightline*, and *Good Morning America* shows to Europe via satellite, where the programs are retransmitted by television stations in Britain, Germany, Spain, and Denmark.[43]

NBC has stepped up its international operations in recent years with investments in Europe, Asia, and Latin America. Its first major overseas project was Super Channel, a satellite-based European regional channel. In Latin America, its operations have included Mexico-based Television Azteca and Canal de Noticias NBC, a Spanish-language news show that reaches over 3 million homes in Latin America and Spain. By 1995, NBC claimed that its overseas programming was reaching 170 million homes worldwide.[44]

American interest in overseas television ventures has been sparked by a new set of players. The best known among them is Ted Turner, who made his Cable News Network an international force in both television and cable TV, with program agreements in over ninety countries. Latin America is a major target for U.S. television and cable broadcasters seeking to supply programming by satellite to the over 70 million households in the region. Rupert Murdoch's News Corporation, owner of the Fox Broadcasting network, has formed a strategic alliance with Globo, Brazil's largest TV network, to provide programs to that country's 33 million TV homes.[45] The deal is part of a larger Murdoch strategy to dominate satellite-delivered television programming throughout Latin America. His partners in this venture include Mexico-based Grupo Televisa, the biggest Spanish-language program provider in the world, and TCI International, a subsidiary of Telecommunications Inc., which merged with AT&T in 1998.

Time Warner has also developed what it calls "strategic partnerships" with foreign firms. The company has made a series of overseas deals in recent years, from constructing movie theaters in Russia to investing in a new Scandinavian commercial television network. Time Warner's biggest strategic partnership deal came in 1992 when two Japanese firms, Toshiba and C. Itoh, each invested $500 million in Time Warner Entertainment, to be used in part to expand the firm's international operations.[46] In 1998, the firm took a 20 percent stake in a project to build and operate the first commercial television station in South Africa. The other 80 percent is held by black investors from South Africa's largest labor unions.[47]

The U.S. networks and other broadcasting firms can expect to find growing opportunities in overseas markets. Nevertheless, international business will remain a relatively minor part of their activities. Their priority is on expanding their operations, and their financial prospects, in the world's largest entertainment market—the United States.

SEEKING OUTSIDE PARTNERS

This possibility was very much on the minds of the corporate groups that took over television networks in recent years. Their opportunities were enhanced by the loosening of regulatory restrictions by the 1996 telecommunications law. The legislation opened up the multimedia strategies of the conglomerates, notably Disney and Westinghouse, that have invested in television networks. Within the media sector, the most logical candidate for deal making has been the cable TV industry. The problem has been the love-hate tension that characterized relations between the two industries for many years. The networks were cozy with cable TV right up to the 1970s, just as long as cable confined itself to small-town operations, retransmitting over-the-air television programs from distant cities. The networks were happy with the extended coverage—and the new audiences—that cable systems supplied.

This compatibility changed, however, when the cable industry developed satellite-based national channels such as HBO, Showtime, and ESPN. Cable was no longer a local mom-and-pop industry. It was now dominated by large conglomerates, which controlled most of the larger local cable systems as well as the more popular entertainment, news, and sports channels. This vertical integration of production and distribution resources gave the major cable firms (known as MSOs—multiple-system operators) both a strategic and a highly profitable advantage over their broadcast network competitors. They were less confined by the kinds of government regulatory restrictions imposed on the networks. There was, for instance, no limit to the number of local cable systems they could control, unlike the networks, which had government-imposed limits on the number of local stations they could own.

The cable industry's power to combine program and distribution resources has been a powerful stimulus to its growth. In seeking alliances with cable, the broadcast networks found themselves the supplicants, asking to break into a booming national industry that a dozen years or so ago was merely a collection of small-town businesses. Moreover, cable is an industry that is a labyrinth of interlocking interests. As a TV executive involved in cable negotiations once noted, "Working with cable is like dealing with the Mob."[48]

THE BIG THREE'S CABLE STRATEGIES

Like it or not, the New York networks had little choice but to deal with cable. Cable programming was one of the few areas where they could exploit their programming and management skills. As noted above, ABC took an early lead, with its investment in the ESPN sports channel in the 1980s. The network was betting that big-time football and baseball games would eventually move to cable lock, stock, and barrel. The first step in this direction was taken in 1987 when the National Football League negotiated a five-year, $1.4 billion contract with ESPN to show thirteen games annually.

The 1987 NFL–ESPN contract was a psychological turning point for both the cable and broadcasting industries. Cable's maverick, Ted Turner, acknowledged the significance of the contract in a speech to cable TV advertisers. The NFL contract was, he declared:

> . . . a milestone, involving the continuing migration of the most important programming to cable. . . . I consider the networks kind of like the Germans were in late 1942: they held a lot of territory very thinly. Two out of three of them are unprofitable now. . . . There has been a basic financial power shift.[49]

It was a crude analysis, but Turner had a point, and the networks knew it. NBC and ABC have been more aggressive in developing strategies to get more directly involved in cable TV. In addition to its investment in the ESPN sports channel, ABC set up an in-house production unit to supply programs both to cable channels and to international markets, a venture that has proved profitable.[50] In 1995, ABC–Cap Cities, now merged with Disney, committed $100 million to a joint programming venture with Dreamworks SKG, a new film studio created by Hollywood insiders Steven Spielberg, David Geffen, and Jeffrey Katzenberg.[51]

NBC was less successful in its initial forays into the cable business. Its woes began with a decision to develop an all-news cable channel, building on its longtime news expertise. In 1987, NBC tried to buy a controlling interest in Ted Turner's CNN, which was then in serious financial trouble. The deal foundered on Turner's refusal to cede editorial control to NBC. NBC's next step was to proceed with an all-news cable channel on its own. It proposed to compete directly with CNN, a reasonable decision given the fact that the Turner channel was a fairly amateurish operation at the time.

On the way, however, NBC bumped into the Byzantine realities of the cable business. Not only did a small group of cable conglomerates control most of the cable TV systems where NBC hoped to place its news channel, but they also owned a significant share of the stock in Ted Turner's far-flung operations, including CNN. It soon became clear that they were not interested in competition from another cable news channel, particularly one run by a television network that would bring superior resources to cable newscasting.

MSNBC: NBC'S SUCCESSFUL CABLE VENTURE

NBC had to give up its plans for a general cable-news channel in favor of a more specialized operation, namely CNBC, the Consumer News and Business Channel, which concentrated on financial news and personal-living features. The cable conglomerates showed their power by setting conditions for CNBC's entry into their local systems, specifying that CNBC could not become a news service in direct competition with CNN, the channel in which they had a financial interest. The cable industry's willingness to sacrifice the principle of program diversity to bottom-line profits was affirmed.[52]

By the mid-1990s, CNBC's mix of business news and celebrity-oriented talk shows had taken a modest but profitable place in cable TV's channel lineup. It branched out overseas with CNBC Asia, based in Hong Kong, and CNBC Europe, a twenty-four-hour cable channel serving millions of subscribers in Great Britain, Ireland, Norway, and Sweden.

CNBC's big breakthrough came in 1995 when NBC agreed to an alliance with Bill Gates's Microsoft Corp. Microsoft made an initial $250 million investment in the joint venture. The newly named MSNBC represented the first major partnership between a prominent television network and the new breed of Internet-oriented "information providers" who are interested in expanding the range of media operations supported by their software. MSNBC is the cable-channel cousin of Microsoft's MSN Internet service. One result of this pairing is that, by 1999, MSNBC began to close in on CNN's formidable lead in cable-delivered news.[53] Collectively, the cable-news channels are seriously eroding the audience share of over-the-air news programs. The 1998 Pew Research Center survey of viewer habits reported that 40 percent of Americans regularly watched cable news, compared to 52 percent who viewed network news broadcasts.[54]

The New York networks have gradually changed their ambivalent attitudes about cable TV competition, moving further away from uneasy confrontation and toward wary cooperation. The change has been spurred by large-scale introduction of digital compression technology in cable systems. Squeezing more channels into existing coaxial cables permits the doubling or even tripling of cable capacity. This development has been a mixed blessing for the networks. On the one hand, it means a further erosion of their traditional over-the-air audience base. However, it also opens up important opportunities to produce programs for the new cable channels. ABC and NBC are both producing programs for cable systems. NBC's strategy for the Olympics in 2000, for example, includes transmitting the event as a PPV program via cable.

Besides pursuing cable-programming ventures, the Big Three networks are looking into owning cable systems, an option opened to them by the liberalization of broadcasting regulations by the FCC and the U.S. Congress. Although networks are now free to invest in cable systems, they face opposition from within the broadcasting industry. Most local television stations including the network affiliates oppose the idea, fearing that it will lead to heavier competition between themselves and local network-owned cable systems for the same advertisers.[55]

COMPETING WITH THE PHONE COMPANIES

Despite their new relationship, the cable TV and broadcasting industries will continue to compete for consumer attention. The two media find common ground, however, in their mutual resistance to telephone industry plans to expand into information and entertainment services for home consumers. Although their respective positions differ in some details, both the cable TV and network television industries lobbied for regulatory restraints on telephone company activities in this area. In the debate leading up to passage of congressional legislation in 1996, they sought assurances that the phone companies would not use their technological and economic power to dominate the information and entertainment services sent electronically into homes.

The telephone industry's plans to provide these advanced services has forced the television networks into a serious discussion of its technological future. For the present, the networks and their affiliated stations are each limited to a single channel. Fifteen years ago, they were confronted with competition from sixty-channel cable systems. Their present prospect is that their single-channel outlets will be swamped by the hundreds of channels that are becoming available to consumers as phone companies and cable TV firms upgrade their circuits. Additionally, the broadcast networks face a serious competitive threat from direct-broadcasting satellites beaming a wide range of program offerings into small household earth terminals.

Where will broadcasters, with their single-channel capabilities, fit into this new technology-driven abundance of channels? Until recently, the industry's strategy was mainly a defensive one, aimed at limiting the competition's role as information and entertainment suppliers by lobbying for continued restrictions on their programming activities. This strategy collapsed in 1996 when Congress ended most restrictions on full competition in media markets.

GAMBLING ON HIGH-DEFINITION TV

The industry's hopes of becoming a multimedia competitor rest largely on the introduction of high-definition television, the first major change in broadcast technology since the introduction of color TV forty years ago. HDTV is a breakthrough toward the computerization of home television sets, leading to their eventual use as multimedia telecomputers. In addition to offering a superior video picture, the HDTV screen itself is a different shape—more rectangular to give a wide-screen effect. Eventually all new television sets in the country will be designed to receive HDTV capabilities.[56]

Broadcast television is only one source of HDTV transmissions, and it may well play a minor role. HDTV can be transmitted by cable TV, telephone fiber-optic circuits, or communications satellites. One disadvantage for broadcasters is that over-the-air television frequencies are technologically inadequate for high-definition transmissions. However, engineers have developed digital compression techniques to squeeze HDTV into existing broadcasting frequencies.[57]

This was necessary also because of the scarcity of usable spectrum bandwidth. An HDTV signal requires a lot of space in the frequency spectrum. Because of the current expansion of all electronic communications, spectrum is a high-demand commodity, particularly in the bands where broadcast television operates. By using digital compression techniques (described in Chapter 3), television broadcasters can offer HDTV services to mass audiences in competition with cable TV, phone networks, or satellites.

The television industry was a major player in a political battle to decide the ground rules for the introduction of HDTV services. The conditions under which the broadcasters could compete depended on decisions by Congress and the Federal Communications Commission The commission's basic position was that there should be a level playing field for all potential HDTV providers, including the broadcasters. It also specified that HDTV standards should be based on digital technology, which permits the transmission of advanced multimedia services—audio and data programming as well as television video.

CHANGING SIGNALS IN THE HDTV GAME

The FCC's insistence on digital HDTV changed the stakes for the television broadcasters. Now they would be dealing with a technology that could deliver a wide range of high-quality (and profitable) services in addition to a TV signal. They lobbied successfully in Congress and at the FCC for so-called spectrum flexibility, the freedom to use the HDTV airwaves for a range of services beyond an enhanced TV signal.[58] Their television programming could be downgraded from HDTV to what the industry called standard-definition TV (SDTV), which would make spectrum space available for profitable audio and data services. This gave broadcasters the technical ability, for the first time, to compete with cable TV, telephone companies, and satellite networkers in providing a full range of inter-active multimedia services to U.S. homes.[59]

Despite this prospect, television broadcasters have been slow to introduce HDTV digital services.[60] The transition from analog technology to HDTV involves very expensive replacement of a large part of their studio and transmitting equipment. The switchover is complicated by an FCC rule that stations must transmit both conventional and HDTV signals during the transition period. The overall cost to broadcasters of providing HDTV services has been estimated at $10 billion.

The broadcaster's reluctance to rush into HDTV also reflects the results of surveys that indicate that most households will balk at the high cost of replacing their old TVs with HDTV-compatible sets. The first HDTV sets, put on the market in 1998, had a price tag of several thousand dollars.

The National Association of Broadcasters, the industry's Washington lobby, mounted a campaign to modify what it regarded as the FCC's tight schedule for introducing HDTV services. The commission eventually backed off from its original deadlines, stretching out the phasing-in period. ABC, CBS, NBC, and the Fox affiliates were ordered to begin broadcasting digitally by May 1999 in the top-10 markets, and to begin operating in the rest of the top-30 markets by the following November. Public television and other noncommercial stations must be on the air by May 2003.[61] A number of larger stations began broadcasting HDTV programs by the end of 1998.

Despite the broadcasters' hesitant steps toward providing digital services, there is little doubt that competition with other digital providers (particularly cable TV operators) will result in a fairly rapid expansion of households with HDTV after the year 2000.[62]

THE INTERNET: TV'S FRIEND OR FOE?

Among other prospects, HDTV digital technology will open the door for multimedia Internet services for the television networks and local stations. How will the industry handle this new prospect? The Internet is already a threat, providing information and entertainment services that have been eroding over-the-air television's traditional audience base. On the other hand, the Internet offers great promise to the industry, given its unique expertise in producing popular programs and delivering them to a hundred million U.S. homes—a record no other mass medium can match.[63]

All of the broadcasting networks have taken active steps to further integrate Internet services into their operations. In a typical deal made in 1998, the Disney Co., owner of the ABC network, bought a 43 percent stake in Infoseek, a California company that operates one of the Internet's most popular "search engines," that helps users navigate the World Wide Web.[64] At the same time, NBC invested in Intertainment, an online service that provides movies, TV programs, and music on demand to personal computers.[65]

The Internet began as a transmitter of data a generation ago. More recently, it has begun to expand into audio and video services. This is done through a technical process known as streaming, which makes possible real-time delivery of digitized audio and video on computer screens. The data arrives in a PC buffer (temporary storage) and is available for viewing a few seconds later. Once a viewer starts watching, the data continues to arrive. The result is a constant flow of video or audio programming thanks to a continuous filling of the buffer. The process is not always smooth, but it provides a reasonable facsimile of a conventional TV program, albeit one that is limited, for the present, to a small part of the computer's screen.

Streaming is already being used by a disparate group of so-called Webcasters who provide a mix of video and audio programming on the Internet. By 1999, there were about 1,200 Webcasters operating on the Web. Looking at Web video has been compared to watching a badly dubbed foreign film reduced to postage-stamp size.[66] Moreover, the program schedule is limited, usually focusing on soft pornography. The Webcasters' hit program in the late 1990s was the *Jenni Show*, a leering peek at the daily activities of its nubile young star.[67]

If television broadcasters begin providing Web services on HDTV sets, they will be adding audio and data material to an advanced video technology vastly superior to the Webcasters' streaming products. Webcasting may prove to be a passing phenomenon of the Internet's early years, eventually overshadowed by the television industry's ability to transmit high-quality HDTV images into a hundred million U.S. homes along with Internet-type digitized voice and print services.[68]

The networks have been moving in this direction cautiously. In part, they are reacting to the challenge posed by CNN, the first major broadcaster on the Net. Launched in 1995, CNN Interactive was an immediate success, with a million "hits" by Web browsers in its first two days of operations. During the 1996 presidential election campaign, its three Web pages received an astonishing 50 million hits in one day. Moreover, the CNN Web operation has been consistently profitable, thanks to an impressive list of advertisers ranging from IBM to Best Western hotels.

The networks have been trying to catch up with CNN. MSNBC, the Microsoft/NBC Web venture, was launched in 1996. Fox Broadcasting started up FoxNews.com at the same time with a service pointedly targeted at a younger audience. Disney began its ABCNews.com pages a year later, with distribution through America Online and ties to ESPN, Sportzone, and other Disney Web sites. Each of these Web sites has been reasonably successful, although collectively they have not been able to match CNN Interactive's audience or its range of multimedia services.

MSNBC and similar network operations will anchor the television industry's future Internet activities. In addition to CNN, they face other outside competitors. One of these is the ubiquitous Bill Gates, whose Microsoft Corp. already has a stake in NBC's Web operation. Microsoft announced in 1998 that the Internet was the next broadcasting network. To back up its statement, the firm has been investing in digital-video companies. In 1998, it bought an equity interest in Thomson Multimedia, a firm that produces advanced television equipment. Microsoft also invested $425 million in WebTV Networks which sells a box that enables consumers to browse the Internet and send electronic mail using their television.

NEW CHALLENGES IN RADIO

Television's problems in coping with HDTV and the Internet are matched in radio broadcasting, which faces similar technological changes. Forty years ago, radio broadcasting was transformed by television's superior ability to attract audiences and revenues. Radio remains a powerful force, however. According to a 1998 Mediamark Research survey, 83 percent of Americans listen to radio regularly, a statistic no other mass medium can match.[69] Radio listening per person averages three hours and forty-five minutes every weekday.

There are two reasons for radio's continued strength. One is the popularity of FM stations, with their superior musical sound. Audience surveys indicate that FM listening accounts for about 80 percent of the radio audience. The second is radio's shift from mass-audience to specialized programming. Today, over 12,000 radio stations use dozens of different formats, from hard rock to classical music. The hot format in the 1990s was talk radio: the number of stations devoting the bulk of their day to talk shows tripled from 405 in 1990s to 1,130 in 1995. By then, Rush Limbaugh's show claimed 20 million listeners each week and generated $30 million in annual advertising revenues.[70]

In their quest for advertising dollars, radio executives pay particular attention to two audience groups: teenagers and commuting automobile drivers. Commuters are the ultimate captive audience. Their listening and buying habits have been studied in exquisite detail by the radio industry. Teenagers are compulsive radio listeners who also represent a $100 billion consumer market. One survey found that 94 percent of all teens aged twelve to nineteen listen to radio regularly.[71]

A major trend in radio broadcasting at the end of the 1990s was the rush by corporations and other investors to buy up stations. Their interest was sparked by the 1996 congressional telecommunications law that abolished rules limiting companies or individuals from owning more than twenty AM and twenty FM stations. The result was a tidal wave of takeovers and mergers in the business. The asking price for radio stations soared. One New York rock station, WAKQ-FM, was sold for $90 million. All in all, about 4,000 of the country's 10,000 stations changed hands by 1998 in deals that totaled an estimated $32 billion.[72] The most aggressive takeover firm was Chancellor Media Corp., whose chairman, Tom Hicks, is a former deejay. By 1999, the firm held interests in 463 stations, making it the biggest radio group in the country.[73]

In the meantime, radio broadcasters face a technological advance that could make their AM and FM operations obsolete. It is digital audio broadcasting (DAB), involving the same shift to digital transmission that television broadcasters are facing. In 1992, the FCC allocated frequencies that permit DAB programs to be broadcast either from satellites or from ground transmitters.

DAB technology is well advanced, but its full-scale application may be delayed for several reasons. One is sharp disagreements within the radio industry on how and when it should be introduced. The industry is, understandably, not keen on the idea of having to spend billions of dollars to replace its AM and FM facilities. Moreover, there are questions about the willingness of radio listeners to switch to DAB. The technology requires replacement of present receivers with more expensive sets. Finally, broadcast DAB has formidable competition from other digital audio services: cable, microwave, compact discs, and digital audio tape. Some industry observers believe it may be a decade or more before DAB becomes a significant force in U.S. radio broadcasting. Its growth may depend on its capability to permit listeners to make crisp, CD-like, high-quality sound recordings at home on minidiscs or digital cassette tapes. The result, according to media consultant Michael Tyler, could be an "armchair record store" with thousands of titles available on demand for home recording.[74]

Despite hesitation by radio broadcasters in adopting digital formats, events are forcing them to move faster. One factor is the prospect of digital broadcasting by satellite. In 1995, the FCC gave initial authorization to a new company, Satellite CD Radio, to construct a two-satellite system capable of beaming thirty national radio channels to subscribers with antennas not much bigger than a silver dollar.[75] Moreover, broadcasters realize that switching to digital radio could bring them significant operating savings by permitting them to tap more easily into national digital program suppliers. It also allows them to operate an entire station on a twenty-four-hour basis with just a few salespeople and a technician or two.[76] Two Washington, DC-area firms, CD Radio and American Mobile Radio, plan to have national satellite-based networks operating in the year 2000.[77]

TELEVISION'S BUMPY TRANSITION

The television broadcasting industry is preparing for a bumpy transition in the coming years. Its major competition, cable TV, is consolidating an already strong position by increasing its channel capacities and moving into Internet services. In addition to cable TV competition, TV broadcasters and their affiliated stations have to share audiences and revenues with direct-to-home satellite broadcasters and, eventually, telephone companies.

As we have seen, TV broadcasters are getting serious about the Internet and other alternate methods for delivering their products. Nevertheless, they remain somewhat cautious about moving into digital program formats, given the high costs and the uncertain consumer response such a strategy involves.[78]

There are signs that the Big Three networks' slide in prime-time audience viewing has slowed down. This has led to renewed optimism throughout the industry about a turnaround and a new cycle of growth in broadcasting operations. Despite its troubles, broadcast television was still the most prosperous U.S. media sector in the 1990s. Advertising revenues on all broadcast networks and local television stations were $34.7 billion in 1997, a figure that is projected to rise to $46.6 billion in 2002, according to the authoritative Veronis, Suhler Communications Industry Forecast.[79]

THE FUTURE OF BROADCASTING

While the broadcasting industry's short-term prospects look generally promising, most industry observers see little chance for long-term improvement in its fortunes. As the *Washington Post*'s Paul Farhi points out:

> No one believes the networks will ever relive their glory days, when they were the nation's "electronic hearth," around which more than 90 percent of the TV audience gathered on a given night. With dozens of existing viewing alternatives, and the prospect of perhaps hundreds of new TV channels through tech-

nological advances, even the most bullish analysts concede the networks will continue to lose audience share.[80]

The inevitable trend is toward mergers and alliances within the media industries in search of successful formulas for combining the traditional strengths of broadcast TV with potential growth in other media products. In the somewhat panicky rush to redefine themselves in this new environment, the worst thing the TV networks could do would be to weaken their most durable stock in trade, namely, good entertainment programs and solid news operations. These are the services they can deliver—when they choose to—better than other media.

THE PBS OPTION

Their model might conceivably be a media competitor whose relevance to their problems would have been dismissed out of hand a few years ago. It is public television, which is also being reshaped to deal with new technological and economic realities. The Public Broadcasting System (PBS) is no small enterprise, with about 350 stations and annual revenues of over $1 billion. Although it has been threatened with cuts in its government subsidy in recent years, the network will survive and thrive as part of the American television mix, with greater attention to the prospects opened up by the Internet and other alternative services.

For decades, PBS operated in what media historian Erik Barnouw has called "safely splendid isolation," wavering between a desire to be popular and a hard-to-shake elitist image. Mike Barnicle, a former *Boston Globe* columnist, once satirized a typical PBS program as "How to Prepare Quiche While Wearing a Bow Tie." Despite its occasional preciousness, PBS has, with relatively limited resources, demonstrated the audience appeal of good programming. After years of hesitation, it has expanded into cable TV and the Internet.[81] In 1999, one of the PBS flagship stations, WETA in Washington, DC, created a public affairs cable channel, supplementing its regular television programs.[82]

Whatever its faults, public television has kept its commitment to high-quality productions, from *Sesame Street* to *American Playhouse*, which cumulatively draw large audiences. It is difficult to imagine a mass conversion of born-again New York television executives to the public broadcasting program pattern. Nevertheless, some variation of this pattern is a viable option for them. Greater commitment to high-quality programming could stabilize their audience base.

The declining fortunes of the old-line networks and their local stations, despite their recent corporate alliances, are something less than apocalyptic events. As *Washington Post* television critic Tom Shales reminds us, God has not specified, as He did with the Ten Commandments, the number of major broadcasting networks. However, what we are losing, Shales suggests, is more than just some highly visible business enterprises:

> Everything is ending. Nothing is beginning. Television as we have known it is unraveling, and when the strands and threads are put back together, it may be all but unrecognizable. . . . For forty years we were one nation indivisible, under

television. That's what's ending. Television is turning into something else, and so are we. We're different. We're splintered. We're not as much "we" as the "we" we were. We're divisible.[83]

NOTES

1. Charles Paul Freund, "Save the Networks!" *Washington Post,* 28 July 1991, p. C-1.
2. Quoted in "And the Tube Shall Make Us Free," *Washington Post,* 24 April 1977, p. H-1.
3. Quoted in "What TV Drama Is Teaching Our Children," *New York Times,* 28 July 1991, p. C-1.
4. Minow's speech was delivered at the annual convention of the National Association of Broadcasters in May 1961. For the text of the speech, and Minow's latter-day reflections on it after thirty years, see *How Vast the Wasteland Now?* Freedom Forum Media Studies Center, Columbia University, August 1991.
5. "Sikes Looks to Strengthen Broadcaster's Hand," *Broadcasting,* 8 July 1991, p. 23.
6. Ken Auletta, *Three Blind Mice.* New York: Simon & Schuster, 1991.
7. James R. Walker and Robert V. Bellamy Jr., "Gratifications of Grazing: An Exploratory Study of Remote Control Use," *Journalism Quarterly* 68, no. 3 (Fall 1991): pp. 422–431.
8. "TV Viewing's No Dating Game," *Variety,* 24 August 1992, p. 15.
9. "Spanish TV Nets a Win," *Washington Post,* 24 April 1998, p. 1.
10. "Murdoch Re-groups Businesses," *Television Business International,* July/August 1998, p. 11.
11. "Media and Entertainment," *Business Week,* 11 January 1999, p. 100.
12. "A Wily Upstart That Did a Lot of Things Right," *New York Times,* 4 January 1998, p. AR-34.
13. "Are Paramount and Warner Looney Toon?" *Business Week,* 9 January 1995, p. 46.
14. "Barry Diller Leaves Home," *Economist* (London), 2 May 1998, p. 61. See also "Barry Owns the Whole Shooting Match," *Business Week,* 15 June 1998, p.120.
15. Quoted in Les Brown, "Reading TV's Balance Sheet," *Media & Values* 40, Summer–Fall 1987, p. 13.
16. "Network TV 'Upfront' Advertising Sales for Next Season Come in at Flat Levels," *Wall Street Journal,* 9 June 1998, p. B-8.
17. "TV's Shifting Balance of Power," *Broadcasting,* 12 October 1987, p. 40.
18. "Cosby Sidesteps Networks in Big TV Deal," *New York Times,* 28 October 1991, p. D-1.
19. The corporate takeover of the three networks has been extensively documented, most particularly in Auletta, *Three Blind Mice.* See also Sally Bedell Smith, *In All His Glory.* New York: Simon & Schuster, 1990. (a study of CBS founder William Paley), and J. Fred MacDonald, *One Nation under Television: The Rise and Decline of Network TV.* New York: Pantheon Books, 1990.
20. For a summary of the networks' cost-cutting activities at the time, see "One of TV's Best Secrets: How ABC, CBS and NBC Have Taken the Bite Out of Program Costs," *Broadcasting,* 9 December 1991, pp. 3–4.
21. "Now That's Funny Money," *Business Week,* 26 January 1998, p. 40.
22. "Shrinking Network TV Audiences Set Off Alarm and Reassessment," *New York Times,* 22 November 1998, p. 1.
23. "The Networks in Play," *Broadcasting,* 11 November 1991, pp. 3–5.
24. For a description of the negotiations leading up to the two sets of mergers, see "Awesome," *New Yorker,* 14 August 1995, pp. 28–32.

25. "The Trophy in Eisner's Big Deal," *New York Times*, 6 August 1995, p. F-1.
26. "The Invisible Manager," *New Yorker*, 27 July 1998, p. 26. See also "Westinghouse RIP," *Economist* (London), 29 November 1997, p. 63.
27. "Media Control Is Narrowing: Should We Worry?" *Business Week*, 14 August 1995, p. 37.
28. "A Goofy Deal," *Wall Street Journal*, 4 August 1995, p. A-8. See also "Mergermania in Medialand," *Forbes*, 23 October 1995, pp. 252–259.
29. Bill Carter, "TV Networks, in a Crisis, Talk of Sweeping Changes," *New York Times*, 29 July 1991, p. D-1.
30. "Broadcasting Network Executives Struggle to Reinvigorate Their Business," *New York Times*, 4 January 1999, p. C-20.
31. "Coveting Cable Strains Affiliate Relations," *Television Business International*, July/August 1998, p. 4.
32. "A $16 Billion Advertising Market," *Television Business International*, February 1991, p. 30.
33. "The Networks and Affiliates May Be Falling Out of Love," *Business Week*, 15 June 1992, p. 41.
34. "Quality TV: Hollywood's Elusive Illusion," *Broadcasting*, 18 November 1991, p. 17.
35. Auletta, *Three Blind Mice*, p. 563.
36. "Internet News Takes Off," Pew Research Center for the People and the Press, Washington, DC, June 1998, p. 1. See also "Stop Press," *Economist*, 4 July 1998, p. 17.
37. "World Series Is a Hit, But CBS Still Loses," *Washington Post*, 29 October 1991, p. D-1.
38. "No NFL PPV Until At Least 1994," *Broadcasting*, 2 September 1991, p. 17. See also Phillip M. Cox, "Flag on the Play? The Siphoning Effect of Sports Television," *Federal Communications Law Journal* 47, no. 3, April 1995, pp. 571–591.
39. "NFL Sunday Ticket," *Via Satellite*, August 1994, pp. 32–33.
40. Tapio Varis, "The International Flow of Television Programs," *Journal of Communications*, 34, No. 1, Winter 1984, pp. 143–152. See also "U.S. Programs Account for 75 Per Cent of International Marketplace," *Radio-Television Age*, 14 May 1984, p. 12.
41. "Stand Aside, CNN. America's No. 1 Export is 'Baywatch,'" *New York Times*, 3 July 1995, p. C-7.
42. "Ready for Prime Time in Moscow," *New York Times*, 22 January 1992, p. D-1.
43. "ABC Dishes It Out," *Broadcasting*, 5 October 1992, p. 18. For an overall survey of current international television trends, see R. Negrine and S. Papathanassopoulos, "The Internationalization of Television," *European Journal of Communications* 6, no. 1, March 1991, pp. 5–32.
44. "NBC Cable Dons Seven-league Boots," *Broadcast & Cable*, 10 October 1994, p. 90.
45. "DBS Hopes to Leave Big Footprint on Latin America," *Broadcasting & Cable*, 28 August 1995, pp. 22–26. See also "Latin Tunes," *Economist* (London), 25 November 1995, p. 64.
46. "That's Not All, Folks," *Economist* (London), 2 November 1991, p. 64.
47. "Black-led Group Wins License for S. Africa's 1st 'Free' TV Station," *Washington Post*, 31 March 1998, p. E-3.
48. "NBC Walks into Cable Minefield," *New York Times*, 10 April 1989, p. D-1.
49. Quoted in Auletta, *Three Blind Mice*, p. 282.
50. "Cable, Overseas Program Markets Targeted by ABC," *Broadcasting*, 8 May 1989, p. 34.
51. "'We'll Take a Hit Show from Attila the Hun,'" *Business Week*, 20 March 1995, p. 34.
52. For a discussion of the CNBC case and similar incidents, see Henry Geller, *Fiber Optics: An Opportunity for a New Policy?* Annenberg Washington Program, Washington, DC, November 1991, pp. 19–20.

53. "This Little Peacock Is Showing Some Pluck," *Business Week*, 17 August 1998, p. 64.
54. Pew Research Center, op cit., p. 3
55. "Networks, Affiliates Still at Odds over Cable Crossownership Ban," *Broadcasting*, 14 October 1991, p. 33.
56. U.S. Congress, Office of Technology Assessment, *The Big Picture: HDTV and High-Resolution Systems*, background paper OTA-BP-CIT-64, Washington, DC, June 1990, pp. 49–59.
57. "Compression: Changing the World of Television?" *Broadcasting*, 11 June 1990, pp. 68–71.
58. "In Your Face," *Economist* (London), 7 June 1997, p. 84.
59. "Your Master's Voice," *Wired*, August 1997, p. 45.
60. "Some Broadcasters Back Away From HDTV Programming Pledge," *New York Times*, 18 August 1997, p. C-7.
61. "HDTV: A Four-Bagger in Texas," *Communications Industries Report*, May 1998, p. 1.
62. "Digital D-Day," *Business Week*, 26 October 1998, p. 144.
63. "Leaping Out of the Box," *Business 2.0*, September 1998, p. 112.
64. "Disney Acts to Widen Role on the Internet," *Washington Post*, 19 June 1998, p. F-1.
65. "NBC Backing an On-line TV Service," *New York Times*, 3 August 1998, p. D-4.
66. "Webcasting: Still a Way to Go," *Interactive Week*, 29 June 1998, p. 43.
67. "A Couple in Sync, Airing Programs on the Internet," *Washington Post*, Washington Business supplement, 10 May 1998, p. 5.
68. "Caught in the Web," *Television Business International*, December 1998, p. 14.
69. "Music From the Spheres," *Washington Post*, 19 May 1997, p. 5.
70. "Everybody's Talkin' to Us," *Business Week*, 22 May 1995, pp. 104–105.
71. "Study Details Teens' Heavy Use of Radio," *Broadcasting*, 1 July 1991, p. 37.
72. "The Great Radio Rebellion: The Turned Off Fight Back," *Washington Post*, 2 June 1998, p. D-1.
73. "CBS to Sell Stake in Radio Business," *Washington Post*, 28 August 1998, p. F-3.
74. "Digital Waves Clear the Air," *Financial Times* (London), 7 July 1992, p. 11.
75. "FCC OKs $10 Million CD Investment," *Broadcasting & Cable*, 11 September 1995, p. 53.
76. "Lone Ranger Meets Howard Stern," *Forbes* (4 December 1995): pp. 49–50.
77. "Music From the Spheres," *Washington Post*, Washington Business supplement, 19 May 1997, p. 7.
78. "Tuned In and Dropping Off," *Economist* (London), 4 November 1995, pp. 65–66.
79. Veronis, Suhler & Associates, *Communications Industry Forecast: Industry Spending Projections 1998–2002*, 12th Annual Edition, New York, October 1998, p. 128.
80. "The Networks Stage a Comeback," *Washington Post*, 17 May 1992, p. H-1.
81. For a useful survey of public TV options, see *Strategies for Public Television in a Multi-Channel Environment*, report by the Boston Consulting Group for the Corporation for Public Broadcasting, Washington, DC, March 1991.
82. "WETA, Media Group to Team Up on Cable," *Washington Post*, 6 January 1999, p. C-1.
83. "TV's Sinking Net Worth," *Washington Post*, 31 July 1991, p. B-1.

Cable Television:
The Perils of Success

Cable television has redefined the U.S. mass media environment in the past two decades. From modest origins as a small-town service, it has expanded into national networks, each serving thousands of communities. Cable TV is the primary media link to the outside world in two-thirds of U.S. households. More important, it has given Americans a preview of a future in which information and entertainment products will be delivered to their homes by a single electronic utility. At the turn of the century, cable is taking on a new role as an important transmitter of Internet and other advanced digital services.

Unfortunately for media historians, there is no defining moment for the beginning of cable television—no Johannes Gutenberg looking at the first book from his multiple-copy printing machine, no Alexander Graham Bell shouting, "Mr. Watson, come here" into his primitive telephone. There are many claimants to the title of inventor of cable TV. If the cable industry decides one day to put up a monument to its founder, it may be dedicated to the Unknown Appliance Store Manager. Sometime around 1947, he or she had a clever idea for selling the store's supply of newfangled black-and-white, nine-inch-screen television sets. The problem was that there was no television station in the community. The manager thought, why not put up a tower tall enough to pick up TV programs from a nearby city and then retransmit the programs on cable wires to local households for a fee? The tower was built and the cable strung, and suddenly television had arrived in small-town America.

TABLE 6.1   Prime-Time Audience Shares

Year	Network-Affiliated TV Stations	Independent TV Stations*	All TV Stations	Basic Cable Programs	Pay Cable Programs	All Cable
1992	65.9%	9.1%	75.1%	20.2%	4.7%	24.9%
1993	65.3	9.4	74.6	20.8	4.5	25.4
1994	64.7	9.9	74.7	20.8	4.6	25.3
1995	58.9	10.6	69.5	25.5	5.0	30.5
1996	56.8	10.6	67.3	27.7	5.0	32.7
1997	52.3	10.9	63.1	31.3	5.6	36.9

SOURCES: Veronis, Suhler & Associates, Wilkofsky Gruen Associates, Nielsen Media Research

*Excludes superstations; includes UPN and WB affiliates for 1995–1997

From these humble beginnings sprang the service known as Community Antenna Television (CATV), the forerunner of today's cable TV industry. CATV developed slowly; by 1950, only 14,000 households in 70 communities had cable television services. It was not until 1966 that CATV services had expanded sufficiently to warrant the first FCC regulation of its activities.[1] By 1970, cable TV was a fixture in most rural and suburban communities, and the first large networks were being installed in cities, where cable provided a clearer signal with less interference than over-the-air transmissions.

CABLE FACES MIDDLE AGE

Today's cable industry is a $40 billion enterprise, the most successful new media business of the past three decades.[2] It has, however, entered the ranks of mature industries—with more and more of the aches and pains that institutional maturity brings. The early symptoms are recorded in economic surveys that indicate a general leveling off of cable TV subscriber growth. From the double-digit growth of earlier years (typically around 15 percent annually), single-digit cable TV growth was the rule in the 1990s.

This reflects the fact that cable TV is approaching a saturation point in the number of households it can effectively serve. Most industry analysts predicted that the penetration rate would top off at about 70 percent by the end of the decade. Despite the fact that cable services are available to fewer households than those of the broadcasting networks, cable TV is steadily eroding the broadcasting audience. (See Table 6.1.) During one week in July 1998, the cable networks topped NBC, ABC, CBS, and Fox in prime time by all conventional media indices—total viewers, rating, and audience shares.[3]

The cable TV business remains strong by any measure, but the first bloom is off its rose. Part of the reason has been consumer dissatisfaction with a system they had earlier embraced. This disenchantment was documented in the 1990s

TABLE 6.2 Homes Passed by Cable and Incidence of Subscription

Year	TV Households (Millions)	Homes Passed by Cable (Millions)	Homes Passed as a % of TV Households	Number of Cable Households (Millions)	Cable Subscribers as a % of Homes Passed	Cable Penetration of TV Households
1984	84.9	58.2	68.6%	32.8	56.4%	38.6%
1985	85.7	62.6	73.0	35.5	56.7	41.4
1986	86.8	67.1	77.3	38.2	56.9	44.0
1987	87.4	71.3	81.6	41.2	57.8	47.1
1988	88.6	75.2	84.9	44.2	58.8	49.9
1989	90.4	80.0	88.5	47.5	59.4	52.5
1990	92.1	84.4	91.6	50.5	59.8	54.8
1991	93.1	87.2	93.7	52.6	60.3	56.5
1992	92.1*	88.9	96.5	54.3	61.1	59.0
1993	93.1	90.0	96.7	56.2	62.4	60.4
1994	94.2	91.1	96.7	58.5	64.2	62.1
1995	95.4	92.2	96.6	60.9	66.1	63.8
1996	95.9	93.2	97.2	62.8	67.4	65.5
1997	97.0	94.2	97.1	64.2	68.2	66.2
1998	98.0	95.2	97.1	65.4	68.7	66.7
1999	99.1	96.1	97.0	66.6	69.3	67.2
2000	100.2	97.1	96.9	67.7	69.7	67.6
2001	101.4	98.1	96.7	68.8	70.1	67.9
2002	102.5	99.0	96.6	70.0	70.7	68.3

SOURCES: Veronis, Suhler & Associates, Wilkofsky Gruen Associaties, Paul Kagan Associates, Nielsen Media Research

*Revised downward based on 1990 census

when Consumers Union surveyed 200,000 households on attitudes toward cable TV. Respondents gave a satisfaction index rating of 60 percent to cable, considerably lower than ratings recorded for other major services tracked by Consumers Union. The respondents' complaints were varied, but there was general dismay with the upward creep of cable subscription fees. There was also criticism of cable programming, poor repair services, and system outages.[4]

Consumer unhappiness expresses itself in what the cable industry refers to as its "churn" problem: the continuing turnover in subscribers. Cable system circuits are available to 90 percent of all U.S. households, yet only two-thirds of those homes actually subscribe. (See Table 6.2.) The higher cost of cable subscriptions accounts for part of this reluctance to sign up. Many householders simply cannot afford the service. Even more unsettling for the industry has been those householders who do subscribe and then cancel all or part of their contracts because of disappointment with cable service.[5] This turnover is a persistent headache for local cable operators. The cancellations are offset, in part, by new subscriptions.

Increasingly, however, many cable systems are beginning to lose customers to new competitors—telephone companies, direct-satellite broadcasters, and wireless-cable operators—all of whom can provide similar programming services.

STRATEGIES FOR CONTINUED GROWTH

The cable industry's strategy for dealing with these market problems is twofold. First, the industry has put together a raft of mergers and alliances designed to strengthen its ability to meet the new competition. Many of these linkups have taken place within the industry. Large companies have been buying up smaller local systems, allowing them to pool financial and management resources to match the new competition. By the late 1990s, ten national cable conglomerates controlled most of the systems serving cable households. This consolidation has effectively marked the end of the era of local mom-and-pop cable systems in small towns and cities.[6]

The second part of the cable industry's strategy is to make alliances with forces outside the industry. An early instance of this occurred in Denver in 1992 when the local cable and phone companies agreed to share a fiber-optic circuit serving several thousand customers. In effect, the two companies agreed to compete with each other on a common circuit carrying both their information and entertainment services.

Since then, the deals have become more complex. This is due largely to the relaxation of regulatory barriers mandated in the federal 1996 Telecommunications Act, described in Chapter 4. The legislation opened the door for mergers and acquisitions within the cable industry as well as with other communications-sector companies. This latter strategy was behind AT&T's 1998 takeover of Telecommunications Inc. (TCI), the country's second-largest cable operator. The $48 billion deal was designed to create a combined telephone/cable infrastructure that is potentially capable of being the leader in providing advanced multimedia products, including Internet services, to over 100 million households. Industry observers are agreed that the TCI takeover opens up a new chapter in the short history of cable TV's impact on American mass media.

Despite the absorption of TCI by AT&T, the cable industry will continue to be a strong sector in its own right. However, future mergers and partnerships within the sector and with outside firms will transform the nature and direction of cable television operations in the early years of the new century. In particular, it will change cable's advantage of having had a monopoly, protected by municipal franchises, in most communities. This monopoly advantage is being inexorably eroded by the entry of competitive systems operated by telephone companies, satellite firms, and wireless-cable entrepreneurs.

Cable TV's other advantage will be its continued success in supplying a broad range of program services to its subscribers. Cable TV has begun to overtake its closest competition—broadcast television—by making itself the preferred channel for both local and network TV programs. All this is a long leap from cable's modest beginnings in the 1940s as a retransmitter of over-the-air television programming. By the 1960s, cable systems had begun providing original programming such as bulletin board announcements of community happenings, local high school football games, and an occasional transmission of city council meetings.

FROM SMALL TOWN TO BIG TIME

In the early 1970s, the age of innocence for the cable industry ended for two reasons: communications satellites and Ted Turner. By 1975, U.S. communications satellite networks had expanded to the point where they could transmit video signals anywhere in the country. Ted Turner, a Georgia advertising executive, saw what this could mean for a small local television station such as WTBS in Atlanta, which he happened to own. In late 1976, he leased a national satellite circuit and informed cable owners that they could retransmit WTBS programs without charge. Hundreds of cable owners installed earth stations to pick up old sitcom programs, which were WTBS's stock in trade. Turner also bought the Atlanta Braves baseball team and added their games to the station's schedule. In a short time, WTBS had a national audience of millions, a great attraction for advertisers. Other "superstation" operations sprang up around the country, giving cable operators more programming choices as well as a strong merchandising tool for expanding their subscriber base.[7]

Ted Turner's superstation gamble has taken on legendary stature in the cable industry over the years. Turner himself is not shy in claiming that he revolutionized cable TV. In a 1989 interview, he declared, "On January 1, 1977, cable penetration was at 14 percent. That's when we went on the satellite with WTBS, and now it's at 55 percent. That's four times as much in only eleven years."[8]

In fact, Ted Turner has to share his cable revolution claim with a lesser-known figure, Gerald Levin. Levin was a vice president of Time Inc.'s video group in the mid-1970s when he proposed that HBO, the company's financially ailing pay-television service, deliver its programs to local cable systems by satellite. Levin's satellite proposal was a bigger gamble than Ted Turner's superstation venture, involving a heavier investment by both Time Inc. and the cable operators. Each operator had to invest $100,000 in an earth station to receive HBO programs. When HBO's satellite services began in 1975, there were only two such stations in place. HBO lost money for several years, but by 1980, over 1,700 local cable systems were receiving its satellite programming.[9] HBO is now a staple offering on almost all of the nation's 11,000 cable systems.

In the process, the cable industry broke out of its small-town mold. More than a dozen major pay-television services now follow HBO's satellite delivery pattern of programming that has brought tens of millions of new customers to local cable systems. As a result, the economics of the business has changed dramatically. Previously, cable subscription rates were calculated on a single monthly charge for all programs. With the arrival of satellite-delivered services, that billing pattern changed. HBO and similar national pay-TV services levied an additional "premium program" charge. This multiple-billing practice, known as "tiering" in the industry, is still the financial underpinning for cable systems and their program suppliers. A third revenue source, pay-per-view (PPV) programming, is now becoming an increasingly important profit center for cable operators.

NEW CHANNELS, NEW AUDIENCES

The national services such as HBO, Showtime, The Movie Channel, and the Disney Channel have the largest audience shares. There are, however, loyal audiences for other channel offerings. An outsized example is MTV, the video-music channel owned by Viacom International, available to an estimated 250 million households in 64 countries and territories worldwide. Its programming is almost cost-free to Viacom, since the record companies that produce the videos are paid only nominal fees.[10] Advertisers flock to the channel and its demographically desirable audiences of teenagers and young adults.

Other channels have settled for "narrowcasting" to smaller audiences. Bravo and Arts & Entertainment are consciously cultural, appealing to an upscale audience that is attractive to many advertisers. Lifetime makes a tidy profit with women-oriented programming. The Nickelodeon channel is probably the biggest producer of children's programming in the world.[11] ESPN is the country's largest single cable network, with its macho collection of sports events, from baseball to truck-pull contests. Time Warner has been successful with Court TV, supplying armchair lawyers with sensational court trials. Other channels reach out to history buffs, sci-fi fans, weather watchers, Hispanics, and junk jewelry buyers.

Not all new cable channels are successful. In the early 1990s, Ted Turner inaugurated Checkout Channel, a network of supermarket monitors that displayed snippets of news, fashion tips, and weather reports, along with advertisements, to shoppers waiting in line to pay for their groceries. The idea may have sounded clever to the Turner organization's marketing department, but it did not catch on with shoppers. The Checkout Channel closed down a year later.

Ted Turner's supermarket venture aside, the hope of striking it rich with a new channel still lures eager entrepreneurs. Dozens of new channels are proposed every year, but most of them get no further than a sales pitch. For those that do manage to get channel space on cable, the chances for success are small. Cable consultant Paul Kagan has estimated that fewer than one-third of the new ventures will break even.[12]

TWO INNOVATIONS: CNN AND C-SPAN

Cable television has contributed two substantial media innovations. One is the Cable News Network (CNN), founded by Ted Turner and merged with Time Warner in 1995. Its stock-in-trade, a twenty-four-hour news service, added a new dimension to electronic news, especially for coverage of fast-breaking events.[13] Some of its most successful weeks were those in which it provided full coverage of the 1995 O. J. Simpson murder trial; in one week, its trial coverage accounted for fourteen of the top fifteen cable-viewer ratings.[14] Despite such successes, CNN has had difficulty retaining an audience during quiet news periods, falling back on a program strategy of call-in shows and other lightweight features.[15] By 1998, its daily audience ratings were down 49 percent from the Simpson-trial highs of 1995.[16] Now owned by Time Warner, it faced increasing competition in the late 1990s from copycat news services such as NBC's MSNBC, ABCNews.com, and Fox's Fox News. It responded by expanding its business-news channel along with a World Wide Web service, CNN Interactive, that included advanced video and voice capabilities.

Despite growing competition, CNN is still the leading cable news channel, reaching over 190 million households in the United States and abroad, as well as providing news feeds to almost 500 American over-the-air TV stations.[17]

CNN changed the nature of news broadcasting at home and abroad.[18] In 1992, its impact as an international news channel was confirmed when eleven state-owned European television organizations announced that they would sponsor a regional satellite news channel, Euronews, that would pointedly compete with CNN's growing presence in Europe. The channel's purpose had less to do with making a profit than with defending European culture. "CNN is an American channel, an American point of view," Euronews executive Pierre Brunel-Lantena declared. "The point of Euronews is to give the viewer back his memories."[19] Euronews never met its initial expectations, and it was unable to match the success of CNN and MSNBC, both of which had set up profitable regional news operations in Europe.[20] In Asia, CNN has competition from the British Broadcasting Company (BBC), which broadcasts a satellite-based television news service to thirty-eight countries.

CNN's techniques are being imitated by a number of local cable news channels in U.S. cities. In Honolulu, a Hawaiian-shirted announcer reports on daily surfing conditions, among other subjects. In Los Angeles, the cable news channel has featured "Dr. Drive," who monitors what he calls snafuskis on the local freeways. A CNN-type regional news channel, New England Cable NewsChannel, serves cable networks in six states. By the late 1990s, there were eight regional news channels across the country. One of the most successful, News 12 Long Island, boasts the biggest television news team in the New York–New Jersey–Connecticut area, covering everything from drunken-driver arrests to school-board meetings.[21]

Cable television's other important program innovation is C-SPAN, the public affairs channel. C-SPAN is the brainchild of Brian Lamb, a former federal government official, who saw in cable TV a means to document the political process for ordinary citizens. Lamb persuaded the U.S. House of Representatives in 1979 to allow gavel-to-gavel coverage of its sessions. In 1986, the network added a second channel, C-SPAN 2, when the U.S. Senate agreed to permit coverage of its sessions. C-SPAN's programming extends to other public affairs forums, including state legislatures and the British and Canadian parliaments. In addition to providing a World Wide Web online service for computer users, C-Span began broadcasting highlights of its cable programming on a Washington, DC, FM radio channel in 1997.

C-SPAN is one of the cable industry's more altruistic projects: It is funded by local cable operators at a monthly cost of only several cents per subscriber. The importance of C-SPAN's public-service function was underscored in 1992 when the Big Three television networks slashed their presidential campaign coverage in favor of more lucrative programs. C-SPAN filled the gap with 1,200 hours of campaign programming.[22]

CABLE TV'S CORPORATE MASTERS

C-SPAN, CNN, and other channel services have transformed cable TV into a truly national medium, more akin to the three old-line television networks than to a collection of separate local systems. In the process, the cable industry has been restructured and redefined. Two decades ago, there was a clear distinction between local cable operators and the firms that supplied their programs. Today the industry is dominated by a handful of companies (known as multiple system operators—MSOs), which are full or partial owners of local cable systems that provide services for most U.S. subscribers. These firms also own, wholly or in part, most of the popular national cable programming services supplied to local systems. In 1998, two of the largest cable conglomerates, Time Warner and Telecommunications Inc., produced 35 percent of all cable programming.[23] The smaller cable groups were responsible for most of the rest.

The MSOs draw from a mixed bag of corporate styles. Some are "pure" cable companies, investing only in local cable systems and the program services supplied to them. Others are diversified communications conglomerates, whose interests often include publishing, broadcasting, filmmaking, and other media operations. The biggest of these conglomerates is the Disney Company, followed by Time Warner. Each conglomerate has a different pattern: Disney is strong in filmmaking and, through its ABC network, in broadcasting. Time Warner's strengths are in filmmaking and publishing. Even before its merger with Warner Communications in 1989, Time Inc. recognized the importance of cable TV as part of its multimedia operations. As Time Warner executive Gerald Levin has noted, "Cable was a hardware business before. Now it is a video publishing business, something our company is more comfortable with."[24]

The executives of these megacompanies are the movers and shakers of a transformation in U.S. media. To the general public, they remain a faceless group with little name recognition: Time Warner's Gerry Levin, Disney's Michael Eisner, Cablevision's Charles Dolan, and Viacom's Sumner Redstone. The exceptional name-recognition winner would be Ted Turner, who promoted CNN against all the odds, was *Time* magazine's Man of the Year in 1991, and married Jane Fonda. Since his company's merger with Time Warner, he has been a top executive at the latter company.

JOHN MALONE: A CABLE-TV ORIGINAL

A less flamboyant, but more powerful, member of the new cable establishment has been John Malone, who was chief executive of TCI until he moved over to AT&T in 1998 following the merger of the two companies. Under Malone's leadership, TCI owned or had financial interest in local cable systems with more than

14 million subscribers—about 25 percent of the nation's cabled homes. A Yale graduate with a double major in economics and electronics engineering, Malone joined TCI in 1973. At the time, TCI was overextended financially and unloved generally, with a reputation for hard-nosed business. At one point, in negotiating cable subscriber rates with municipal authorities in Vail, Colorado, TCI closed down its local cable programming for a weekend and transmitted only the names and home phone numbers of the mayor and city manager. The harried local officials hastened to conclude the negotiations on terms favorable to TCI.[25] Malone once summarized the firm's philosophy when he told an interviewer, "This is not touch football, this is tackle."

Malone also changed the direction of the firm by making it a major player in national program services, beginning in 1987, when he led a consortium of cable conglomerates that invested $568 million in Turner Broadcasting. At the time, the Turner firm was in danger of going under as a consequence of Ted Turner's expensive purchase of a large part of the MGM studio's film library. (Characteristically, Turner's MGM gamble, which included such gems as *Gone With the Wind*, turned out to be a financial winner.) TCI held a 22 percent interest in Turner Broadcasting, including its Cable News Network. John Malone also invested in other channels, including Black Entertainment Television, Discovery, and American Movie Classics.[26] His firm's investment in Ted Turner's operations resulted in a financial bonanza when Turner Broadcasting was merged with Time Warner in 1997.

Malone made TCI a significant player in the satellite field, with a 20 percent stake in Primestar, one of the new national satellite-broadcasting networks. In 1995, he built a $100 million digital television studio in Littleton, Colorado, designed to deliver hundreds of channels of programming by satellite to its cable systems across the country.[27] The following year, Malone's TCI teamed up with MCI Corporation and Rupert Murdoch's News Corporation to bid successfully in an FCC auction for the last remaining license to operate a national satellite television service.

John Malone also tried to position TCI to compete in the convergence of cable and telephone services. This led in 1993 to a proposed $35 billion TCI merger with Bell Atlantic, the regional phone company. It was an audacious plan, particularly given the fact that TCI was $11 billion in debt at the time. The deal collapsed a few months later, however, partly because the financial plan was shaky and also because the idea of melding the corporate cultures of a media company and a phone company was slightly ahead of its time. Malone himself attributed failure of the plan to "a fundamental problem between two philosophies."[28] Five years later, he closed the philosophical gap with his 1998 AT&T deal.

During his years at TCI, Malone led the company into such areas as fiber-cable installations, home shopping, data networking, and PPV programming. TCI's cable systems have been outfitted with addressable converters designed for PPV reception. Through negotiations with the Fox Television Network, Malone has arranged to make TCI the first formal broadcast network affiliate in the cable industry. In the process, he became the leading advocate for making cable an all-purpose provider of telecommunications and information services for homes, including telephone and interactive multimedia circuits.[29] TCI took its first step into Webcasting with the 1997 purchase of Sonicnet, a New York firm that has been a pioneer in Internet broadcasting operations.[30]

Malone has also been the leader in recognizing the potential to media companies of providing Internet services. TCI's first venture into this area was a 1992 linkup with IBM to develop a cable-based interactive network to deliver these services.[31] More recently, the company invested $125 million for a 20 percent stake in the Microsoft Network, which, since its debut in 1995, has developed into a serious challenger to America Online, Prodigy, and other interactive services.

All this experience served him in good stead in the bare-knuckle negotiations that led to TCI's merger with AT&T in 1998. The phone giant's technological and economic prowess will be major factors in assuring TCI's role as a dominant presence in the cable TV sector. At the time of the merger, AT&T announced plans to spend $4.4 billion to add high-speed Internet access and enhanced video capabilities to the TCI network and up to $500 per household to add telephone capabilities as needed.[32]

THE MSOS' EXPANSION PLANS

Large multiple-system operators now dominate the cable television business. The top twenty-five MSOs control the circuits to over 75 percent of all cable subscribers. This ratio rose in the late 1990s as the big MSO conglomerates continued to buy out smaller MSOs as well as the remaining independent systems. Their general strategy is "clustering," buying as many systems within a given region as they can. In addition to strengthening regional programming and advertising prospects, clustering also positions these operations for eventual entry into telephone and other local services. Time Warner has been the most successful of the cable-cluster strategists, with over three-quarters of its 12 million subscribers located in thirty-four areas around the country. The company's New York metropolitan area cluster is the largest in the world, with over a million subscribers.

These MSO acquisitions will result in an even tighter consolidation of cable TV transmission and programming resources in the hands of a very small group of companies, in effect an oligopoly of vertically integrated enterprises. The big conglomerates already exercise a greater degree of control over the cable industry than do their counterparts in any other U.S. media industry.

The cable industry's rationale for this development is that consolidation is necessary to finance and manage the planned expansion of each of its local systems to 150 channels or more, together with the new programming that will be carried on those channels. What has been generally downplayed by cable executives is their aim of blocking incursions by telephone companies and other new competitors into the field of home entertainment and information services following the relaxation of regulatory restrictions in the Telecommunications Act of 1996.

The threat of outside competition is only one of the cable industry's concerns. Another is that the industry will soon peak in terms of subscriber growth and in the willingness of subscribers to spend more on new cable services. These are critical considerations as cable systems pursue their costly expansion of channel capacity and program services. Cable television will have to adapt its present strategy to these new realities if it is to maintain its profitable momentum.

INTERACTIVE SERVICES: CABLE'S NEW STRATEGY

The best hope for the industry probably rests in expanding on-demand delivery of PPV (pay-per-view) movies and sports events. The idea is to capture a significant part of the $20 billion spent annually by Americans on videotape rentals. The industry's strategy has been to market PPV as the "video store at home," emphasizing that cable subscribers can avoid the inconvenience of leaving the house to rent tapes one day and going out again the next day to return them.[33]

However, the PPV market has developed slowly. Fifteen years ago, a major PPV experiment in Columbus, Ohio, failed because subscribers found the technology for ordering programs awkward to deal with and because its programs were similar to those already available on HBO and other pay-TV channels. It became obvious that PPV would be economically viable only when more efficient, user-friendly systems for viewing special programs were developed. By the mid-1990s, this began to happen. In 1998, PPV access was available in over one-third of all U.S. cable households, and spending for its programs was doubling each year.

To access PPV easily, a subscriber needs a special device that has, in the industry's phrase, "full addressability"—that is, equipment that allows easy two-way communications between the viewer and the program supplier. Originally, a subscriber had to make a phone call to order a program. Advanced versions of converter boxes now allow a subscriber to use a keypad to scan a menu of current PPV offerings and then to select a program by punching in the program's number. The program appears on the video screen. At the same time, the subscriber's account is debited. This kind of quick access to programs is essential, since surveys have shown that most PPV viewers are impulse buyers.

TIME WARNER'S INTERACTIVE EXPERIMENTS

Time Warner was the first cable company to install the new PPV technology. Its earliest test was a 150-channel cable network, located in an affluent section of Queens, New York. The system, known as Quantum, delivered up to fifteen different movies on fifty-seven PPV channels in addition to regular cable TV service. Initial subscriber costs for PPV showings ranged from $1.95 to $4.95, low enough to discourage visits to the local video rental store. Quantum also offered a full menu of cable TV fare, from the Prayer Channel ("reverent contact with God throughout the day") to channels programmed in Greek, Hindi, Korean, Cantonese, and Mandarin.[34]

Time Warner followed its Quantum experiment with a more advanced system in Orlando, Florida, that went well beyond conventional cable TV technology. Dubbed the Full Service Network, the 500-channel Orlando facility relied on a video server, essentially a high-capacity computer that stores a vast amount of voice, text, and video images that can be retrieved and transmitted on demand via digital switches and fiber-optic circuits to subscribers. "We're creating a TV architecture that gives people what they want when they want it. It is channel-less," Greg Holmes, Time Warner's technology director, declared.[35]

Announced with great fanfare in 1992, the Orlando project was slowed down by technical glitches in its early years. It also had trouble attracting customers: by 1995, fewer than 4,000 Orlando-area households had been connected to the system. After spending hundreds of millions of dollars, Time Warner cut back the project drastically. Three regional Bell phone companies—Bell Atlantic, Nynex, and Pacific Telesis—promoted a similar network, designed to put viewers in control of what they watched and when they watched it. The project, known as Tele-TV, turned out to be a costly flop, as well as a warning to other cable networkers about the perils of rushing into advanced interactive operations.

"At least these trials accomplished one thing: we know what does and doesn't work," says Richard Green, president of Cable Television Laboratories. "They were expensive lessons for the industry to learn."[36] In the late 1990s, cable operators took a new look at interactive programming, including the Internet and PPV. In part, they realized that they had to move quickly into the field to match similar plans by competitors such as the telephone companies and direct broadcasting satellite firms. Moreover, a new generation of technology had been developed that went beyond delivering video-on-demand to include electronic shopping, music, quick access to the Internet, and other services. The new systems also offer consumers easier ways to point-and-click through their various program menus.

Intertainer, a California company promoting the new technology, teamed up with Microsoft and Sun Microsystems to incorporate high-speed chips into advanced digital set-top boxes. Working with Comcast, a cable company, and US West, a regional phone firm, Intertainer began marketing its technology in selected cities in 1998. A competitor, Diva Systems, made similar moves at the same time in other cities.

THE NEW PUSH FOR INTERACTIVE SERVICES

Cable TV's future is tied to its success in expanding into advanced digital services. As noted above, this expansion is, in part, a defensive move to match similar strategies by TV broadcasters, DBS satellite operators, and telephone networkers. Moreover, there are clear indications of potentially strong consumer demand for interactive programs, particularly sports events and new Hollywood films. Surveys have shown that the average consumer would be prepared to pay almost $6 extra monthly for interactive services, which could mean billions of dollars in added revenues for the cable industry.[37] The major uncertainty for cable operators is determining which interactive services subscribers want. When Time Warner polled subscribers to its high-tech Orlando network, it found that the service the customers valued most was the convenience of ordering stamps from the post office without having to wait in line. Another interactive service that many subscribers like, although few will admit it, is online delivery of so-called adult films. In the late 1990s, channels like Playboy and Spice earned about $200 million annually, roughly a third of the pay-per-view market at the time.[38]

PAY-PER-VIEW'S FUTURE

Sports is the other pay-per-view service that clearly attracts viewers, and profits, for cable operators. Interest in PPV sports was kicked off in the early 1990s by three world championship boxing matches. Local cable networks charged home viewers premium rates of up to $40 per match, which brought in total gross revenues of a quarter-billion dollars for the three events.[39] In 1992, the summer Olympics were made available to PPV viewers under joint arrangements between NBC and cable companies. The venture was a programming success and a financial failure; NBC reportedly lost $100 million on the project.[40] Nevertheless, NBC's expectations for a financial bonanza from its contract to cover the summer and winter Olympics in the year 2000 are based on anticipation of heavy PPV revenues.

Most industry observers believe that PPV will expand rapidly when National Football League and Major League Baseball games, now only partly available on cable, are all routinely shown as PPV offerings. Both leagues are moving toward this goal in their negotiations with cable operators.

Until that happens, the bread-and-butter programming of the PPV services is new Hollywood films. The film industry is well aware of this potential for new revenues. A survey by Goldman Sachs, the New York investment house, notes that, for PPV showings, the studios get about fifty cents of every subscriber dollar collected, while they get only twenty cents of every videocassette dollar and fifteen cents of every pay-cable movie dollar.[41] In the late 1990s, all the big Hollywood studios began examining the prospect of getting direct control by opening their own PPV channels, thus eliminating the cable middlemen altogether.

As the cable industry moves into expensive new PPV operations, it needs to maintain a high level of profitability. As noted earlier, the rate of subscriber growth is leveling off. The industry also continues to have problems with churn, a persistent turnover in subscribers. At one point in the 1990s, cable systems across the country had more disconnects than new subscribers, reversing a forty-year trend.[42] Another problem for cable companies is their heavy debt load, inherited from the high-riding 1980s when they were expanding their systems. Cable systems were being traded like baseball cards in a schoolyard, often at dizzying prices. It took many cable operators a decade to recover at least partially from this financial frenzy.

SEARCHING FOR ADVERTISING DOLLARS

Although the cable industry overall is in good financial shape, it needs to pursue new revenue opportunities. The most immediate increase in revenue may come from advertising. Cable advertising has already increased to the point where subscribers are objecting to "clutter": too many commercials interfering with programs they have already paid for with subscription fees. One study has indicated that cable has significantly more clutter than the television networks in prime time.[43]

The cable industry has introduced a new twist in electronic advertising with infomercials, thirty-minute advertisements that often masquerade as talk shows and provide viewers with a toll-free phone number for ordering the featured products. (Infomercials are also broadcast regularly on many television channels.) They are the fastest-growing segment of the multibillion-dollar TV direct-response industry, which also includes the shop-at-home channels such as the Home Shopping Network. Cable operators hope to expand this service when more subscribers are equipped with digital "black box" equipment that will allow them to sample, shop, and pay for a wide range of products electronically. Their model is the growing success of shop-at-home pages on the Internet's World Wide Web pages.

The trend in cable advertising favors local cable channels, not the big national program providers. On local channels, business firms can reach the specialized audiences they want, a benefit not usually available on the national channels. Furthermore, cable ad rates are considerably lower than those charged by broadcasting stations. A thirty-second prime-time advertisement on a cable channel often costs about one-fourth the broadcast rate, a distinct attraction for small, local advertisers. Overall, national and local cable operators earned over $9 billion in advertising revenues in 1998.[44]

CABLE AS AN EDUCATIONAL RESOURCE

Advertising will continue to be an increasingly profitable revenue source for cable operators as they add more channels to their systems through digital compression technology. The operators are looking for new programming opportunities to fill the expanded channels. One relatively unexplored area is programming for school classrooms. Public television's school programs have served as an educational resource for decades, but these programs are usually limited to a single channel in a community. As a result, it has been difficult to tailor educational TV programs to meet diverse curriculum needs. In a 150-channel cable environment, that difficulty will be easier to overcome. Fifteen or 20 channels could be made available during the day for curricular or enrichment programming. The prospects for greater cable TV involvement in educational programming have been strengthened by Cable in the Classroom, a clearinghouse for school projects funded by the cable industry.[45]

A unique cable TV educational service, the Mind Extension University, was created by Denver cable executive Glenn Jones in the early 1990s. The Mind Extension University quickly became one of the fastest-growing basic cable services in the country, available to over 23 million households. Local cable operators paid three cents a month for each of their subscribers to carry the channel. Originally developed for high schools in remote areas, the channel has also been used by city schools.

CABLE'S GLOBAL OUTREACH

Cable television is essentially a local business that extends no farther than the end of its community network. However, some large cable conglomerates have found profitable business opportunities abroad. The ESPN sports network delivers programs by satellite to Latin America and Europe. USA Network has teamed up with several Latin American cable companies to sponsor USA America Latina, supplying Spanish-language versions of such programs as *Entertainment Tonight* and *Murder, She Wrote*.[46] Time Warner has also been aggressive in seeking overseas business. In the early 1990s, the company entered the European cable market as a partner in a joint venture to manage a system in Hungary. Its HBO subsidiary has operated a successful program distribution network in Central and South America since 1988.[47]

Cable News Network offers a Spanish-language service to Latin America. Moving beyond the network's English-language programming and seen in over seventy countries, this Latin American service was CNN's first attempt at foreign-language broadcasting. Some cable companies are making coproduction arrangements with foreign producers for programming that can be marketed worldwide. Time Warner transmits several of its most profitable and popular services to European viewers via the Luxembourg-based Astra satellite. A company executive sees such projects as steps toward transforming the firm into a "vertically integrated global company that will produce and distribute programming around the world."[48]

Among smaller channel networks, MTV has been aggressive in expanding its successful brand of music videos overseas. In addition to being available on cable systems in dozens of countries abroad, MTV began webcasting music videos to personal-computer owners in Europe in 1998.[49]

Meanwhile, at home, the cable industry is looking to a digitized future as the best means of improving its product offerings and profits. The Internet and other advanced services will not be viable revenue sources for most cable systems until their channel capacity is expanded.[50] On the other hand, PPV revenues are needed to pay for the cost of installing digital-compressing equipment. Further channel expansion will involve time, money, and a gamble on consumer tastes. "Channel rebuild," to use the industry's phrase, costs about $300 per subscriber and will take years to accomplish.[51]

These costs, adding up to billions of dollars, are one reason that cable systems have generally been moving slowly in upgrading their facilities. By 1999 cable modems—the key equipment for interactive services—had been installed in fewer than a quarter of U.S. cable households. The pace of modem installation has been stepped up since then, but it will be several years before modems for advanced services become generally available in U.S. homes. (See Table 6.3.)

TABLE 6.3   The Outlook for Cable Modems

Year	Number of Online Households (Millions)	Cable Modem-Capable Households (Millions)	Subscribers (Millions)	Penetration of Cable Modem-Capable Households	Monthly Fee	Aggregate Spending ($ Millions)
1997	23.0	2.0	0.2	10.0%	$40.00	$ 96
1998	28.5	3.0	0.6	20.0	35.00	252
1999	32.5	5.0	1.2	24.0	30.00	432
2000	36.0	8.0	2.2	27.5	30.00	792
2001	39.0	12.0	3.5	29.2	28.00	1,176
2002	42.1	15.0	5.0	33.3	25.00	1,500

SOURCES: Veronis, Suhler & Associates, Wilkofsky Gruen Associates

THE INTERNET FACTOR

Advanced Internet products will be an important marketing tool in expanding interactive services. Emily Green, a cable analyst at Forrester Research, thinks cable modems will be the dominant method of access to the Internet. Microsoft's Bill Gates agrees with her to the point of investing $1 billion in Comcast, a leading cable firm, in 1997.[52] Comcast will be competing with other cable conglomerates in Internet and other online offerings. Time Warner's system, Road Runner, has been operating since 1996. The most technologically ambitious project is At Home, a channel developed by TCI to deliver, among other options, Internet programming to cable households.[53]

An advanced cable service with high potential is digital radio. Industry pundits believe that it will do for home stereo systems what cable has done for TV. In a cable radio system, the cable TV wire is split in half; one half is linked, as before, to home TV sets, and the other half is connected to stereo systems. In this way, hundreds of compact-disc-quality sound programs can be accessed for a relatively modest monthly fee. Cable companies that have offered digital cable radio services have found strong consumer acceptance.[54]

CHALLENGING THE NEW COMPETITION

In summary, the cable TV industry is rebuilding its infrastructure and its product offerings. Besides supplying more revenue sources, these moves will position the industry to meet marketing challenges from other media competitors in the next decade. Cable operators prospered for forty years on assurances of municipally granted monopoly franchises for their local networks. There is, however, a growing trend among city councils and other local franchise authorities to license competing cable TV systems. The most formidable competition, however, will come from three sectors that have already begun to offer advanced consumer services: the telephone companies, DBS operators, and "wireless cable" networkers. A fourth sector, over-the-air broadcasters, may also become a competitive threat in the near future when multimedia HDTV service is available in most American homes.

Of these three potential competitors, the least threatening is probably wireless cable, which uses over-the-air microwave channels to deliver programming to homes. (The technology is described in Chapter 3.) The Federal Communications Commission has issued operating licenses to several hundred wireless cable systems. (The Commission is involved because it has legal authority over the allocation of the radio frequency spectrum, including microwave.) These wireless networks originally served outlying rural districts, beyond the urban and suburban area where most cable TV systems are located. More recently, wireless cable entrepreneurs have moved into metropolitan areas where they compete directly with cable TV. Wireless cable has certain advantages in the competition. Installation costs are much cheaper—about $600 per subscriber versus $3,000 for an average cable wire installation—and subscription fees are also generally lower. Nevertheless, the wireless-cable business is not yet a significant competitor of conventional cable TV. However, wireless technology was given a new lease on life in the late 1990s as the result of renewed interest by telephone companies and other networkers planning to supply homes with the Internet and other advanced services.

THE SATELLITE BROADCASTERS

A more significant long-term threat to cable TV systems are information and entertainment programs transmitted by direct-broadcast satellites (DBS). The cable industry is well aware that satellites can deliver such programming to every household in the country, including the 25 million or so that could receive cable TV services but do not subscribe. In the early 1990s, cable TV operators tried to slow down DBS development by refusing to sell most of the popular cable programming, which they controlled, to companies promoting DBS networks. A federal antitrust decision forced the cable TV operators to make the programs available to DBS operators.[55]

National DBS networking became a reality in the mid-1990s when several companies began satellite-broadcast operations. The leading network is DirecTV, a venture sponsored by Hughes Communications. DirecTV offers over 100 home information and entertainment channels beamed into small, customer-owned earth stations. Most of these services are identical with cable TV offerings, although DirecTV and its competitors also offer additional services that could lure away cable TV subscribers. They contracted with Major League Baseball to broadcast hundreds of games not available to viewers.[56] DirecTV offered access to more than fifty PPV channels, including new Hollywood films and a National Hockey League "Center Ice" package that included more than twenty games each week.[57] DirecTV has been the leader in upgrading its system to deal with HDTV and advanced Internet offerings.[58]

By 1999, DirecTV and its DBS competitors had signed up over ten million subscribers and were adding over 100,000 new customers a month.[59] Industry observers expect that the number of DBS households will exceed 10 million at the turn of the century. This growth will come primarily at the expense of the cable TV industry.[60] On the other hand, the old-line television networks benefit from the new satellite services, since DBS channels extend network programming to several million homes in remote areas previously inaccessible to over-the-air broadcasters.

The DBS networks' strongest threat may be several years away, when digitized HDTV services come on the market. As noted earlier, satellite broadcast networks could have a technological advantage. Broadcasting directly into small household "dishes," they avoid the expensive cost of wiring (or rewiring) houses. Equally important, satellites can reach into every household in the country with HDTV services, unlike cable TV systems, which currently serve only two-thirds of American homes.

Competition within the DBS industry will increase as new entrants are attracted to the market. Lockheed Martin Corp., the aerospace giant, announced in 1998 that it would set up a joint venture with General Electric to launch a satellite system offering Internet access and other advanced services.[61]

THE PHONE COMPANY CHALLENGE

For the present, the broadcast networks and cable TV are focused on a more immediate threat: the expansion of the telephone companies into home information and entertainment services. The Telecommunications Act passed by Congress in 1996 lifted most of the restrictions that kept the phone companies out of this business. As outlined in Chapter 5, the legislation was the culmination of a decade of acrimonious debate and lobbying, pitting the phone companies against the media industry.

The phone companies had won a limited victory in 1991 when the FCC issued its "video dial tone" proposal, which allowed phone subscribers to call up a menu of video services in much the same way as they phoned friends and neighbors. Cable and broadcasting executives correctly saw this as the first step by the telephone industry to invade their territory. Their fears were confirmed in 1993 when Southwestern Bell, a regional phone company, announced it was buying three cable systems in the Washington, DC, area for $650 million. It was the first instance of one of the Baby Bell companies moving into the cable TV business. However, they were still constrained by federal regulations limiting their cable activities.

LOOKING TO THE FUTURE

Most of these regulatory limits were lifted by the telecommunications act passed by Congress in 1996. The legislation, in effect, put the stamp of approval on almost any plans for the cable TV and phone industries to enter each other's business. It was designed primarily to accommodate the competing interests of these two major players. In doing so, it set the stage for major developments in the U.S. media marketplace. The most dramatic result was the AT&T/TCI merger in 1998 that integrated the cable and telephone network resources of two of the largest communications firms in the country. The merger set a pattern of consolidation that will be repeated in various forms over the next few years.

Predicting the eventual pattern of these media-market changes is, for the present, a very risky business. The 1996 legislation was a compromise, based largely on reconciling the opposing views of the major industries involved, particularly the phone companies and cable TV operators. Future technological developments can alter many of the assumptions on which the law is based. One such factor is the growing role of DBS networking, a technology that has the potential of outmatching cable TV and telephone capabilities for reaching every U.S. household with advanced information and entertainment services.

For the next few years, the odds seem to favor the cable companies. By upgrading many of its present coaxial cable circuits to a hundred or more channels, cable TV can provide a broader range of information and entertainment services in ways that will satisfy a majority of its customers.[62] The telephone companies will gain less in the short run, primarily because they will not be able to compete fully with cable TV's expanding channel capacity in the near future. The phone companies' plans to wire all U.S. households for advanced multimedia services may take longer to complete. When it is finished, however, such a network could be capable of delivering a much higher level of advanced services to homes than cable TV or satellite circuits. The question is whether cable TV, even with its lesser capabilities, will not have preempted the consumer market, particularly for entertainment programming.

Nevertheless, the phone companies should not be counted out. They are a ubiquitous presence in every American community, reaching into virtually every business and household. They have access to the deep-pocket financing needed to complete an advanced information structure.[63] Their primary deficiency lies in experience in dealing with entertainment products. However, despite the wisecracking wisdom that no one wants to rent a film from AT&T, the phone companies are prepared to move vigorously into entertainment services well beyond their typical preoccupation with voice and data telecommunications.

SERVING THE MARKETPLACE OF IDEAS

Media market developments involve more than business issues. They also concern the U.S. marketplace of ideas. The debate leading up to the passage of the 1996 telecommunications legislation by Congress was dominated by large corporations, each extolling the virtues of open competition leading to a wider variety of services. On the dark side, however, the legislation could give undue license to a relatively few large conglomerates to consolidate their marketing power by buying up smaller companies. Consolidation was already well under way before the Telecommunications Act was passed, and the new legislation accelerated that trend, as we have seen.[64]

This could put at risk the principle of open access for all citizens to a broad range of competitive information resources. The electronic marketplace of ideas could be less free, and the evolution of a diverse national information utility could be impeded. That utility should be kept open for all communications—voice, video, and text—as a fundamental First Amendment principle. It should, in effect, have the basic characteristics of the present telephone system. In regulatory terms, the phone companies are common carriers, required to provide access so that any customer may send or receive a message. Phone companies are, moreover, regulated as to the rates they charge in order to ensure nondiscriminatory economic access.[65] The new national information utility should be organized under comparable rules.

The debate on these issues has just begun. Their resolution will determine the future of the cable industry as well as other media in the new digital environment.

NOTES

1. Federal Communications Commission, *Cable Television Information Bulletin*, January 1990, p. 2.
2. Veronis, Suhler & Associates, *op. cit.*, p. 42.
3. "Cable Ratings Top Networks," *Washington Post*, 7 August 1998, p. C-5.
4. "Television," *Consumer Reports*, September 1991, pp. 576–585.
5. In recent years, the cable industry has taken active steps to improve customer relations. See "Cable Industry Tries Guarantees of Better Service to Polish Image," *Wall Street Journal*, 1 December 1994, p. B-1.
6. "Cable Clustering Makes for Active Market," *Broadcasting & Cable*, 6 June 1995, p. 53.
7. See Porter Bibb, *It Ain't as Easy as It Looks*. New York: Random House, 1993, pp. 97–108, for a lively account of Ted Turner's entry into the cable TV field.
8. "Ted Turner, on Top of the World," *Washington Post*, 13 April 1989, p. C-1.
9. "Time Marching On With Video," *New York Times*, 2 January 1980, p. C-1.
10. "MTV International: Brand On the Run," *Broadcasting & Cable*, 6 April 1995, pp. 34–36.
11. "Is Redstone Studio-Prone?" *Variety*, 13 January 1992, p. 85.
12. "Not Now, Darling," *Economist* (London), 3 September 1994, p. 63.
13. Barbara Zelizer, "CNN, the Gulf War, and Journalistic Practice," *Journal of Communication* 42, no. 1 (Winter 1992): pp. 60–81.
14. "Top Cable Shows," *Broadcasting & Cable*, 6 March 1995, p. 29.
15. "As Ratings Languish, CNN Faces Identity Crisis," *New York Times*, 22 August 1994, p. D-11.
16. "CNN: No Longer Exactly On Top of the News," *Washington Post*, 2 September 1997, p. D-9.
17. *Washington Post*, ibid.
18. "The People's Network," *New Yorker*, 3 August 1998, p. 28.
19. "Top of the News," *Economist* (London), 9 May 1992, p. 89.
20. "Unsnoozing the News," *Economist* (London), 22 November 1997, p. 56.
21. "Cable With a Local Twist," *New York Times*, 24 July 1995, p. D-1.
22. "C-SPAN Picks up Network News Slack," *Variety*, 17 February 1992, p. 32.
23. "Cable's Hold On America," *Economist* (London), 24 January 1998, p. 61.
24. "Time Marching On With Video," *New York Times*, 2 January 1980, p. C-1.
25. "Television's Real-Life Cable Baron," *Business World*, special supplement to the *New York Times*, 2 December 1990, p. 38.
26. "Fear, Loathing and Respect for Cable's Leader," *Washington Post*, 23 January 1992, p. 1.
27. "TCI's Digital Satellite Headend," *Via Satellite*, September 1995, pp. 58–62.
28. "Infobahn Warrior," *Wired*, July 1994, p. 86.
29. "A Man to Watch," *Barron's*, 16 March 1992, p. 10.
30. "Malone: TV's New Uncrowned King?" *Business Week*, 5 October 1998, p. 118.

31. "The King of Cable Scrambles to Shore Up His Fortress," *Business Week*, 27 July 1992, pp. 74–75.
32. "AT&T: Who Needs ILECs," *Tele.com*, August 1998, p. 44.
33. "Blockbuster's Fired-Up Mr. Fixit." *Business Week*, 9 February 1998, p. 100.
34. "Quantity Time On Cable," *Washington Post*, 2 February 1992, p. C-1.
35. "Interactive In Orlando," *Washington Post*, 13 December 1994, p. A-1.
36. "That's Intertainment," *Business 2.0*, September 1988, p. 74.
37. "A New Yardstick For Interactive TV," *Broadcasting & Cable*, 23 May 1994, p. 6.
38. "An Adult Affair," *Economist* (London), 4 January 1997, p. 64.
39. "PPV Bolstering Weak Pay TV Performances," *Broadcasting*, 22 July 1991, p. 11.
40. "Advantage: Pay-per-View? Don't Count on It," *Business Week*, 28 September 1992, p. 44.
41. "Cable Battles Stir PPV $ Lust," *Variety*, 23 March 1992, p. 1.
42. "Gone With the Cash," *Economist* (London), 3 November 1990, p. 73.
43. "Cable Faces C Word: Clutter," *Broadcasting*, 21 October 1991, p. 45.
44. Veronis, Suhler & Associates, *op. cit.*, p. 122.
45. "Cable Carves a Niche as a Classroom Tool," *Business Week*, 26 August 1991, p. 33.
46. "USA Network Boosts Latin American Slate," *Broadcasting & Cable*, 24 October 1994, p. 28.
47. "Cable Industry Wants World On a Wire," *Broadcasting & Cable*, 24 January 1994, p. 37. See also "U.S. Cable Networks Go Global Via Satellite," *Via Satellite*, September 1995, pp. 44–54.
48. "Cable Networks' Future: Original, International," *Broadcasting*, 2 December 1991, p. 42.
49. "MTV Guide," *Wired*, September 1998, p. 65.
50. "Television and the Internet: Set-top Boxing," *Economist* (London), 29 September 1997, p. 67.
51. "High Speed Access Kicks Into High Gear," *Communications News*, August 1988, p. 98.
52. "Enter God, With $1 Billion," *Economist* (London), 14 June 1997, p. 68.
53. "Media and Entertainment: Prognosis 1999," *Business Week*, 11 January 1999, p. 100.
54. "Cable's New Frontier: Wiring the Wireless," *Business Week*, 2 July 1990, p. 36.
55. For background, see Leland L. Johnson and D. R. Castleman, *Direct Broadcasting Satellites: A Competitive Alternative to Cable Television?* report R-4047-MF/RL Santa Monica, CA: Rand Corporation, 1991.
56. "More Baseball for Satellite Viewers," *Broadcasting & Cable*, 21 August 1995, p. 12.
57. "PPV On the Offensive in New Orleans," *Broadcasting & Cable*, 10 April 1995, p. 48.
58. "DirecTV Signs Deal to Partner With Rural Cable TV Operators," *Satellite News*, 17 August 1998, p. 5.
59. "Will Murdoch Land a Starring Role at Primestar?" *Business Week*, 10 August 1998, p. 31.
60. "U.S. Satellite TV," *Via Satellite*, November 1995, pp. 46–50.
61. "Lockheed Plans Unit for Satellite Services," *Washington Post*, 12 August 1998, p. C-9.
62. "Cable's Secret Weapon," *Forbes*, 13 April 1992, pp. 80–81.
63. The timetable for construction of the telephone fiber network and the policy implications are discussed in Henry Geller, *Fiber Optics: An Opportunity for a New Policy*, Annenberg Washington Program, Washington, DC, November 1991, pp. 23–25.
64. David Waterman, "Vertical Integration and Program Access in the Cable Television Industry," *Federal Communications Law Journal* 47, no. 3 (April 1995): pp. 511–534.
65. For a useful survey of the evolution of cable TV policy, see "Defining Cable Television: Structuration and Public Policy," *Journal of Communication* 39, no. 2 (Spring 1989): pp. 10–26.

Hollywood: Remodeling the Dream Factory

Like most of its films, Hollywood is a fiction. No major motion pictures are made these days in Hollywood, a generally run-down district on the northern edge of Los Angeles. The film industry moved its operations long ago to other parts of the Los Angeles area, to other U.S. cities, and overseas. About 20 percent of the industry's annual production takes place outside the United States.

The word *Hollywood* is, however, a convenient shorthand for describing an industry that has been the lodestar of the U.S. entertainment world for almost a century. Besides motion pictures, Hollywood produces most of the entertainment products used by the television, cable TV, videocassette, and music recording industries. Its unique quality over the years has been its ability to attract a broad range of creative talents. When Orson Welles, a young theater and radio director, first saw the RKO Radio studio in 1939, he described it as the greatest electric train set a boy ever had.[1] He proceeded to use his toy to write, direct, and act in *Citizen Kane*, arguably the best film ever to come out of Hollywood.

Citizen Kane was an artistic success, but it was initially a commercial failure—a reminder that Hollywood is also a business, dominated in its day-to-day decisions by bottom-line economics. Hollywood studios and other production units earned almost $34 billion from filmed entertainment in 1997 (see Table 7.1). This is a small segment of the $300 billion global entertainment business but an inadequate measure of Hollywood's overall impact as an economic and cultural force.

TABLE 7.1   Growth of U.S. Spending on Entertainment

	Filmed Entertainment	Recorded Music	Interactive Entertainment	Total
1997 Expenditures ($ Millions)	$33,878	$12,237	$3,626	$49,741
1992–1997 Compound Annual Growth (%)	6.2%	6.3%	8.5%	6.4%
1997–2002 Projected Compound Annual Growth (%)	6.3%	5.5%	5.1%	6.0%
2002 Projected Expenditures ($ Millions)	$45,924	$15,999	$4,654	$66,577

SOURCES: Veronis, Suhler & Associates, Wilkofsky Gruen Associates, Motion Picture Association of America, Adams Media Research, Paul Kagan Associates, McCann-Erickson, Recording Industry Association of America, NPD Group, Electronic Industries Association, Software Publishers Association, PC Data

The tensions between hard-line economics and artistic creativity are more pronounced in the film business than in any other media sector. After a century, there is still no agreement, inside or outside the industry, on how these two factors combine to make Hollywood what it is. William Goldman, the screenwriter, observed that the defining rule in explaining Hollywood is that nobody knows anything.[2] The industry's chief Washington lobbyist, Jack Valenti, has described it as a business that "flies on gossamer wings." Hollywood is the land of the hunch and the wild guess. An idea that is creative (and many that are not) must survive a tortuous process of assembling money, scripts, production facilities, actors, and distribution arrangements before it is realized on film. Once the process is completed, and the product is put to the ultimate test of attracting an audience, six out of ten Hollywood feature movies end up in the red.

BLOCKBUSTERS AND LOSERS

In any normal business, such a record would be a formula for instant failure but not so in Hollywood. In part, this is because of the industry's arcane bookkeeping procedures. Even a film that makes a lot of money over and above its production and distribution costs can still end up on the books as a financial loser. The most controversial example in the past decade was an Eddie Murphy film, *Coming to America*, which cost $48 million to make. In a court case about the allocation of the film's $300 million gross profits, Paramount Pictures claimed that the film lost $18 million—a claim that was rejected by the court.[3] Hollywood economics are based on the gamble that a few blockbuster movies will cover whatever losses a film studio suffers on the rest of its products. In fact, this often happens. The 1997 blockbuster *Titanic* grossed nearly $1.5 billion in its first year of distribution, providing Paramount and Twentieth Century Fox (the studios that invested in the film) with the financial cushion to absorb losses from their less successful productions.[4]

Nevertheless, most studios are constantly squeezed between the profits generated by the occasional blockbuster success and the losses incurred by other films. In the 1990s, the average cost of all films, including their marketing, was over $50 million. This reflected, among other factors, the wildly escalating salaries negotiated by superstars like Harrison Ford, Tom Cruise, and Leonardo DiCaprio, whose presence in a film usually assures its success. A record of sorts was set by comedian Jim Carrey when he was paid $20 million for starring in *The Cable Guy.*[5]

Despite its convoluted ways of doing business, the film industry has shown remarkable staying power over the decades. Predictions of Hollywood's decline and fall have been a recurrent theme for most of its history. However, the industry is more prosperous now than at any time in the past, in large part because it has expanded beyond feature films into a panoply of new revenue sources ranging from videocassettes to Disneyland-type theme parks. Hollywood is, in fact, very big business. It was a key factor in the economic comeback of Southern California following cutbacks in the aerospace industry a decade ago. By the mid-1990s, over 112,000 workers were working in motion picture and TV production in Los Angeles county alone.[6]

While it has branched out into all kinds of related ventures, the industry has a problem with its traditional bread-and-butter business: people sitting in a movie theater watching shadows on a screen. A customer looking at network TV or a rented video, surfing the Internet, or playing a video game is a customer who is not going to show up at the local neighborhood multiplex. As recently as 1980, 80 percent of the film industry's income came from U.S. ticket sales. Now less than 20 percent does; the rest is earned largely from home video and television sales. There are fewer U.S. moviegoers now than at any time in recent decades, with the annual number of tickets sold falling below the billion mark. (By contrast, over 4 billion tickets were sold to a much smaller population in 1946.) There has also been some falling off in Hollywood's traditionally strong hold on overseas audiences. Moreover, that audience loss, both at home and abroad, has involved mainly younger filmgoers, the industry's primary target.

The industry is undergoing major structural changes. For most of its history, Hollywood has been largely a business unto itself, with few outside connections. This is no longer true. Six of the eight largest studios have become parts of large corporations, each of them involved in other entertainment products they hope to merge with their new film interests. The industry's new owners have brought a different style of management and operations that are changing the way Hollywood does business and the kinds of products it churns out.

CHANGING WITH THE TIMES

These business innovations are one way of dealing with the threat posed by new media technologies. Hollywood has dealt with similar challenges in the past, most notably in the 1950s when it began to lose audiences to television viewing. At first, the studios tried to check the loss by limiting TV showings of their vast stock of old feature films. Within a few years, however, the studios realized that they had more to gain by joining forces with the television industry than from fighting a losing battle. The old films were rereleased, and Hollywood became the largest single producer of new television products for both the domestic and foreign markets.[7] The film industry was thus able to co-opt television technology to its own advantage. However, it may have a harder time coming to terms with its current challengers such as HDTV, DBS, PPV cable programming, and the new mix of multimedia computer products.

The most striking example of the impact that the new technologies have had on the film industry is videocassettes. By 1998, home video sales and rentals were a $17 billion business; this is more than double anticipated box office revenues.[8] People are watching Hollywood entertainment at home rather than in a theater. By the mid-1990s, American households with videocassette recorders were renting an average of fifty tapes a year; by the end of the decade, over 85 percent of U.S. households were equipped with video recorders (see Table 7.2).

The impact of this change on the film industry was documented in a Louis Harris survey. In one month, Americans rented 197 million videocassettes. Assuming, conservatively, that there were two viewers for each rental, this adds up

TABLE 7.2   VCR Households

Year	Television Households (Millions)	VCR Households (Millions)	VCR Penetration of TV Households
1984	84.9	12.2	14.4%
1985	85.7	20.7	24.2
1986	86.8	30.9	35.6
1987	87.4	40.8	46.7
1988	88.6	49.6	56.0
1989	90.4	56.4	62.4
1990	92.1	61.5	66.8
1991	93.1	66.5	71.4
1992	92.1*	70.3	76.3
1993	93.1	72.4	77.8
1994	94.2	74.4	79.0
1995	95.4	76.4	80.1
1996	95.9	78.7	82.1
1997	97.0	80.5	83.0
1998	98.0	82.3	84.0
1999	99.1	84.0	84.8
2000	100.2	85.7	85.5
2001	101.4	87.3	86.1
2002	102.5	89.0	86.8

SOURCES: Veronis, Suhler & Associates, Wilkofsky Gruen Associates, Paul Kagan Associates, Adams Media Research, Nielsen Media Research
*Revised downward based on 1990 census

to a cumulative audience of almost 400 million home viewers in two weeks, or about 40 percent of the total U.S. movie theater audience for the whole year.[9] With movie theater audiences falling off, Hollywood had become increasingly dependent on the videocassette business, which in turn is almost totally dependent on film industry products.

There are signs that the home videocassette market is leveling off after years of double-digit expansion. Blockbuster and other video distributors are confronting competition from newer services that meet consumer needs more conveniently. The major challenger is pay-per-view (PPV) offerings, delivered by cable or satellite. Promoted widely as "the video store in the home," PPV exploits the fact that its programs are available simply by pressing numbers on a TV-set keypad. PPV services also provide a wide range of "live" programming such as sports events, concerts, and other entertainment features, all competing for consumer dollars that, in past years, went largely to Hollywood.

The Hollywood studios are also affected by other shifts in consumer entertainment patterns. The decline in broadcast television viewing is affecting the industry, since it is the largest single supplier of entertainment programs to the New York networks. Their economic problems give the networks good reason to balk at the rising costs of the programs they buy from Hollywood.

Finally, the film industry still has to come to terms with emerging technologies that alter both their products and the ways they are distributed. High-definition television, for example, will affect the products that Hollywood supplies to television and cable networks. Also, multimedia computers and advanced compact discs are already pushing the film industry into new kinds of production. All the major studios have created special production units to develop program materials for these technologies.

Meanwhile, the industry is taking another look at its traditional audience: the people who pay to watch a film in a theater. There has been relatively little change in the way movies are shown since the introduction of wide-screen technology forty years ago. Films are still delivered in large reel cans to theaters and then projected from a booth in the rear of the hall.

The biggest current change in film distribution is the rapid increase in what the industry calls multiplexes. The traditional one-screen theater is giving way to multiscreen structures. A decade ago, the multiplexes offered three or four different movies. More recently, a 30-screen multiplex has been built in Ontario, California. This escalation is changing the way consumers pick and watch their movies. With each of the new super-multiplexes costing up to $30 million, it's a game for giants, according to a *Business Week* survey, which notes that, in the late 1990s, 3 percent of the film-distribution chains control over 60 percent of the nation's screens.[10]

The Hollywood studios are considering new ways of controlling film distribution on their own. They might, for example, transmit films from a central point by satellite to earth stations on theater roofs or even directly to households. The studios are also planning to replace traditional 35mm prints altogether with devices that project digitized signals. The first generation of these digital products will be installed in theaters by 2002.

The industry is also looking at another innovation: theaters designed to show special films on giant screens that are often four or five stories high. By the late

1990s, there were over a hundred theaters with these big-screen facilities in the United States and abroad. A more elaborate innovation is the "leisure simulator," a moving platform that uses the same technology as an aviation flight simulator. Reconfigured as a small film theater rather than an airplane cockpit, the movements of the six-axis platform are coordinated with a wide-screen film, giving the audience the impression that they are moving with the film's action. Dozens of leisure simulators had been installed around the world by a British firm, Hughes Rediffusion Simulation.[11]

REACHING OUT TO NEW AUDIENCES

The film industry is also revamping its traditional product: movies shown in ordinary theaters. This includes a production shift to films that are computer-generated in whole or in part. The effects may be consummately artificial, but they are often stunning. Hollywood has learned that digitization and other computerized effects bring in cash at the box office. By the mid-1990s, seven of the ten biggest-grossing movies ever made were "effects" films such as *ET* and the *Star Wars* sagas. More often than not, the digital effects share top billing with the stars.

The film industry is on the edge of a sweeping transformation in what it produces and how it distributes the product. Previously it has had to cope with one innovation at a time. Now the industry has to deal with a range of new technologies, each of which represents both a threat and an opportunity for its future operations. Acronymically, these innovations include DVD, HDTV, and PPV, among others. As noted earlier, one relatively simple device—the videocassette—has eroded theater ticket revenues while at the same time providing a new source of profits. However, the industry's chances of recouping its lost theater audiences in the United States are slim, given the current competition from videocassettes and the prospect of even more sophisticated home-delivered entertainment resources in the future.

Can Hollywood make a profitable adjustment to these new realities? The industry has not been noted for taking the long-range view. Its operating mode is frenetic, hypersensitive to current entertainment trends, and given to shifting enthusiasms that can lurch overnight from cowboy epics to horror films to intergalactic space adventures. Fortunes are made or lost betting on whether the newest money-making trend can be exploited further or whether the time is ripe to launch a new trend. Hollywood has always been about winners and losers in this gamble.

The film industry will not easily shake off its addiction to betting on film trends. Nevertheless, it is slowly changing some of its high-stakes gambling habits, in part because the large corporations that now control the studios are looking at production and distribution costs with a colder eye. Most of the global media conglomerates, such as Time Warner and News Corp., now have direct or indirect interests in Hollywood, along with their publishing, television, and cable TV holdings.

In the film industry's so-called Golden Age (roughly from 1930 to 1950), the big studios were independent and functioned with little financial oversight, except from the New York bankers who put up the money for their films. The studios controlled their own production facilities, and they each kept their own stable of writers, actors, and directors. The bigger film companies also controlled many of the theatrical outlets where their films were shown until federal antitrust laws forced them to end the practice. The studios were run by strong personalities who decided, for better or for worse, what pictures would be made. Studio heads such as Walt Disney, Louis B. Mayer of MGM, Darryl Zanuck of Twentieth Century Fox, and Adolph Zukor of Paramount all put their own distinctive imprints on their studios and on the industry at large.

By the 1970s, Hollywood's golden years were a romanticized memory. Outside financial interests were now buying into film companies. The Coca Cola Company was a major investor in Columbia Pictures. Many of the old-line companies lost both control of their production facilities and much of their individual style. As director Billy Wilder noted ruefully at the time, "Studios are nothing but the Ramada Inn: you rent space, you shoot and out you go."[12] Despite these changes, Hollywood continued to be generally successful in producing feature films for itself, and video products both for broadcast television and, more recently, for the cable TV networks.

INVASION OF THE CORPORATE CONGLOMERATES

Inevitably, Hollywood's moneymaking formulas attracted the attention of the corporate conglomerates that began to dominate the U.S. media sector after 1975. The idea of integrating its products with other media operations was not entirely new to the film industry. In 1911, publisher William Randolph Hearst expanded his newspaper and magazine empire by setting up Cosmopolitan Films, an important feature-film studio in early Hollywood history.[13] Hearst did not shrink from using his print publications to publicize Cosmopolitan films, but his attempts to use his various media holdings to support each other, however successful, were amateurish compared to the strategies adopted by present-day media conglomerates. Today's code phrase is "information packaging." The emphasis is on establishing synergy among the conglomerates' various media holdings, with each supporting the others in the production and marketing of their products.[14]

One Hollywood production company learned how to create synergy among its products long before any of the new media conglomerates had ever moved into the industry. The Walt Disney studio has been exploiting the multimedia possibilities of Mickey Mouse, Donald Duck, Bambi, the Lion King, and the other denizens of its cartoon bestiary for over half a century. Disney operations have changed dramatically in recent years, but the company has not lost its founder's touch for using diverse media outlets—from comic books to theme parks—to publicize its film products and boost its revenues. Disney's ability to spin off products from its films is one of the perennial wonders of the industry. Within a few years after its release, the studio's animated blockbuster, *The Lion King*, has produced revenues of over $1 billion. Only $730 million came from box office receipts; the remainder came from videocassette sales, toys, clothing, and other products tied to the picture. Over 25 million videocassettes of the film were sold in the first year after its theatrical release.[15] Despite its diversification into other entertainment areas, films are the key generators of Disney revenues.

THE DISNEY EXCEPTION

Disney is the only major Hollywood studio that has resisted the recent wave of corporate takeovers in the industry. It is, in effect, its own media conglomerate.[16] In recent years, it has pursued a strategy of acquisitions and alliances that made it, by far, the most extensive multimedia operation in the entertainment business.

Industry analysts have been studying the reasons for "Disney magic" for over a half-century. However esoteric their analysis, it all comes down to what the movie business once called tie-ins and now goes by the more sophisticated name of multimedia synergy. It began in the 1930s when Walt Disney sponsored Mickey Mouse Clubs to build up loyalty for his cartoon products. In 1938, *Snow White and the Seven Dwarfs*, its first feature-length cartoon, was also the first film to have a complete merchandising campaign in place. By the mid-1940s, the Disney organization was marketing about $100 million of film-related merchandise a year.[17]

Walt Disney had a somewhat undeserved reputation of marketing scrubbed-up products, celebrating the virtues of an idyllic capitalistic America. In fact, as Steven Watts points out in his study of Walt Disney's impact on American culture, the *Snow White* film satirized big business and industrial efficiency, with the dwarfs fiddling with the hands of a clock so they could get off work early. Donald Duck was in a constant battle with dehumanizing technology from robot butlers to mechanical barbers.[18]

At the turn of the century, Disney's multimedia properties include hockey's Mighty Ducks as well as a 25 percent stake in baseball's Anaheim Angels. These teams are part of a Disney sports operation that includes a dominant role in sports television broadcasting. All told, the company spent $11.1 billion on acquiring television rights for national football, hockey, and baseball games in the late 1990s. This is twice the amount spent in the same period by any of its rivals in sports broadcasting, including Fox, CBS, NBC, or Time Warner's Turner Sports.[19]

Disney's Televentures unit was created in 1995 to produce and market products to be used by telephone companies and other new entrants into the home-entertainment field. Another unit, Disney Interactive, produces CD-ROM games, many of which are spinoffs of its animated films. Two of its best-selling CDs are *Lion King Activity Center* and *Aladdin Activity Center*.[20] In addition to its cable TV Disney Channel, the firm supplies programming to DirecTV, the largest U.S. satellite broadcaster. It has moved into overseas satellite distribution with an agreement with CLT, the biggest European networker, to provide Disney-style programming.[21] The Disney Publishing Group markets publications that are tied to its film productions. It also operates a separate unit, Hyperion, which issues general-interest books.[22] All these enterprises are tied into its oldest, and most profitable, business—producing and distributing films that now cover the gamut from family-oriented G-rated to raunchy R-rated productions.

Disney's biggest acquisition was the 1995 takeover of Capital Cities–ABC for $19 billion in cash and shares. Disney was already an important player in the television industry, producing its own Disney shows as well as prime-time serials such as *Home Improvement*. The Cap Cities linkup gave Disney formidable assets for expanding its U.S. operations and for expanding abroad, where it had been something of a TV novice compared with ABC. An important part of the assets Cap Cities brought to the merger was its 80 percent stake in the ESPN cable-sports channel, which had audiences in over a hundred countries abroad. Sports will be half of Disney's ammunition in its assault on international markets. The other half will be its film products, especially its cartoons, which have the virtue of being just about the safest global programming around, given their lack of political controversy and the ease with which they can be dubbed into foreign languages.[23]

Disney gave new meaning to the phrase "entertainment conglomerate" in the mid-1990s when it announced plans for Disney Cruise Lines. By 1998, the venture was conducting one-week cruises aboard ships that feature Disney movies, Disney-themed staterooms, and ports of call that include a Disney-owned private island as well as a stopover at a resort located near Disney World in Florida.

Occasionally even the mighty Disney organization slips. A decade ago, its theme park in France almost suffered financial disaster due to misjudgments about European entertainment tastes. The company was able to recoup most of its losses in the late 1990s by changing many of the theme park's attractions to accommodate local tastes. Disney also misjudged foreign sentiments in 1995 when it signed an exclusive marketing agreement with the Royal Canadian Mounted Police to license the Mountie image around the world in toys, T-shirts, and other products. Although the proceeds were to be used for the Mounties' charitable projects, the uproar in Canada was immediate and intense. Canadians regarded the deal as a crass commercial sellout of a beloved national institution. "Canada's symbols are not commodities," thundered the *Toronto Globe and Mail*. "The country's identity is not something that can be packaged and sold at Wal-Mart. . . . Walt Disney, wonderful as it is, is as American as handguns." The Disney organization beat a hasty retreat.[24]

CORPORATE HOLLYWOOD

As noted above, Disney remains the exception to the Hollywood pattern of outside corporate takeovers. The other big studios have all become parts of larger enterprises. In the early 1980s, Gulf & Western Inc. bought Paramount Pictures, one of the most consistently successful studios in the film business. At that time, Gulf & Western also owned the largest U.S. book publisher, Simon & Schuster, as well as a number of independent television stations. The firm later became known as Paramount Communications until its $18 billion takeover in 1994 by Viacom Inc., which added the MTV cable channel, Blockbuster Entertainment Inc., and the United Paramount television network (UPN) to the conglomerate's multimedia mix.

In 1986, Rupert Murdoch, then known primarily as a newspaper publisher, added momentum to the acquisition trend by buying a half-interest in Twentieth

Century Fox. Later, he gained full control of the studio. The Twentieth Century Fox deal made Murdoch's firm, News Corp., the world's largest and most extensive media conglomerate, with holdings that include newspapers, magazines, television, and other media enterprises.[25]

The Murdoch group lost its primacy, however, when Time Inc. and Warner Communications negotiated a stock merger to form Time Warner Inc. in 1989. At the time of the merger, the two firms had combined annual revenues of $13 billion, putting them easily into the lead as the largest global media conglomerate. Time Inc. brought to the merger its extensive magazine and book publishing expertise as well as cable TV properties that included the Home Box Office network and a large number of local systems. Warner brought its experience in film production and distribution along with its ownership of one of the world's largest record companies. The merged companies expanded their operations significantly in the mid-1990s by acquiring the Cable News Network and other Ted Turner enterprises. The Time Warner merger also involved a $12 billion debt load that hampered the firm's ability to expand synergistic entertainment packaging plans as fast as it had hoped. Largely as a result of this heavy debt, Time Warner did not make a profit in its early years.[26]

THE JAPANESE TAKEOVERS

There are no typical entertainment conglomerates. The film industry is too diverse and too spread out for any cookie-cutter patterns. This was proven conclusively with the unexpected arrival of Japanese companies on the Hollywood scene in the late 1980s. It is useful to take a closer look at the so-called Japanese invasion of Hollywood because it illustrates both the opportunities, and perils, of attempting to fit the film business into the multimedia synergistic mold that has dominated media industry strategy in recent years.

The Japanese-Hollywood saga began in 1988. In quick succession, two major electronic manufacturers—Sony and Matsushita—took control, respectively, of Columbia Pictures and MCA, the owner of Universal studios. Foreign investment in the film industry was not unknown before these takeovers. There was little reaction when Rupert Murdoch's News Corp., a firm with strong British ties, bought Twentieth Century Fox, or when TVS Entertainment, a British television firm, paid $320 million for MTM Enterprises in order to acquire its large library of old television programs such as the *Mary Tyler Moore Show* and *Hill Street Blues*.[27]

Attitudes toward the Japanese takeovers were different. When Sony assumed control of Columbia Pictures, there was an outcry about "buying the soul of America," together with dark hints by some industry observers that Sony and Matsushita would turn their studios into Japanese propaganda outlets. A *Newsweek* magazine poll reported that 48 percent of Americans saw the Sony acquisition as "a bad thing." The Japanese takeover of the two studios was the motivation for a congressional bill that proposed a 50 percent cap on foreign ownership of U.S. "cultural business enterprises," pointedly including film studios. The proposal was roundly criticized by the film industry. Hollywood's attitude was summarized at the time by film producer Freddie Fields: "Sony isn't going to orientalize the movies at Columbia. . . . This is business, and the infusion of foreign money is exciting."[28]

Why did the Japanese come to Hollywood? A Japanese plan to mount an assault on American culture, if it ever existed, is the most far-fetched explanation. A more plausible explanation is simply that several film studio properties were ripe for takeover—part of the overall shakeout that has characterized all parts of the U.S. entertainment industry in recent years. The two Japanese firms saw advantages in investing in an industry with good economic prospects. Sony and Matsushita made it clear from the start that they were investing for the long run. "We Japanese plan and develop our business strategies ten years ahead," Sony chairman Akio Morita declared in 1989, "while Americans seem to be concerned only with profits ten minutes from now."[29]

Moreover, the Japanese brought cash to the table. The Sony takeover of Columbia involved an outlay of $3.4 billion, plus $1.3 billion in assumed debt. It was the largest single Japanese investment in any U.S. company at the time. A year later, Matsushita went higher with its $5.7 billion purchase of MCA, the company that owned Universal Pictures, record labels, a television studio, and a string of amusement parks.[30] As far as Hollywood is concerned, money is money, whatever its nationality. Both the Sony and Matsushita deals were friendly takeovers, unlike many other entertainment industry acquisitions.

VERTICAL INTEGRATION, JAPANESE STYLE

The strategies of the two companies went beyond the goal of developing an integrated global production and media distribution capability. This had been the game plan adopted by Gulf & Western, Rupert Murdoch's News Corp., and Time Inc. in their studio acquisitions. The Japanese firms had a broader objective. Both companies are major producers of CD players, video recorders, and other consumer entertainment equipment. (Matsushita is best known in the United States for its Panasonic products.) Their declared intention in buying up major film studios was to promote and protect sales of the electronic equipment they made or planned to make. They wanted an assured supply of the entertainment software that could be used with their machines. As one Sony executive noted at the time of the Columbia studios takeover, "Hardware and software are parts of the entertainment industry that can no longer be talked about separately."[31]

Sony had made its first move in this direction a few months before buying Columbia Pictures when it paid $2 billion for CBS Records, then the world's largest recording company. The next logical step was to invest in Hollywood, the production source for the most popular (and profitable) film, television, cable TV, and videocassette programs. In addition to having direct access to new productions, the two companies also acquired the studios' vast libraries of old movies; Sony's purchase of Columbia included an inventory of 2,700 feature films, from *Rambo* to *Lawrence of Arabia*, as well as 23,000 episodes of situation comedies and other television series.

The Sony and Matsushita takeovers were the first in the entertainment industry that attempted to vertically integrate operations at all levels, from equipment production to distribution of the final media product. Their strategy has turned out to be less than successful, in part because both companies were too caught up in the hubris of thinking that Japanese-style management, plus the infusion of large amounts of money, could work wonders anyplace on earth. The formula, which usually worked in other industries, came to grief when it hit the exotic, often bizarre, operating styles that have made Hollywood successful for over a century. "They thought they could crank out movies the way they cranked out any commodity. They looked at it as another item on the assembly line," according to Harold Vogel, a film industry analyst.[32]

Although the two studios owned by the Japanese companies made some very successful products—notably MCA's *Jurassic Park*, which earned $1 billion—they have not been able to avoid the cyclical ups and downs of Hollywood economics. By 1996, Sony had sunk an estimated $6 billion in Columbia Pictures.[33] Matsushita was, however, the first company to beat a retreat from Hollywood, in 1995, selling 84 percent of its share in MCA to Seagram Co., the Canadian beverage conglomerate. Meanwhile, Sony has fared better. After a series of reorganizations, its film operations (now called Sony Pictures Entertainment) have stabilized the firm's position as a major Hollywood presence.[34] In 1997, Sony released thirty-eight films, five more than second-place Disney. As a result, Sony had the top market share of films revenues (20.8 percent) in the industry that year.[35]

NEW MERGERS, NEW PATTERNS

Mergers and takeovers will continue to be common occurrences in the film industry as it adjusts to the changing patterns imposed by new technologies and by economics. The big studios have already been folded into larger organizations. Now they are being challenged by new enterprises that may be better attuned to changing realities. One example is Dreamworks SKG, an entertainment company set up in 1994 by three of Hollywood's most successful entrepreneurs: Steven Spielberg, David Geffen, and Jeffrey Katzenberg. Dreamworks set out to defy film industry wisdom by proposing to be a multimedia company from the start, producing a wide range of products: films, TV shows, CD-ROMs, interactive games, and music, among others. The Dreamworks strategy is based on alliances with outside organizations: In its first year, it had established links with Time Warner's Home Box Office, Cap Cities–ABC, Microsoft Corporation, and Silicon Graphics, the computer graphics company.[36] Despite this impressive support, Dreamworks has been less than successful, particularly in its television projects. After failing with a succession of TV series, the company learned, as one media observer put it, that television is a humbling business, where the evil sorcerer shows up far more often than the genie from the magic lamp.[37]

Dreamworks may eventually be a big winner, but not all of the new high-powered deals work out. In the mid-1990s, Creative Artists Agency (CAA), Hollywood's most powerful talent agency, put together a $300 million joint venture, Tele-TV, with three regional phone companies—Nynex, Bell Atlantic, and Pacific Telesis—to supply programming for household entertainment services planned by the phone companies. The agreement collapsed soon after, primarily because CAA's chief, Michael Ovitz, left the agency to become president of the Disney Company, which had its own rival $500 million production venture with four other large phone companies. The failed deal was only one in a long line of examples proving that Hollywood agreements are not written in stone.[38]

The old-line studios and their new rivals both share a perennial problem: how to anticipate the public's tastes and what entertainment products it will pay to see. Dore Schary, a film executive in the 1950s, once declared that America is a "happy ending" country. Acting on that assumption, he produced happy films that made a lot of money for MGM, his employer. Formulas for success are more complicated now. The U.S. demographic pattern is changing radically, along with the ways Americans allocate their time and money for leisure activities among a constantly lengthening list of options. These variables are enough to daunt even the most intrepid Hollywood strategists.

There are also troublesome, if unofficial, censorship problems. Filmmaking was inhibited for decades by the Motion Picture Production Code, which rated films on a morality scale. The Code was eliminated in the 1960s, replaced by a more lenient rating system. Recently, however, new calls for censorship have come from a wide assortment of interest groups, including Native Americans, African Americans, animal rights proponents, and the gay community. Each is intent on registering disapproval of alleged slights to their interests in the hope of shaping (or reshaping) their public images as displayed in films.[39] The Disney studio found its family-oriented image challenged in 1997 when the Southern Baptists, at their annual convention, called for a boycott of all Disney films, TV shows, and theme parks as a protest against Disney's alleged "gay-friendly policies."[40]

LOOKING FOR GOOD STORIES

Although the urge to follow the newest trend is strong, the studios usually fall back on tried-and-true formulas. The most enduring and successful of these is the big, visually exciting blockbuster film with a strong story line. Original scripts are still important, but the best of these films tend to be based on an old reliable: the novel. At a time when people have less time to read fiction, they depend on the film industry to bring it to them in a quicker and more easily digested form. Independent producer Frank Price has noted, "Movies have become the short stories of the video age."[41] The search for good stories can be a gold mine for writers. Novelist Michael Crichton was paid $1.5 million by Universal Studios for the rights to *Jurassic Park*. The bidding for filmable books reached an apogee in 1995 when an independent studio owned by actor Robert Redford, together with Hollywood Pictures (a Disney operation) paid $3 million to a little-known British writer, Nicholas Evans, for the screen rights to an unfinished first novel, *The Horse Whisperer*, which was eventually made into a moderately successful film in 1998.[42]

Mr. Evans's bonanza is symptomatic of the industry's struggle with rising costs. As one Hollywood wag put it, there is a tightening of the Gucci belts throughout the movie business. The industry's primitive financial structure is not much help. With some exceptions, new films are financed one at a time. As noted earlier, six out of ten Hollywood films don't make a profit. This means that a profitable movie must gross upwards of $120 million in order to pay its own costs and help make up losses on other films. Nevertheless, most Hollywood studios are profitable, primarily because they can usually recoup their feature film failures with television program and videotape revenues plus the occasionally lucrative blockbuster hit.

Despite these fiscal complexities, Hollywood's basic product is still the standard feature film, a consumer item that depends for its success on the fickle whims of an ever-shrinking theatergoing audience. This fickleness is magnified by the influence of a relatively small group of film critics, whose opinions can often make or break a film in the first few days after its release. As one critic, Nigel Andrews, notes:

> It is a demented cultural-economic climate. Critics are sometimes asked why they express negative or carping opinions about a work of cinema. The answer is: because they are the only people allowed to do so. No one else connected with the industry, when assessing a film, is permitted to point out that the Emperor is naked; or even to offer hints that the weather is a little chilly, your majesty, and you may want to throw on a scarf.[43]

CUCKOO-CLOUDLAND ECONOMICS

Given the risks involved, financing a film is an exercise in cuckoo-cloudland economics. The takeover of the big studios by cash-rich corporations has given some stability to the process, but the risks remain. As noted earlier, over half of the industry's film productions do not earn enough to pay their production and distribution costs. The rate of return demanded by outside investors is often in excess of 20 percent—a requirement that would be regarded as highway robbery in any other industry.[44]

Nevertheless, investors keep taking risks on film projects, intrigued by Hollywood's perennial ability to come up with the occasional financial blockbuster. Big successes happen often enough to keep investors coming back for more. One blockbuster, *Batman Returns*, cost about $105 million to produce and publicize. It earned $106 million in box office receipts during its first two weeks of showings.[45] The blockbuster success of the 1990s was *Titanic*, which promises to gross over to $1.5 billion in box office receipts, videotapes, and other spinoffs before it runs its course.

Popular films can also be solid long-term investments. The low-budget cult film *The Rocky Horror Picture Show* has earned Twentieth Century Fox $37 million at domestic box offices since its release in 1976. The long-run investment champion is the 1937 Disney cartoon classic *Snow White and the Seven Dwarfs*, which had taken in over $62 million in theater receipts—more than thirty times its original production costs.[46] Additionally, Disney has sold over 20 million *Snow White* videocassettes in recent years.

HOLLYWOOD'S GLOBAL MARKETS

The international market has always been a critical component in Hollywood's financial success. By the 1930s, overseas receipts accounted for more than half of the industry's revenues. There are film industries in over sixty countries, but typically they restrict themselves to local subjects in their productions. It was Hollywood that invented the international film. The names of such stars as Clint Eastwood, Tom Hanks, and Arnold Schwarzenegger are as familiar in New Delhi and Paris as they are in Boston and Des Moines. Unlike their overseas competitors, the Hollywood studios hired foreign directors, actors, and writers and then proceeded to make films in all parts of the world.

But it is Hollywood's portrayal of life in America that has had the most influence. The impact has not always been flattering. In 1967, when an American cowboy film was being shown to Vietcong prisoners of war, the audience cheered for the Indians.[47] Among most moviegoers abroad, however, the reaction is more sympathetic. For journalist A. M. A. Aziz, who grew up in India, cowboy films depicted a heroic America:

> It is sweet to recall those movie impressions of America—the America of the cowboys and their adventures. . . . Of course, there were villains and crooks in the movie stories. But the villain did not typify the average American in the boyhood image. On the other hand, the hero did. Then came the more serious type of American. He was the village sheriff, wore a top hat, and gathered some half a dozen other top-hatted persons around a table to discuss a grave problem. The gathering of the top-hats inspired confidence that the problem, however grave, would be solved; and so it was.[48]

AMERICAN FILMS: GLOBAL BOX-OFFICE HITS

The world's continuing fascination with U.S. films is such that Hollywood is the biggest single contributor to the U.S. net trade surplus in media exports. U.S. films account for only about 15 percent of annual global production, but that is a poor measure of Hollywood's artistic and marketing influence. U.S. films consistently dominate the lists of popular films being shown in theaters overseas. Many American films are financially more successful abroad than they are at home. Disney's *Who Framed Roger Rabbit?* earned $189 million overseas in its initial showings, compared to $157 million domestically.[49] *Titanic* is an even more dramatic example of Hollywood's economic dependence on overseas markets. By the middle of 1998, the film had grossed $543 million in the United States and about $933 million more in the rest of the world.

Hollywood's foreign earnings have been erratic in recent years, in part because of political restrictions in the form of quotas designed to protect local film producers. In 1989, the twelve European Community countries established a 50 percent quota on foreign (i.e., Hollywood) entertainment programs on their television stations. The French government set its quota at 60 percent, which was officially explained as an action to preserve the integrity of the French language and the French film industry.

The fact is that the European film industries have a hard time competing with American products. About 80 percent of all European box office receipts go back to America. The French, in particular, are inclined to take intellectual refuge in Hollywood's alleged lack of high-minded cultural standards. This explanation is challenged by Guillaume de Verges, a Paris film executive:

> If movie attendance in France has fallen from 200 million per year to 130 million per year since 1980, it's not because American films are better but because ours are worse. We should have some self-criticism and recognize that we don't make films people want to see.[50]

Overseas markets now figure equally with the American market in Hollywood's plans. The chief difference between the two, according to film executive Sam Golden, is that "domestically, we're facing consolidation, contraction and network erosion; in most of the rest of the world, we're dealing with expansion, with more customers and more outlets." Even with restrictions on its products abroad, Hollywood's overseas box office receipts topped $5 billion in 1997.[51]

Large parts of the world that were previously off-limits to Hollywood—such as China, Eastern Europe, and the former Soviet Union—are now potentially huge markets. Buena Vista International, a Disney company, has a multiyear barter deal with a Moscow TV company, giving the Russians the option of showing six hours of Disney programming a week in exchange for exclusive rights to sell advertising to accompany the programs. The Disney studio began marketing its cartoons to Chinese television in 1986, attracting 300 million viewers a week.[52] The company halted the arrangement in 1990, in part to protest the fact that Disney-trademarked products were being counterfeited by Chinese industries. Disney has since resumed its operations in China with a schedule of television programs as well as a Chinese-language Disney magazine and twenty stores that sell Disney T-shirts and other products.

Another factor favoring Hollywood export marketing is the rapid expansion of movie theaters abroad. The new emphasis, particularly in Europe, is on multiplexes, a phenomenon largely unknown overseas until recently. American companies are drawing on their experience with domestic multiplexes to invest in them abroad. In the mid-1990s, Time Warner budgeted $224 million to increase the number of its Warner Brothers movie houses in England.[53]

VIDEOCASSETTES AND PAY-PER-VIEW

The Hollywood studios are also paying more attention toward what the industry calls its peripherals, products that are spun off from the basic filmmaking activities, from Disneyland-type theme parks to music recordings. Pending the full adoption of DVD discs that can play an entire feature film, the most important of these spinoffs is the videocassette. Consumer surveys show how videocassettes are changing consumer entertainment habits. An Electronic Industries Association survey has indicated that consumers prefer home video screenings to theater outings by a margin of more than 3 to 1. Only 22 percent of the respondents, given a choice, preferred to leave home for a movie. The survey also indicated that a substantial majority of the tape-renting public takes home more than two movies a month, while the majority of moviegoers get to a theater less than twice a month.[54]

As noted earlier, Hollywood is a major beneficiary of cassette sales and rentals because it supplies most of the programming. Rentals account for most of the industry's cassette revenues, although sales have provided a rising portion of the take in recent years. Disney cartoons are consistent favorites, accounting for the top five all-time videotape best sellers. Films with live actors come in well behind in the videocassette sweepstakes.

Despite their present strong position, videocassette revenues can be expected to decline slowly but steadily in the coming years. Home viewers are beginning to order pay-per-view showings of new Hollywood movies and other attractions on their cable TV channels. As noted in Chapter 6, PPV was slow to develop in the 1990s primarily because its early technology could not deliver programs quickly on demand. With that problem largely resolved, PPV usage is expanding, with channels capable of serving tens of millions of homes. The number of PPV services will increase as cable companies install advanced modems that permit quick and easy access to current films and to sports events (see Table 7.3).

Hollywood is ambivalent about the changeover from videocassettes to PPV services. Clearly, the industry stands to make a lot of money by offering films and other programs to PPV channels. The question is whether the studios should develop their own channels or at least invest in the currently operating channels. This latter strategy was first tested in the early 1990s by Paramount Pictures and MCA, which made a joint investment in TVN, a ten-channel PPV distributor.[55] Paramount also negotiated agreements that allowed it to license PPV rights directly with cable systems, bypassing the normal PPV middleman vendors.[56] More recently, other Hollywood studios have become involved in PPV operations, usually as part of the strategies of the large multimedia conglomerates that own them.

Pay-per-view is still a minor factor in Hollywood's calculations. The number of households subscribing to PPV services is still relatively small. The studios' at-

TABLE 7.3   Growth of U.S. Spending on Subscription Video Services

	Basic Services	Premium Channels	Pay-Per-View	Advertising	Total
1997 Expenditures ($ Millions)	$22,402	$6,766	$1,424	$7,860	$38,452
1992–1997 Compound Annual Growth (%)	10.2%	5.5%	28.7%	18.7%	11.1%
1997–2002 Projected Compound Annual Growth (%)	11.8%	4.8%	10.7%	15.9%	11.6%
2002 Projected Expenditures ($ Millions)	$39,080	$8,545	$2,362	$16,450	$66,437

SOURCES: Veronis, Suhler & Associates, Wilkofsky Gruen Associates, Paul Kagan Associates

titude about controlling distribution of their own products could change as PPV's audience increases. The economic advantages of bypassing the current PPV channels and initiating their own services would then be hard for the studios to resist.

MAKING MUSIC—AND MONEY

A more immediate opportunity for increasing studio revenues lies with another entertainment business: music recording. Hollywood has always had close ties to the record industry, beginning with the days when record companies promoted 78 rpm recordings of such film-song staples as Bing Crosby's "White Christmas." Records are big business, with over $12 billion in U.S. sales in 1997.[57] Moreover, it is an expanding industry; currently, it is experiencing a growth spurt due in part to the popularity of MTV, the music-video cable channel, which has given popular music new exposure in recent years. The slow but steady growth in advanced DVD recordings adds another potentially profitable dimension to the music business.[58]

Hollywood is now more involved with the record industry than ever before. Three of the biggest takeovers of major film studios in the past decade have involved companies with significant record operations—Time Warner, Sony, and Matsushita. Time Warner owns Warner Records, and Sony has its Sony Record label. In 1998, Seagram Co. completed a dramatic transition from a liquor company to a global entertainment corporation by paying $10.6 billion for the Polygram Group, a European film and music conglomerate. Because Seagram already had a majority stake in the MCA film studios as well as the Geffen record label, the Polygram acquisition put the firm in the top ranks of multimedia conglomerates, with projected 1988 sales of $18 billion worldwide.[59]

Along with its Hollywood competitors, Seagram sees the record business as an important part of a strategy to develop multimedia voice, video, and print packages. In the process, their record operations will face new competition from non-Hollywood companies that have plans to deliver digitized music to customers via cable TV, satellites, and the Internet. In 1997, Microsoft and AT&T each announced plans for marketing and purchasing music on line.[60] About $35 million in disc sales were generated over the Internet in 1997.[61]

These and similar deals have whetted the interest of other Hollywood studios in the record business. The Disney studios, which had a small children's record division, created an adult-oriented record label, Hollywood Records. Morgan Creek, an independent studio, launched its own Morgan Creek label. The Fujisanki Communications Group, Japan's largest media conglomerate, entered the market when it bought a 25 percent stake in a major British label, Virgin Records. These moves sharpened the already aggressive competition within the record industry, dependent as it is on the whims of young people who buy fully half of its products.[62]

The risks were dramatized in Sony's deal with its resident superstar, Michael Jackson, in the early 1990s. Mr. Jackson's early albums, *Bad* and *Thriller*, were big hits. *Bad* sold over 45 million copies. In contract renegotiations, Jackson demanded and got a new record label of his own, along with arrangements to create his own feature films, theatrical shorts, and other media products. Sony officials confidently predicted that the new contract could generate $1 billion in sales. (Record companies deal in round numbers.)

The arrangement ran the very real risk that Michael Jackson's particular talents might cease to attract a new generation of his youthful audiences. The contract went against the industry's accepted truism that every new musical trend takes the record business by surprise, including the rise and inevitable decline of its big stars. As it happened, Michael Jackson did trip over that truism in 1995 when a long-awaited album, *HIStory*, turned out to be a marketing failure despite a $30 million promotional campaign by Sony.[63]

TAKING ON THE NEW TECHNOLOGIES

Hollywood's rekindled love affair with the record business is helping to push the major film studios into new technologies. The recording industry has already gone through one major technological change recently, with compact discs replacing long-playing records and cutting deep into the audiotape market. As noted above, the industry has come to terms with more advanced high-technology products, including multimedia discs that combine music, video, and text capabilities.

The film studios, record companies, and every other media industry will be increasingly involved in new kinds of mass-consumer information and entertainment products. The next step is exploiting the prospects of home telecomputers, living room machines that will function as a combined television set and computer, with programming delivered by television stations, CD-ROMs, fiber-optic cable, or direct-broadcasting communications satellites. Hollywood has high hopes for digital video disc technology (DVD), which is capable of storing a full-length film on a compact disc with superior picture quality and stereo sound. The industry is betting that DVD will eventually displace today's videocassettes and their recorders, opening up a profitable new market for this industry.

HOLLYWOOD LOOKS TO THE FUTURE

Will Hollywood become a major production center for multimedia programs? The answer is not yet clear. The film industry's primary expertise is in making movies. The new multimedia technologies are only partly about making movies. They are also about new ways of integrating sound, video, graphics, and print. Hollywood has focused primarily on applying the new technologies to its staple product, the feature film.[64] Digital technology allows the studios to edit their films more efficiently and to create breathtaking effects that fill movie theater seats and increase videocassette sales. Digital technology has given us striking images of Jurassic Park dinosaurs, the *Titanic* disaster, and Tom Hanks as Forrest Gump shaking hands with President John Kennedy. The Disney studio has been the leader in using computer-generated imaging (CGI) techniques in its recent cartoon features. *Toy Story*, one of Disney's early CGI hits, was put together by twenty-seven animators, far fewer than the seventy or so who had worked on a Disney animated film, *Pocahontas*, a few years earlier.[65]

Hollywood's role in the multimedia environment will largely be determined by the industry's new owners: Time Warner, Rupert Murdoch, Sony, and Dreamworks, among others. Each has reorganized its operations to produce and distribute multimedia entertainment products. This is in the industry tradition of successfully adapting to technological changes over the past century. The introduction of sound movies in the 1920s forced the industry to turn around in a few months. The Internet will require similar changes. Every studio is examining ways it can exploit the Internet's resources to promote its films and, perhaps eventually, to display them directly on home screens. This was part of the Disney Co.'s motivation in 1998 when it invested $900 million in Infoseek, a World Wide Web service.[66]

Disney later became the first Hollywood studio to establish a full-scale Internet presence. In 1999, it created the Go Network, which combined the company's many Web sites into a single service that markets its multimedia products. Disney had already been a formidable presence on the Internet, with as many as 15 million monthly inquiries a month to its Web pages. The integration of these sites into a single network gave the company a strong advantage in competing with other major online services—such as America Online and Yahoo—in the race to amass audiences and to sell its wares.

The transition to new multimedia products will take a few years, given the costly production, marketing, and distribution problems involved. The technology is ready, poised to change the way the industry produces and distributes its products.[67] Hollywood will still make movies, but they will be different. The industry's reputation as the world's premier dream factory will remain. Hollywood is a survivor. As one of its legendary film directors, Billy Wilder, once boasted, "I can assure you that, on the day the world ends, somebody will be out there shooting second unit."[68]

NOTES

1. Barbara Leaming, *Orson Welles: A Biography*. New York: Viking Penguin, 1985, p. 212.
2. William Goldman, *Adventures in the Screen Trade*. New York: Warner Books, 1983.
3. "Buchwald vs. Paramount: Coming to a Conclusion," *Washington Post,* 2 March 1992, p. B-1.
4. "Why *Titanic* Conquered the World," *New York Times,* 26 April 1998, p. AR-1.
5. "Stars' Salaries Skyrocketing," *New York Times,* 18 September 1995, p. D-1. See also "Costly Flops, Rising Budgets Give Hollywood Its Own 'Crimson Tide,'" *Washington Post,* 2 January 1996, p. B-10.
6. "The New Business Boom in Hollywood," *Washington Post,* 19 May 1996, p. H-1.
7. Wilson Dizard, *Television—a World View*. Syracuse, NY: Syracuse University Press, 1966, p. 118.
8. Veronis, Suhler & Associates, *op. cit.,* p. 212.
9. "Sales, Rentals Hit Highs," *Variety,* 27 January 1992, p. 19.
10. "Now Playing on Screen 29," *Business Week,* 7 July 1977, p. 46.
11. "In Tomorrow's Motion Picture Theater, the Theater Is Also in Motion," *Intermedia* (London), March–April 1993, p. 46.
12. Chris Columbus, "Wilder Times," *American Film,* March 1980, p. 28.
13. Leo Bogart, *The American Media System and Its Commercial Culture,* occasional paper 8, Gannett Foundation Media Center, March 1991, p. 4.

14. "Big vs. Little: Surviving in a World of Media Giants," *Television Business International* (London), October 1990, pp. 54–66.
15. "Lion King Success Is the Pride of Disney," *Financial Times* (London), 26 April 1995, p. 12.
16. Ron Grover, *The Disney Touch: How a Daring Management Team Revived an Entertainment Empire*. New York: Business One Irwin, 1991. See also Kevin Maney, *Multimedia Shakeout*. New York: John Wiley & Sons, 1995, pp. 162–168.
17. "America's Sorcerer," *Economist* (London), 10 January 1998, p. 71.
18. Steven Watts, *The Magic Kingdom: Walt Disney and the American Way of Life*. Boston: Houghton Mifflin, 1998.
19. "Disney Now the Biggest Player in Football," *Washington Post*, 6 September 1998, p. 1.
20. "Disney Interactive Lays Off 40, But Denies Strategy Change," *Cowles/Simba Media Daily*, 17 August 1998.
21. "Disney and CLT Agree on Euro Venture," *Television Broadcasting International*, September 1994, p. 82.
22. "Disney's Hyperion Book Arm to Launch Mass-Market Paperback Publishing Line," *Wall Street Journal*, 12 January 1994, p. B-6.
23. "Prime-time Passions," *Economist* (London), 5 August 1995, pp. 55–60.
24. "Canada Sees Red over Disney Marketing Link to Mounties," *Financial Times* (London), 5 July 1995, p. 1.
25. "How Murdoch Makes It Work," *New York Times*, 14 August 1988, p. F-3.
26. The Byzantine negotiations involved in the Time Warner merger and its aftermath are described in Connie Bruck, "Deal of the Year," *New Yorker*, 8 January 1990, pp. 66–89; also Connie Bruck, "Strategic Alliances," *New Yorker*, 6 July 1992, pp. 34–56. For an account of the merger that emphasizes the alleged loss of editorial independence by Time Inc. publications, see Richard Clurman, *To the End of Time*. New York: Simon & Schuster, 1992.
27. "Invasion of Studio Snatchers," *Business Week*, 16 October 1989, p. 53.
28. "Valenti Hits Foreign-Ownership Bill," *Variety*, 11 November 1991, p. 20.
29. "Chief of Sony Tells Why It Bought a Part of America's Soul," *Financial Times* (London), 4 October 1989, p. 6.
30. For an interesting description of the political as well as economic factors involved in the Matsushita acquisition, see Connie Bruck, "Leap of Faith," *New Yorker*, 9 September 1991, pp. 38–74.
31. "The Entertainment Industry," special survey, *Economist* (London), 23 December 1989, p. 10.
32. "MCA, Sony: Why Mergers Didn't Work," *Washington Post*, 8 April 1995, p. D-1.
33. "Retreat from Tinseltown," *Economist* (London), 8 April 1995, pp. 58–59.
34. "For Sony's Studios, a New Mood," *New York Times*, 28 July 1997, p. C-15.
35. "For the Movie Industry, Silver Screen Has Been Golden in '97," *Washington Post*, 30 December 1997, p. 1.
36. "Dream Team Plans TV, Film Mega-merger," *Broadcasting & Cable*, 17 October 1994, p. 6.
37. "Media," *New York Times*, 2 June 1997, p. D-9. See also "How Well Mr. Spielberg Wears a Suit," *Economist* (London), 1 August 1998, p. 58.
38. "3 Baby Bells Drop CAA Contract," *Washington Post*, 24 August 1995, p. B-11.
39. "Hollywood's Sensitivity Training," *Washington Post*, 28 December 1991, p. C-1.
40. "Duck, Goofy," *Business Week*, 1 September 1997, p. 38.
41. "Loved It, Darling, Let's Shoot," *Economist* (London), 12 October 1991, pp. 94–95.
42. "The Media Business: Publishing," *New York Times*, 6 February 1995, p. D-6.

43. Nigel Andrews, "Stop Mugging the Paying Public," *Financial Times* (London), 1 January 1992, p. 21.
44. "Venturing into Capital," *Television Business International*, April 1991, p. 40.
45. "A Big Weekend for Batman," *New York Times*, 25 June 1995, p. D-6.
46. "Top 100 All-Time Film Rental Champs," *Variety*, 6 January 1992, p. 86.
47. "Viet Cong Weeps for Redskins," *Variety*, 25 January 1967, p. 2.
48. A. M. A. Aziz, *A Pakistani Journalist Looks at America*, Dacca: Al-Helat, 1960, p. 7.
49. "Studios Look to Foreign Markets," *New York Times*, 7 March 1990, p. D-1.
50. "Sacre Bleu! French Films a la Hollywood," *New York Times*, 8 January 1996, p. 33.
51. '97 Saw Boffo Box Office Abroad," *Washington Post*, 1 January 1998, p. B-9.
52. "Disney Co. Cartoons Are Going to China in Commercial Foray," *Wall Street Journal*, 23 October 1986, p. 1.
53. "Time Warner to Invest $220 Million in Cinemas," *Financial Times* (London), 21 January 1995, p. 7.
54. "No Place Like Home," *Washington Post*, 23 January 1992, p. D-7.
55. "Hollywood Tries to Fit PPV into Its Game Plan," *Broadcasting*, 29 April 1991, p. 37.
56. "Paramount to Make Its Own PPV Deals," *Broadcasting*, 2 November 1992, p. 51.
57. Veronis, Suhler & Associates, *op. cit.*, p. 199.
58. "Farewell, the Quaint, Old-Fashioned CD," *New York Times*, 7 September 1997, p. H-76.
59. "Seagram to Acquire Music Firm Polygram," *Washington Post*, 22 May 1998, p. D-3. See also "Size Does Matter," *Economist* (London), 23 May 1998, p. 57.
60. "The Sound of Money," *Business 2.0*, September 1998, p. 114.
61. Veronis, Suhler & Associates, *op. cit.*, p. 226.
62. "Can These Upstart Record Labels Survive?" *New York Times*, 5 January 1992, p. F-5.
63. "History Catches up with Sony Music," *New York Times*, 17 July 1995, p. D-1.
64. "Hollywood 3.0," *Wired*, October 1998, p. 148.
65. "Out of the Inkless Well," *Business Week*, 30 October 1995, p. 46.
66. "Disney Will Invest in a Web Gateway," *New York Times*, 19 June 1998, p. 1.
67. "Hollywood: the People Who Are Reinventing Entertainment," *Wired*, November 1997, p. 201.
68. "The AFI Life Achievement Award," *American Film*, July 1987, p. 22.

Gutenberg's Last Stand?

"Networked computers will be the printing presses of the twenty-first century."[1] That prediction, made in the early 1980s by communications scholar Ithiel de Sola Pool, was dismissed at the time by most publishing industry experts as a futuristic fancy. Professor Pool's prediction, however, is being realized faster than even he might have anticipated. The traditional publishing sectors—newspapers, magazines, and books—are adjusting their operational styles to computer realities, as well as coping with competition from a growing number of new electronic information providers.

The changes do not, however, signal the end of print. Johannes Gutenberg lives on in familiar morning newspapers, in weekly magazines, and in the 50,000 books published annually in the United States. The U.S. printing and publication sectors remain comfortably profitable. The idea that computers and other electronic devices might transform America into a "paperless society" has been turned on its head.

An environmental experiment in the early 1990s confirmed the tenacity of our paper habits. Eight "bionauts" volunteered to live in a sealed glass dome in the Arizona desert for two years, communicating with the outside world only electronically. The experiment was a limited success. The bionauts soon realized their reliance on e-mail and fax messages generated considerable paper use among their correspondents outside their glass abode. "We discovered that true paperless living required a lot of people outside who are also paperless," bionaut

Linda Leigh explained. "You can't really be an island of paperless life." She and her companions wanted something to read—on paper. (Their most requested item was *TV Guide*.) By the second year, the paper ban had to be modified to permit the introduction of printed materials into their otherwise enclosed habitat.[2]

Computers and photocopiers have, ironically, created a glut of printed paper, simply because so many people want to store computer-generated information as hard copy in old-fashioned file cabinets. It is one of the reasons the computer-rich United States accounts for one-third of the more than 200 million tons of paper produced annually around the world. A 1998 survey by computer maker Hewlett-Packard estimated that around 860 billion pages were being spewed out of copiers, fax machines and computer printers in America during one twelve-month period.[3]

OLD PRINT AND NEW TECHNOLOGY

Paul Saffo, research fellow at the Institute for the Future, predicts a new synergy between traditional printed information and its electronic versions:

> Paper won't disappear, but paperless media will soak up more of our time. We will eventually become paperless the same way we once became horseless. Horses are still around, but they are ridden by hobbyists, not commuters. . . . Now it is cheaper to store information electronically. Paper has become an interface—an increasingly transient, disposable medium for viewing electronically compiled information. We are entering the future where information is reduced to paper only when we're ready to read it, and then the paper is promptly recycled.[4]

Meanwhile, the electronification of print is taking hold. Media scholar Anthony Smith compares this trend to two earlier communications upheavals: the invention of writing and the Gutenberg printing press.

> The computerization of print is truly a third revolution in communications of similar scale and importance, in that it raises comparably fundamental issues concerning the social control of information, the notion of the individual creative function, the ways in which information interacts with human memory.[5]

The computer, Smith says, calls for a complete reorganization of the concept behind the print medium. Although computers were used initially by publishers to turn out products in their traditional form, print computerization opens up innovative possibilities for collecting, storing, and marketing information for mass audiences.

As has happened in every other media sector, print publishers have been generally slow to understand these implications. For years, they used computerized technologies as cost-cutting operational aids while they continued to produce their traditional products in the old ways. The prospects opened to publishers by digital multimedia devices are only beginning to be understood. The pioneer in this field was Sony, the Japanese electronics manufacturer. The company's Electronic Book Player, introduced in the early 1990s, was a portable machine that fitted in the palm of the hand. Each of the player's discs stored and displayed 100,000 pages of text, 32,000 graphic images, or a combination of both. "It weighs eight million pounds less than your average library," Sony's advertisements proclaimed.

EARLY ELECTRONIC PUBLISHING FAILURES

The publishing industry's reluctance to branch out into computerized products stemmed in part from disappointing experiences with electronic publishing two decades ago. Those early projects generally failed, bedeviled by limited technology, poor marketing, and disinterested consumers. The few projects that succeeded were those that identified a specialized audience with the interest, and the money, to make good use of electronic information targeted toward their specific needs. An early success was the LEXIS data network, introduced in 1973, which gives lawyers quick online access to court decisions in ways that have made printed law digests largely obsolete.

Eventually, electronic publishing will require massive restructuring of the print industries. This will involve a psychological shift on the part of publishers. As Times-Mirror executive Jerome Rubin puts it:

> Growth in publishing—and, in some cases, survival—will lie in our ability to work in multiple dimensions. . . . Gutenberg provided a means of creating identical multiple copies. Electronic technologies, on the other hand, provide a means of creating infinite variations of the same material. Different versions are thus created continually, and each one can be stored in the computer. There is no one "author," nor is there any "definitive version" of the material. We are returning in spirit to Plato's Academy and the pre-copyright world of oral dialogue.[6]

DEALING WITH THE NEW DEMOGRAPHICS

Progress toward the computerization of print is influenced by other developments affecting the future shape and direction of the American publishing industries. The most important one is the changing profile of U.S. society. The prosperity of the media industries after World War II was stimulated by unprecedented population growth. The postwar baby-boom generation developed into a large, affluent, and receptive audience for traditional print products—newspapers, magazines, and books—as well as for television and other electronic media. Demographic patterns were relatively stable for several decades. White families with several children were the norm, the personification of the cottage-with-white-picket-fence American dream. This pattern, however, is eroding, according to a 1998 U.S. Census Bureau study of the postwar baby-boomer generation.[7] Population growth in the 1990s averaged about 7 percent, the slowest rate in the country's history. That change is accompanied by a major transformation in the U.S. population profile. Married couples with children now account for about 25 percent of all households; almost 30 percent of married couples have no children; another 25 percent of the adult population is unmarried.

These changes are having a major impact on newspapers, magazines, and other publications. A special factor is the new importance of ethnic minorities.

About 80 percent of the U.S. population increase projected between now and the year 2010 will occur in the African American, Hispanic, and Asian communities. The Census Bureau estimates that Hispanics will become the nation's largest minority by 2005.[8] One result of this shift is the growth of ethnic publications, similar in pattern but greater in volume than the surge experienced earlier in this century when many immigrant groups had native-language newspapers and other publications. The Washington, DC, area has five weekly Spanish-language newspapers. It also has a lively Korean media sector, which includes five daily and three weekly papers, three radio stations, and two television production units.[9] Altogether, the Washington area has more than two dozen foreign-language newspapers.

Along with these demographic changes are shifts in work and leisure patterns, which affect reading habits. A study by the Washington-based Economic Policy Institute found that the average U.S. worker puts in about 140 more hours on the job every year than the worker of two decades ago. Commuting time has also increased, so that Americans annually have almost 160 fewer hours—or one month less—for leisure activities.[10]

Demographic shifts and lifestyle changes affect the form, content, and distribution of print-media products. For example, big-city afternoon newspapers in the United States are disappearing as middle-class readers move to the suburbs and rely on the evening television news for a quick review of the day's events.[11] Between 1950 and 1997, the number of afternoon papers dropped from 1,450 to 816.[12]

These trends have also transformed the publishing industry's financial prospects. In the past, publishing revenues were based largely on products aimed at broad general audiences centered around family households. As older lifestyles erode, newspapers and magazines have fewer readers whose interests can be met with general information. Mass publications are losing readers to other print products that appeal to the ever-narrowing specialized interests of select audiences—scuba divers, Barbie doll collectors, or Corvette drivers, to name a few of the many groups that now have their own publications.

Special interest publications are not new, of course, but their widespread popularity is. Collectively, they have overtaken general interest newspapers, magazines, and books as the dominant growth sector in U.S. publishing. Newspapers have responded with special editions, edited for particular audiences. General magazines are dividing up their readerships by zip codes and income groups in order to satisfy advertisers who are no longer willing to pay for an undifferentiated mass readership. These are expensive efforts and have escalated production and distribution costs. Since the mid-1980s, single-copy magazine prices have increased by over 70 percent; book and newspaper prices are not far behind.[13]

SHRINKING ADVERTISING PROSPECTS

Advertising revenues are still the financial mainstay for newspapers and most magazines, but they have been under siege in recent years. Beginning in the mid-1970s, these publications, along with television, benefited from an extraordinary expansion in the amount of money spent on advertising. Total U.S. advertising expenditures grew by an average of 13.5 percent annually from 1975 to 1984, most of it spent on television, newspaper, and magazine ads.[14] Since then, general advertising spending in the printed media has been reduced to the point where, in many cases, it barely keeps pace with inflation.

In addition to tightening their print-media budgets, advertisers are refining their strategies at the expense of the print media. Instead of saturating consumers with sales messages, they are targeting their efforts more directly toward particular markets with the best prospects. This strategy includes greater reliance on direct mail campaigns, telephone marketing, sweepstakes, shop-at-home catalogues, and Web pages. These alternative advertising techniques have been expanded recently to also include specially prepared videocassette presentations. The Chrysler Corporation was one of the early adopters of videocassette advertising. In the early 1990s, it mailed out 400,000 cassettes promoting a new minivan model to a targeted list of potential customers.

THE TELEMARKETING CHALLENGE

The fastest-growing type of alternative advertising is telemarketing, the selling of products or services by telephone. Telemarketing techniques include unsolicited sales calls to customers as well as 800- and 900-number calls initiated by customers. There are over a million 800-number services operating throughout the United States. The newer 900-number industry is a billion-dollar enterprise whose primary service is not pornography pandering, as popularly believed, but the dispensing of practical information.[15]

The telemarketing industry did not exist twenty-five years ago. The industry's success is based on a combination of advanced telecommunications technology and computers. Increasingly, its telephone operations are carried out by robotic machines using computerized speech to process orders. One such device, developed by a British company, can handle up to 120,000 calls a day, compared with the 2,000 previously handled by a staff of sixteen telephone attendants.[16] Despite this and similar automation techniques, the Direct Marketing Association, the industry's trade association, expects telemarketing sales employment to top 2 million by 2001, with sales at that time totaling $250 billion.[17]

Taken together, telemarketing and the other alternative marketing sites are a significant economic threat to newspapers and magazines. A *Business Week* analysis of major consumer industries in the mid-1990s found that traditional media advertising accounted for only 30 percent of marketing budgets, down 13 percent from ten years previously.[18] General print publications will continue to be attractive outlets for many advertisers, particularly those offering products (soft drinks, cigarettes, etc.) aimed at large consumer groups. The overall trend in advertising, however, increasingly is to bypass mass-audience newspapers and magazines.

Diminishing advertising revenues have forced a retrenchment throughout the print publishing sector. A large number of magazines and newspapers, including some of the best and most venerable, have disappeared entirely. Many of the surviving publications have turned to mergers and buyouts to ease their financial troubles. These takeovers are usually carried out by big media corporations, intent on incorporating published materials into multimedia operations that often include television, film, and cable TV resources as well as newer, computer-driven technologies.

In summary, the publishing industry is undergoing major changes, brought on by demographic shifts, financial upheavals, and the pressure of new technologies. Instability and reassessment are common to all parts of the industry—newspapers, magazines, and books—but the situation in each sector is distinct enough to warrant examining them separately.

THE CHANGING NEWSPAPER INDUSTRY

First, let's look at newspaper publishing, which is still the centerpiece of U.S. print media activities. Historically, it is the industry that has defined the standards and responsibilities of media in U.S. society, long before radio, television, and the other mass-communications services came along. Newspapers are woven into the warp and woof of the U.S. experience, from Ben Franklin's *Pennsylvania Gazette* to present-day publications like the *New York Times* and the *Unterrified Democrat*, which has been flaunting its defiant title in rural Missouri every week for over a century.

No other medium has the capability to collect, record, and distribute information at so many different levels, from the daily activities of small towns to national and international events. In aggregate, newspaper files contain the most complete written memory of American society. When the *Boston Globe* decided some years ago to catalogue and upgrade its century-old newspaper morgue, it discovered that it had 9 million clippings in 700,000 folders, along with 800,000 photographic prints. The *Globe's* files document, in raw form, the history of modern Boston and its surrounding area.[19]

For all its past glories and lapses, U.S. print journalism is now in a period of massive transition, challenged by present-day electronic media on the one hand and by newer, computer-driven information resources on the other. The debate is already under way about how (and even whether) newspapers can withstand the assault. There is no simple answer. Newspapers will continue to be a major presence in U.S. media for a long time to come. To survive over the long run, however, they must continue to adjust their production and editorial styles to the new computer-based competition and to the changing demographics and life patterns of their readers.

Fifty years ago, newspapers were still the primary sources of news, opinion, and light entertainment for most Americans. More important, they were the preeminent institution for setting the nation's political and social agendas. The only competitive mass medium was radio, whose news influence at the time was spotty. Many homes received both a morning and an afternoon paper. Newspaper market penetration in 1945 was 135 percent, meaning that more papers were sold every day than there were households. Circulation continued to climb until the early 1960s and then began to level off. Market penetration did not keep pace with the postwar baby boom. By 1970, newspaper circulation had fallen below the total number of households.

The accepted wisdom in the industry at the time was that circulation would rise again as baby boomers grew up and became, like their parents, regular newspaper readers. This did not happen. The baby boomers turned to television for their news. More women (who composed a disproportionately high share of home newspaper readership) went to work outside the home. By 1989, newspaper penetration of households had fallen to 67 percent, less than half the percentage at the end of World War II.[20]

LOSING THE NEWSPAPER HABIT

Many Americans began to lose the newspaper habit. That decline has been recorded in many studies of newspaper readership, particularly those carried out by the American Society of Newspaper Editors (ASNE). The surveys went beyond the well-known facts about overall readership losses. They also probed the habits of individual groups, including regular and occasional readers as well as nonreaders. One study identified a solid core of loyal readers, about 55 percent of U.S. adults, who regard newspapers as an important part of their life. Then there are the "at-risk readers," who pick up a paper several times a week but find little value there. As one ASNE report noted wryly, "They are not our fans. They are primarily interested in news that helps them cope with everyday living."[21] Finally, there are the nonreaders or very occasional readers, who are unlikely to take up the newspaper habit.

The most disturbing trend in newspaper readership is the defection of young adults. The majority of at-risk and potential readers are in this group, the critical age category for the future of U.S. journalism. A 1998 media-audience survey by the Pew Research Center for the People and the Press indicated that only 28 percent of young respondents had read a newspaper the day before, compared with 69 percent of seniors. The under-thirties make up a high proportion of the one in five Americans who turned regularly to Internet news sources in 1998—a threefold increase in just two years.[22]

The newspaper industry is finding it increasingly difficult to attract younger readers. In part, this is due to the recent proliferation of alternative news sources, particularly cable-news channels and Internet Web pages. However, it also reflects the fact that lifestyles of young adults tend to be fast moving and volatile, unsuited to regular newspaper reading habits. They are caught up in constantly shifting patterns influenced by job changes, two-income households, child care, divorce, and frequent household moves.

In an effort to reach young adults, newspapers are adopting flashier page formats and features that focus on personal-living issues. Overall, however, newspaper executives are not optimistic about stemming readership losses. The problem was summarized by Lou Heldman, an official in the Knight-Ridder newspaper chain:

> We know how to win Pulitzers. We know how to topple politicians. We know how to do gut-wrenching stories. What we don't always know is how you get people to read serious journalism.[23]

Some newspaper executives dispute the importance of the overall decline in readership. They argue that newspapers are retaining their most important reader groups, the middle class and the affluent, who have the most buying power and are therefore most sought after by advertisers. True as this may be, it has not prevented a general decline in newspaper advertising revenues in recent years. Newspaper ad revenues did benefit from the 1980s economic boom, but by 1990, they had turned sharply downward.[24] That year, for the first time in decades, the American Newspaper Publishers Association (ANPA) reported no increase in ad revenues. Newspaper advertising rebounded in the 1990s, increasing by 7.3 percent in 1994, its largest jump since 1987.

Readership losses and the challenge of new information technologies raise concerns about the future of the newspaper business. For the present, however, the business remains basically healthy.[25] Advertisers and readers spent a total of $56.7 billion on newspapers in 1997 (see Table 8.1). Daily newspapers were still ahead of all other media in advertising revenues, with about a 25 percent share. Television ranked second, with 22 percent, and direct mail was third, with 18 percent.

THE NEW NEWSPAPER CONGLOMERATES

Historically, the industry's pattern has been a mix of many independent papers in smaller cities, together with national chains, which dominated the big-city markets. This mix still characterizes the industry, but the composition of the mix is changing. Unlike most of their predecessors, many of the larger newspaper chains now belong to conglomerates with multimedia holdings. The most striking example is the Gannett Company, which in the late 1990s owned *USA Today* and eighty-six other daily newspapers, making it the largest U.S. newspaper company. Gannett also controls twenty television stations, cable TV systems in five states, the Louis Harris polling organization, its own news service, and the largest billboard advertising group in the country. The New York Times Company is more than the *Times*: It is the owner of the *Boston Globe* and thirty-two smaller papers, seventeen magazines, six television stations, a radio station, and a thriving data information service, and it has a half-interest in the Paris-based *International Herald-Tribune*. Newspaper firms with extensive holdings in other media operations include the *Washington Post, Chicago Tribune, Los Angeles Times-Mirror,* and

TABLE 8.1 Growth of U.S. Spending on Newspapers

	Daily Newspapers	Weekly Newspapers	Total
1997 Expenditures ($ Millions)	$51,407	$5,365	$56,772
1992–1997 Compound Annual Growth (%)	5.3%	7.4%	5.4%
1997–2002 Projected Compound Annual Growth (%)	6.4%	8.2%	6.6%
2002 Projected Expenditures ($ Millions)	$70,068	$7,939	$78,007

SOURCE: Sources: Veronis, Suhler & Associates, Wilkofsky Gruen Associates, Newspaper Association of America, Paul Kagan Associates, *Editor & Publisher*

the Gannett and Knight-Ridder chains. There are very few newspaper-only chains left: One of the largest is the little-known MediaNews Group, with fourteen dailies in nine states, including the *Denver Post*. Another relatively unknown newspaper owner is Conrad Black, the Canadian media entrepreneur who controls 437 newspapers worldwide, of which about 250 are in the United States, including the *Chicago Sun-Times*.[26]

Many media observers believe editorial independence is threatened by chain ownership,[27] and there are enough documented examples of such threats to justify these concerns. More characteristically, however, the new multimedia groups are led by corporate executives who are not inclined to interfere in editorial policy; they are more interested in bottom-line profitability. They are generally more cost conscious than owners of independent papers, and they tend to invest heavily in improving product quality.[28] However, editorial independence often comes under heavy pressure from a paper's business managers. This happened in 1997 at the *Los Angeles Times*, where management decided to organize its marketing staff around the same editorial sections as its journalists. The idea was that the two sides would work together to attract readers and manage their brands.[29] The proposal was loudly denounced by reporters and editors as a violation of the so-called "Chinese Wall" principle of separation of editorial and marketing staffs.

The potential loss of editorial independence by chain-owned newspapers should not be underestimated. As media critic Ben Bagdikian has warned:

> The problem is not evil media empires. Nor is it the nature of any one corporation. The real problem is that more and more of the country's mass media is being controlled by fewer and fewer corporations. . . . Economists know perfectly well what happens. When a handful of companies have most of the business and the remainder is divided among hundreds or thousands of small companies, it is market domination. The dominant companies control prices and the nature of the product. But in this case, the product happens to be the country's reservoir of news, information, ideas and entertainment.[30]

The new conglomerate owners of newspapers are reshaping the industry. About 75 percent of U.S. daily newspapers are owned by chains. The extent of this change has been summarized by Richard Harwood, the media critic of the *Washington Post*:

> Our 25 leading newspaper corporations own a third of all American newspapers, control two-thirds of the circulation and have more than $30 billion in annual revenues, half of which comes from non-newspaper sources: television, radio and cable stations, magazines, book publishing, newsprint mills, billboards and various cyberspace enterprises including way stations on the electronic "superhighway" that lies ahead. In 98 percent of our cities, newspapers have achieved monopoly status.[31]

Faced with declines in readership and revenues, the newspaper industry is looking for ways to maintain its competitiveness. Increasingly it is turning to new technologies, both to upgrade its present products and to improve production and marketing efficiency.[32] For two decades, newspapers have been moving toward computerization of their internal operations. Newspaper production is now almost totally automated, from newsroom word processing to computerized delivery programs. Technology is changing the ways reporters cover stories; in particular, it has vastly increased their ability to tap into computerized information resources.[33]

Meanwhile, publishers are redesigning their newspapers in order to increase their appeal, particularly for younger audiences. Even the *New York Times*, a long-time holdout against flashy journalism, has redesigned itself in recent years, using more graphics and adopting magazine-style layouts.[34] The *Times* also devotes more space to local news, an acknowledgment that, despite its journalistic pre-eminence, it reaches only about a tenth of the households in the New York area. The *Times*'s transformation was accelerated by the addition of an automated $450 million printing plant in Edison, New Jersey, where computers and robots perform most of the tasks previously done by humans.

USA TODAY: SETTING A NEW COURSE

The most dramatic attempt to create a new kind of newspaper was the launching of *USA Today* by the Gannett chain in 1982. The paper was the brainchild of Allen Neuharth, one of the more flamboyant figures in recent U.S. journalism. (His autobiography is entitled *Memoirs of an SOB*.) Neuharth deliberately set out to offer a print version of television news and features—short, eye-catching, and light on details. With its editorial material delivered by satellite to printing plants throughout the United States and abroad, the paper's weekday editions are bought by 1.7 million people, the largest circulation of any American daily. *USA Today* has been an expensive effort to find out how a newspaper can attract audiences in a media-saturated environment. Although the paper did not turn a profit until 1993, by the late 1990s it was comfortably in the black.[35]

In part, this financial turnaround was due to the paper's decision to offer more substantive news reporting, a distinct change from its earlier emphasis on lighter and brighter journalism. *USA Today* now provides better coverage of national and international affairs and of economic developments affecting its readers.[36] That change is part of a larger trend in the newspaper industry, reflecting the realization that its primary strength is in providing substantive, detailed information on a wide range of current events.

EXPERIMENTING WITH ELECTRONIC JOURNALISM

Newspapers have also turned to technologies that enable them to deliver timely information in more innovative and profitable ways. Their early attempts at electronic delivery were trial-and-error experiments.[37] In the late 1980s, dozens of newspapers began marketing selected summaries of their editorial products to subscribers with fax machines. As noted in Chapter 3, these experiments had only limited success. The most successful sellers of fax-delivered news have been newsletter publishers, whose stock-in-trade is providing specialized groups of customers with news of fast-breaking events in their professional fields.

The *New York Times* began the first major experiment in computerized news access in the mid-1970s. Its New York Times Information Bank provided summaries and full texts of current and past articles from its daily editions for subscribers with personal computers. In 1980, an Ohio paper, the *Columbus Dispatch*, made its entire daily editorial content available for a fee to home computer owners, using the CompuServe network.[38] Viewers could call up a news menu from which they could select the stories they wanted to see.

Other newspapers adopted different strategies for going on line. The *Raleigh* (NC) *News & Observer* had its own dial-up electronic bulletin board systems that users could access for a fee. *USA Today* brought its snappy, news-nugget style to the CompuServe network, specializing in sports information.

The pioneer in this field was the *San Jose Mercury News*, which began supplying news summaries via America Online in 1994. It later expanded the service to include the full text of the hard-copy edition of the newspaper, available on the Internet's World Wide Web. Initially offering the service for free, the paper's publishers decided to charge for access to its contents. Other papers formed alliances to provide online services on the Internet. One such group, created in February 1995, consisted of two Philadelphia papers, the *Inquirer* and the *Daily News*, collaborating with the *Newark Star-Ledger* and the *Jersey City Journal* in a jointly operated regional World Wide Web news service.

The most extensive effort to create a nationwide Internet-based news network was also launched in 1995. The organizers were eight of the country's largest newspaper companies: Gannett, Tribune, Cox, Hearst, Knight-Ridder, Advance, Times Mirror, and the Washington Post. Their New Century Network was a joint venture, designed in part to help smaller newspapers start online services, linking them to services provided by the large newspaper chains. The organizers of the network saw their project as a way to better position the newspaper industry to meet competition from other online providers. According to Peter Winter, a Cox Newspapers executive who was in charge of the project, there was a sense of urgency about the venture: "We thought it wasn't in anyone's interest to hang around and wait. The Internet is a place where commerce is going to happen, and therefore all of us have to be there."[39]

The project did not succeed in its effort to become a profitable online presence, competing against America Online and the Microsoft Network. Although it had enlisted 140 newspaper affiliates in four years, New Century cut back its news operations sharply in 1998, restructuring its operations to serve as an advertising sales network for its sponsors.[40]

Despite this setback, individual newspapers are making heavy use of Internet Web pages to display their wares, seek subscriptions, and gain advertising revenues. In 1995, only a hundred daily papers sponsored Web pages. By the turn of the century, all large-circulation papers were represented on the Web, along with hundreds of smaller publications. Increasingly, they are playing to their strength, which is local information.

Hundreds of newspapers have developed local entertainment-guide Web pages as well as online versions of Yellow Page directories. Many of them have signed up with companies like CitySearch Inc., a local content developer that also helps the papers sell advertising on their Web pages. By 1998, the *Washington Post* had a twenty-person staff working with City Search to sell ads.[41] The newspapers' strategy is to leverage their local information expertise in ways that attract corporate advertisers who have developed their own Web pages both for a dvertising their products as well as for direct sales.

Other newspapers have moved ahead with different versions of online services. The most successful of these has been the *Wall Street Journal*'s interactive edition, established in 1996. By 1999, the *Journal*'s electronic edition had over 250,000 paid subscribers, making it one of the few newspapers earning a profit from its online operations.[42]

"DIGITAL INK ON SILICON PAPER"

The most advanced experiment in creating a new kind of electronic newspaper was conducted in the mid-1990s by the Knight-Ridder chain. The company set up an "information design lab" in Boulder, Colorado, to test an experimental hand-held tablet, somewhat similar to a notebook computer. The Knight-Ridder tablet translated newspaper stories into "digital ink on silicon paper," according to Roger Fidler, director of the project. The tablet's screen displayed what looked like a condensed version of a well-designed newspaper, with sharp color graphics "pages." The tablets did not have a keyboard. Instead, readers touched the screen to turn pages, see advertisements, and browse through other information resources. They could download specific items, which were delivered over telephone lines.

The Knight-Ridder project created a stir in the newspaper industry, but it soon ran into trouble. No electronics manufacturer was able at the time to produce a tablet with ten-inch screens that has enough processing power to create the graphics-filled pages the project required. Moreover, the cost of such a device, initially at least, put it out of the range of most potential customers. The project was described by one newspaper consultant, Mary Modahl of Forrester Research Inc., as a "highly impractical futuristic vision that has not been grounded in any sort of need or market economics."[43] By the late 1990s, Knight-Ridder had cut back most of the funding for the project.

Like other newspaper conglomerates, Knight-Ridder has had trouble adjusting to the Internet's role in electronic publishing. In 1997, the company reportedly spent $27 million on its thirty-two Web sites, but it earned only about $11 million in revenues from them. In the same year, Knight-Ridder sold its database unit, Knight-Ridder Information, to a British business information publisher for $420 million.[44]

Knight-Ridder's problems underline the fact that economic and technological limitations will control the pace and direction of advanced electronic newspaper publishing. Millions of dollars have been spent on less ambitious projects, with few signs of a profitable return. As noted above, the *Wall Street Journal*'s interactive edition is one of the few exceptions.

Many publishers are relying on simpler electronic strategies to link themselves with their customers. One of the most successful of these approaches is the use of 800- and 900-number telephone networks to offer information products to consumers. The range of services they supply is already wide and spreading rapidly. The *Washington Post* developed over forty free 800-number services, ranging from sports scores to current mortgage rates. The *Post*'s services averaged over 6 million calls annually in recent years. The *Los Angeles Times* began offering 800-number access to its editorial contents and then shifted to pay-per-call 900-number access at $1.50 per minute. The *Atlanta Journal and Constitution* offered advance snippets of weekend sermons, a service paid for by the city's churches and synagogues.

COMPETING WITH THE PHONE COMPANIES

Useful as these services are, they have had relatively little impact on the problems that newspapers face in adjusting to new electronic competition. A major issue for the industry concerns the growing role of the telephone and cable TV industries in supplying video, text, and voice services via electronic circuits to U.S. homes. Newspaper executives see this as a long-term threat to their own role as information suppliers. Their concerns have been summarized by George W. Wilson, chairman of a newspaper industry task force on telephone competition:

> The flood of new electronic products and services that the regional Bell telephone companies are creating will be nothing less than tomorrow's system for distributing information to every American home. . . . Depending on how they are used, these distribution systems will strengthen or shatter the traditional links between newspapers, their advertisers and their readers. In short, the phone companies could reshape the media triangle.[45]

Mr. Wilson and his fellow publishers worry that the phone companies will replace printed classified advertising—an important source of newspaper revenues—by offering customers cheap, easy-to-use electronic Yellow Pages. In response to this threat, the newspaper industry mounted a lobbying campaign in the early 1990s, designed to convince Congress that limits should be placed on phone company involvement in information services. Their efforts failed. As we have seen, Congress passed comprehensive legislation in 1996, which lifted almost all restraints on the ability of phone companies and cable TV networks to compete with newspapers as suppliers of electronic information, including classified ads.

More recently, newspapers have taken direct steps to protect their interests in the $15 billion classified market. The most important of these initiatives was a 1997 partnership of ten newspapers in major markets, including the *Los Angeles Times*, the *Washington Post*, and the *Chicago Tribune*. The partnership, New Ventures, initially offered an America Online service that promoted new-car sales—a critical ad market for the papers.[46] In part, the service is designed to match a trend among auto manufacturers to advertise and even market their cars on the Internet. In part, the New Ventures project is reacting to the fact that the car manufacturers are investing large resources in electronic marketing: By 1998, General Motor's Web site had 500 pages and 300 links.[47]

These online efforts by newspapers to attract advertisers and readers faced a formidable new competitor in 1998. It was Microsoft that inaugurated a national network of free consumer services. Known as Sidewalk, the network includes electronic Yellow Pages, an entertainment channel and a shopping service offering reviews and other information about a wide range of products from bicycles to cookware. The latter allows people to make side-by-side comparisons of products and search by Zip code to find the stores that carry the specific item they want. Initially, about 6,000 advertisers signed up with Sidewalk, which gives them such options as stand-alone Web sites, enhanced Yellow Page listings and targeted ads placed next to relevant features.[48]

Despite electronic inroads into traditional publishing, most industry observers are skeptical about any sudden transition from traditional print to electronic modes. The cost to consumers of making the switch to electronic services is often a deterrent. As Walter Baer, a media expert at the Rand Corporation, has noted:

> When you're dealing with high-value information for business and professional people, electronic information is workable. But most consumers don't find information so valuable that they want to pay more than 50 cents for the newspaper. Newsprint will be around until well after the turn of the century.[49]

ASSESSING THE NEWSPAPER'S FUTURE

Another view is offered by newspaper analyst William Blankenburg of the University of Wisconsin. In the current evolution that the industry faces, he writes:

> The comprehensive daily newspaper is not viable. Only pieces of it will survive, probably in targeted combinations, perhaps for a very long time. Some of its functions will be carried out by other means in the converged megamedium. The vertical integration of the newspaper industry will end, and with it, presumably, the local monopoly that allowed economies of scale in production. In the hazy future, the optimist will see the public freed from the shackles of old monopolistic media that constricted the flow of information vital to democracy. But the pessimist worries that a huge information utility controlled by mammoth venal corporations will widen the gaps between rich and poor, invade privacy, and destroy the communities of interest that shared the comprehensive daily newspaper.[50]

Whether through traditional print or by means of the new electronic techniques, the newspaper industry will be a force in the new-media environment. Newspapers bring unique experience and strong resources to the production and distribution of information for both business and home consumers. The industry stands to benefit greatly if it exploits this advantage and becomes a central player in new forms of electronic journalism during the coming decade. Still, this scenario may be too optimistic, according to a survey of newspaper industry prospects by the London *Economist*:

> Even putting aside the much-hyped information highway, the situation for newspapers is fairly grim. The first and longest-term problem is that it is no longer plain that people need to seek their information from ink on paper. Many

still like doing so, of course. But television gets news faster, and covers the sensational stuff more sensationally; magazines cater to every taste, however peculiar. No surprise, then, that Americans are reading newspapers less. In 1970, almost four-fifths of adults read a paper every weekday. That figure has shrunk to three-fifths.[51]

MAGAZINES IN TRANSITION

The magazine industry is also in a state of transition, sharing with newspapers the problems created by demographic shifts, the competition for advertising dollars, and challenges from electronic technologies. Newspapers have a certain advantage in the new environment in that they usually operate within a limited geographic area and so can adjust their content on a daily basis. Magazines deal with larger, more varied national audiences, whose attitudes and preferences are often harder to define.

General magazines such as *Time*, *Newsweek*, and *Reader's Digest* still have, collectively, the largest share of readers. The major trend in the magazine business, however, is the division of its audiences by interest groupings. Almost every conceivable group, from bird-watchers to sky divers, has one or more magazines targeted toward their particular interests. The industry is fragmented into thousands of national, regional, and local special-interest publications.

Many magazines are edited and distributed in different editions, with targeted editorial content and advertising in segmented editions. *Farm Journal*, for instance, publishes different editions for dairy, hog, beef, and high-income farmers. Some industry strategists foresee the day when magazines will be routinely personalized for subscribers, with no two copies alike.

JOINING THE MULTIMEDIA MIX

In common with other media, the magazine industry flourished in the 1980s, when over 2,500 new publications were launched. Most of them had disappeared by the mid-1990s. The more enduring legacy of the 1980s was the scramble by multimedia corporations to buy up successful magazine properties. In one single spectacular sale, Rupert Murdoch's News Corporation paid $3 billion for *TV Guide* in 1988. The deal of the decade, however, was the 1989 merger of Warner Communications and Time Inc., resulting in the world's largest media conglomerate. Their corporate marriage began with high hopes. Nicholas Nickels, a Time Inc. executive, declared at the time, "By the year 2000, when we have access to every home in the world on a direct-to-consumer basis, that's when the big numbers kick in."[52]

On paper, Time and Warner were the perfect multimedia fit. Warner was a major film, television program, and music record producer. Time Inc. had a stable of highly successful magazines, including *Time*, *Fortune*, *People*, and *Sports*

Illustrated. It was also a major book publisher, one of the largest investors in cable TV systems, and owner of HBO, the leading networker of satellite-delivered cable programming. The Time Warner deal was a bizarre financial arrangement, tied to an exchange of stock, which left the merged company with over $10 billion of debt.

The deal also raised some serious questions about a mismatch between a pop entertainment conglomerate and a major U.S. publisher, and especially about preserving the editorial integrity of the latter. These doubts were validated during the merger's early years when the two partners had difficulty in establishing the synergistic pattern they both had hoped for, in part because of the cultural gap separating the two halves of the organization.

THE FLOWERING OF SPECIAL-INTEREST MAGAZINES

In the late 1990s, the magazine industry continued its shift away from general-interest publications toward more specialized ones. Special-interest readers could choose from a wide range of publications, from *Cats Quarterly* to *Christian Motorsports Illustrated.*[53] In particular, new magazines emphasizing personal health, sports, and financial planning flourished. Computer magazines proliferated, offering self-help guidance to millions of new personal computer owners. A San Francisco-based magazine, *Wired,* established itself successfully as the monthly handbook for computer users trying to understand the new information-driven culture.[54] There has also been a new emphasis on publications for retirees and older readers in general. Circulation skyrocketed for *Modern Maturity,* the publication of the American Association of Retired Persons. Bridal magazines have also flourished as the marriage rate increased and formal ceremonies came back in style. One issue of *Bride's and Your New Home* made the Guinness Book of World Records as "the weightiest publication ever," at 1,024 pages.

THE NEW ECONOMICS OF MAGAZINE PUBLISHING

The 1990s were shakeout years for the magazine industry. Most new publications that had started up during the previous decade disappeared, as did many of the older ones. Despite these losses, the industry remains basically healthy, but many of its products are having a difficult time fitting into the new information environment. The search is still on for flexible editorial formulas to fit the shifting demographics and lifestyles of their readers. Meanwhile, the economics of magazine publishing continue to change. Magazines, like newspapers, are affected as advertisers turn to direct mail and other so-called alternative advertising techniques. One result is that subscription rates loom much larger as revenue producers. In the 1970s, advertising produced two-thirds of magazine revenues; in the 1990s, subscription revenues became the chief revenue producers.[55]

MAGAZINES FOR A WORLD MARKET

Another trend has been the steady globalization of the magazine business. *Time*, *Newsweek*, and *Reader's Digest* have each published international editions for over forty years. The *Digest's* forty-eight editions are issued in nineteen languages and sold to over 27 million readers abroad.[56] More recently, other publications have expanded abroad. *Business Week* publishes English-language European and Asian editions as well as foreign-language editions for China, Russia, and Poland. *Cosmopolitan* proclaims the gospel of the *Cosmo* Girl in thirty-three international editions. In 1994, *Cosmo's* publisher, the Hearst Corporation, launched a Russian-language edition in Moscow to compete against local women-oriented publications with such earthy titles as *Factory Worker Lady* and *Peasant Lady*.[57] Within a year, the Russian *Cosmo* reached a circulation of a quarter-million copies. International Data Group, a Boston firm specializing in information technology journals, publishes over 140 magazines in 55 countries.[58] Meanwhile, foreign publishers have been moving into the U.S. market. They include Hachette, a major French publisher, Rupert Murdoch's News Corporation, and Britain's Reed Elsevier group. Reed's American affiliate, Cahners Publishing, specializes in trade journals, with a list of over 60 publications ranging from *Variety*, the show business journal, to *Modern Materials Handling*.

ADAPTING TO THE COMPUTER AGE

Magazines publishers have made the shift to new technologies to improve their editorial content and their revenues. Most magazine production is now computer driven, from desktop layouts of editorial copy to the final printed product. Computerization has made it easier to produce segmented editions, with subscription lists categorized by income level, geographic location, or other specialized characteristics. *American Baby*, a monthly with a circulation of 1.1 million, is often segmented into 100 different versions of a single issue.

New printing techniques make it possible to tailor issues to fit the interests of individual customers. Time Warner began testing individualized printing with three of its magazines in the 1990s. In one project, each subscriber to *Time*, *Sports Illustrated*, and *People* found his or her name in an advertisement for Isuzu automobiles, together with a special insert listing the Isuzu dealer nearest to the subscriber's home.[59] *Forbes* magazine added an electronic touch to its advertising strategy when it included a bound-in floppy disk in an issue sent to 700,000 subscribers. The disk offered interactive ads, with animated color graphics, from ten advertisers.

Not all new electronic magazine ventures succeed. *Newsweek* was one of the first general-interest magazines to offer editorial material on a CD-ROM. The *Newsweek* Interactive disks were sold by subscription four times a year. Each disk was devoted to an in-depth review of a single subject. The project was not a success. *Newsweek* shifted to another strategy already adopted by *Time*, its major competitor: putting the contents of the magazine online.

THE INTERNET OPTION

The Internet has become a useful channel through which magazines can display their wares and secure subscribers. Every mass-circulation magazine, and most of the smaller ones, now has a Web site. Time Warner created Pathfinder, an advertiser-supported Internet site that provides text, photos, and graphics from its eight magazines. The Conde Nast publishing house established a Web presence for its fourteen magazines, served by a special subsidiary called Condenet. In a typical use, *Conde Nast Traveller* offers a vacation-planning service for Web surfers, which includes making hotel and airline reservations, checking the local weather at the vacation site, and introducing subscribers online to other travelers who have already been there.[60]

In summary, the magazine industry is adapting to the new world of electronic multimedia information and entertainment, with formats that will be quite different from the familiar ones. Computer-generated publishing has become the norm in the magazine business, expanding beyond its uses in producing newsletters and other specialized publications. Most general circulation magazines already rely heavily on desktop computers, interacting with other electronic equipment to produce high-quality, graphics-filled products.

BOOK PUBLISHING: ALIVE AND WELL

The most venerable of the media industries is book publishing. For all the many advantages of new electronic media, none has improved on the book for its practical attributes as an information storage device: portability, affordability, expansive range of subject matter, and security against costly repairs.

The U.S. book industry is big and diverse. Americans continue to spend more on books than on almost any other medium. (See Table 8.2.) About 50,000 books are published annually in the United States. Educational and professional books account for over half of this volume. Trade books—those sold for general consumption—are a smaller part of the industry's output; fewer than 5,000 fiction books are issued every year. Over 20,000 firms publish one or more books annually. New, less

---

TABLE 8.2   Growth of U.S. Spending on Consumer Books

	Consumer Book Expenditures
1997 Expenditures ($ Millions)	$15,430
1992–1997 Compound Annual Growth (%)	3.5%
1997–2002 Projected Compound Annual Growth (%)	5.0%
2002 Projected Expenditures ($ Millions)	$19,734

SOURCE: Sources: Veronis, Suhler & Associates, Wilkofsky Gruen Associates, Book Industry Study Group

expensive production techniques, such as desktop publishing, make it easier for new entrants to break into the field. Most of them remain minor operations.

The book trade is dominated by a half-dozen major publishers. Significantly, five of these six big firms belong to large media conglomerates. The takeovers of old-line publishing houses over the past twenty years have irrevocably changed the industry's staid, literary-oriented image. The distinctive styles of such firms as Charles Scribner, Viking, Grove Press, and Doubleday have been either lost or diluted. No longer is Random House defined as the publisher of William Faulkner, W. H. Auden, and Sinclair Lewis. Alfred A. Knopf once enjoyed an outstanding reputation as a publisher of high-quality literature, particularly works by foreign authors. In recent years, Knopf's high-style image has been diluted by such products as *Miss Piggy's Guide to Life* and the voyeuristic sex surveys of Shere Hite.

The largest and most successful U.S. publishing house in the 1990s was Simon & Schuster. The firm was taken over in 1975 by Paramount Communications, a multimedia conglomerate with extensive Hollywood and television holdings. Simon & Schuster flourished under Paramount, shedding its long-time image as primarily a trade book house to become an eclectic publisher of educational and professional books in both print and electronic forms. By the mid-1990s, its annual sales had reached $2.5 billion, of which only 10 percent was accounted for by trade books. The firm became the largest publisher of computer books, and 40 percent of its titles included CD-ROMs.

Simon & Schuster was acquired by Viacom Inc. in 1994 as part of its massive ($18 billion) takeover of all of Paramount's media properties. Viacom's chairman, Sumner Redstone, made it clear that his interest in Simon & Schuster, as with Paramount's film and television properties, was to exploit their software—books, films, and other products. "Software is king, was king and always will be king," he declared. "It would have taken us several lifetimes to have built up all the businesses of Paramount. Simon & Schuster has 375,000 copyrights in the software business, adding thousands every year."[61]

In the late 1990s, however, Simon & Schuster was in trouble, mainly because of Viacom's debt problems. In 1998, Viacom sold off most of the publishing firm's assets to London-based Pearson PLC for $4.6 billion, the largest deal ever in the book business. Viacom retained control of Simon & Schuster's consumer division, which publishes the works of such popular authors as Stephen King and Mary Higgins Clark.[62]

THE NEW CONGLOMERATES

Other large media conglomerates with publishing interests include Time Warner (Little, Brown, and others), Rupert Murdoch's News Corp. (HarperCollins), and the Reader's Digest Association, with its perennial condensed books editions. They see their book-publishing activities as an integral part of the marketing synergy they are trying to develop among all their media properties. This has led to fierce competition among them for books by big-name authors who can, they hope, guarantee large sales and multimedia exposure. In 1995, Random House reportedly paid General Colin Powell an advance of $6.5 million for his autobiography, *An American Journey*.

Foreign media companies have substantially expanded their publishing interests into the United States. Doubleday and Bantam Books were bought up in the 1990s by Bertelsmann A. G., a German conglomerate, which began as a publisher of Bibles two centuries ago. The firm is now an international media power, third only to Time Warner and Disney in the size of its multimedia holdings.[63] Bertelsmann's global presence was enhanced in 1998 when it bought Random House, one of the most venerable of the American publishing houses.[64] In addition to acquiring a large share of Simon & Schuster's assets, Pearson PLC, the British publishing, banking, and industrial group, owns a number of other U.S. publishing houses, including Penguin, Viking, New American Library, E. P. Dutton, and Addison Wesley Longman.

The U.S. book industry today is, in many ways, stronger and more successful than at any time in its history. Like all the other print industries, however, book publishing is feeling the pressure of new information technologies that are making its traditional print formats obsolete.[65] The industry has succeeded in automating its internal operations in ways that have lowered production and distribution costs.

Book production is now mostly computerized, from the author's word processing to final printing and distribution. The process, known in the trade as electronic manuscript management, tracks a book's production on a day-by-day basis. Tallies on costs, work hours, and production schedules are kept continuously current. Despite these improvements in production efficiency, the industry is still bedeviled by expensive, obsolete practices. This was a factor in the HarperCollins 1997 decision to cut costs by reducing its publishing list by 463 titles.[66]

ELECTRONIC PUBLISHING: THE PROSPECTS

Economics and technology are creating a new type of publishing house whose output consists solely of electronic books. The earliest all-electronic publisher was a Santa Monica firm, Voyager, which began marketing its publications on laser discs in the early 1990s and has since graduated into CD-ROM formats. The firm's initial list included a science fiction trilogy, Douglas Adams's *Hitchhiker's Guide to the Galaxy*; *Jurassic Park*, by Michael Crichton; and an annotated version of *Alice in Wonderland*. Each was produced with Apple Computer's Macintosh software, integrating print copy with animated drawings, sound effects, and hypertext links that let readers readily locate materials of particular interest to them. According to Voyager executive Bob Stein, "Apple, completely unintentionally, created the first electronic book."[67] By the mid-1990s, Voyager had evolved from obscurity in Santa Monica to a growing presence on the New York publishing scene, with a large catalogue of interactive CD-ROM titles.[68]

The big publishing houses were initially wary about moving into electronic books. By the late 1990s, however, they had all set up special units to explore the market for electronic products. A few made more substantial commitments. Random House issued its *Modern Library* books in electronic formats so they can be read on a computer. It also teamed up with Broderbund, a California software developer, to produce an interactive line of Dr. Seuss children's books.[69] Simon & Schuster invested in Computer Curriculum Corporation, a small firm specializing in computer-based curricula for schools. It also produced an array of electronic computer games based on books it has published. One of Simon & Schuster's biggest hits was the *Star Trek Interactive Technical Manual*, a CD-ROM product that sold more than a quarter-million copies.

Most publishers still restrict their electronic products to reference materials such as dictionaries and technical manuals. Encyclopedias are big sellers in compact-disc formats, primarily because the price is right for a mass audience. Microsoft's *Encarta* sells for under $100, weighs less than an ounce, and provides a lot of video and voice extras. The venerable *Encyclopaedia Britannica* has supplemented its twenty printed volumes with a disk version that contains all of its 65,000 articles, totaling 44 million words. In 1997, Britannica editors inaugurated Britannica Internet Guide, a search engine that allows subscribers to filter out marginal Web pages and leads them directly to useful sites on such topics as geography, history and sports.[70]

THE AMAZON INVASION

The Britannica's use of the Internet as a direct publishing outlet is still unusual in the industry. The primary beneficiaries of the Internet's ability to store and transmit large amounts of printed materials have been the academic and scientific communities, both of which have experienced the high costs of printing materials for a small audience. Hundreds of scientific journals are now published electronically, increasingly without a supplemental printed edition. The result is that new research gets out quicker, production costs decline, and subscription rates go down.[71] In 1997, the Columbia University Press started a new Web site, Columbia International Affairs Online (CIAO), which publishes everything from journal articles and working papers to entire books.[72]

These academic forays into the Internet represent a very small part of the American publishing industry. The biggest opportunity—and threat—posed by the Internet to the mainline publishing industry is the Internet's role in marketing their products. For years, the industry dismissed the Internet, questioning whether its customers were ready (as one wag put it) to "curl up with" a computer terminal.[73]

These attitudes changed in the late 1990s. Suddenly, the Internet became a looming presence in the business, not as an alternative channel for publishing books but as a very effective tool for selling them. The shift was summarized in one phrase: Amazon.com.[74] Amazon's electronic bookstore emerged in the late 1990s as one of the most successful Internet "e-commerce" sites, part of a trend that (according to Forrester Research Inc.) will gross $327 billion in online sales early in the new century. Amazon.com's not-so-secret formula is convenience— offering easy access to 3 million titles, often at cut-rate prices, with fast delivery. In its internal operations, Amazon carried only $17 million in inventory in 1998, just 2 percent of that carried by Barnes & Noble. Moreover, the Ingram Book

Group, Amazon's chief supplier, has been developing technology to print books one by one as orders come in.[75]

Despite its initial success, Amazon.com was still a small player in the U.S. bookselling business in the late 1990s, with just under 1 percent of the market in 1997. However, Keith Benjamin, a media analyst with BancAmerica Robertson Stephens, thinks that Amazon will have a 5 to 10 percent market share early in the new century.[76] At that time, it will also have a lot of competition. As noted in Chapter 3, Barnes & Noble and other big book chains have moved into the online sales market, along with Web site newcomers such as Books Now, which offers deep discounts for selected titles and has a special service that tracks down out-of-print books.[77]

THE FUTURE OF BOOK PUBLISHING

In addition to the problems raised by online marketing, book publishers need to come to terms more directly with the prospects opened by electronic publishing. Many of them still doubt whether there will be a significant market for computer-based books in the near future, beyond reference works and other professional publications. Other industry observers continue to be optimistic about the long-term prospects for electronic publishing. "We see this marketplace really growing as a business-to-business marketplace," says Stephen DiFranco, manager of new applications development for Sony Corp. "Trying to change how we culturally read and entertain ourselves is not as easy and will take a little longer."[78]

Whatever the industry's hesitations, electronic book publishing is here to stay.[79] The technical ability to add sound, graphics, and animation to the printed word is creating a new kind of literature that will take us beyond the linear story-telling of traditional books. Some experts foresee "books" that will only remotely resemble the traditional product. Researchers at Xerox Corp.'s Palo Alto labs and at other facilities are working on new forms of electronic books. In one proposal, book pages will each have their own onboard microprocessor built up out of ink. As one researcher, physicist Joe Jacobson, describes it, "Unlike a laptop, it wouldn't need memory, just a little CPU powered by a couple of AA cells in the spine. Unlike a screen, you could actually remember where your place was, and instantly flip to anything you needed."[80]

Computer expert George Landow observes that "movement from the tactile to the digital is the primary fact about the contemporary world." He envisions a cultural transformation in the ways we deal with the kinds of information presently encapsulated in printed books:

> Electronic text processing marks the next major shift in information technology after the development of the printed book. It promises (or threatens) to produce effects on our culture, particularly on our literature, education, criticism and scholarship, just as radical as those produced by Gutenberg's movable type.[81]

As they make their plans for electronic products, old-line book publishers are confronting competition from some formidable outsiders. These include the major computer and software companies such as IBM, Apple, and Microsoft, all of which have set up electronic publishing subsidiaries. Competition may also come from electronics manufacturers, such as Sony and Matsushita, which are interested in controlling the publications software needed to support their CD players and other consumer equipment.

Decisions that book publishers must make in the new electronic environment are similar to those facing managers in newspaper, magazine, and other print enterprises. Each sector of the publishing industry brings special strengths and vulnerabilities to the job of expanding the exchange of information far beyond the powers of Gutenberg's great invention.

NOTES

1. Ithiel de Sola Pool, *Technologies of Freedom*. Cambridge, MA: Harvard University Press, 1983, p. 224.
2. "The Electric Paperless Prototype," *Wireless*, June 1994, pp. 44–45.
3. "Bad News for Trees," *Economist* (London), 29 December 1998, p. 48.
4. "The Electronic Future Is Upon Us," *New York Times*, 7 June 1992, p. F-13.
5. Anthony Smith, *Goodbye, Gutenberg*. New York: Oxford University Press, 1980, p. 41.
6. Jerome S. Rubin, "Publishing as a Creature of Advanced Technology," in *Toward the Year 2000: New Forces in Publishing*. Gutersloh, Germany: Bertelsmann Foundation, 1989, p. 41.
7. "The Millennium Generation Is Making Its Mark," *Washington Post*, 29 June 1998, p. 1.
8. "Hispanic Youths Outnumber Blacks," *Washington Post*, 15 July 1998, p. A-2.
9. "Korean Media Clamor to Deliver News from Home," *Washington Post*, 2 December 1991, p. C-1.
10. Juliet Shor and Laura Leete-Guy, "The Great American Time Squeeze: Trends in Work and Leisure, 1969–1980," research report, Economic Policy Institute, Washington, DC, February 1992.
11. John Morton, "40 Years of Death in the Afternoon," *Washington Journalism Review* 13, no. 1, November 1991, p. 50.
12. "No More Media Elite," *Washington Post*, 8 July 1998, p. A-17.
13. Jib Fowles, "The Upheavals in the Media," *New York Times*, 6 January 1991, p. D-13.
14. For the evolution of changes in the advertising industry, see Martin Mayor, *Whatever Happened to Madison Avenue?* Boston: Little, Brown, 1991.
15. "For 900 Numbers, the Racy Gives Way to the Respectable," *New York Times*, 1 March 1992, p. F-8.
16. "Robots Pick up the Call," *Financial Times* (London), 23 February 1992, p. 14.
17. "Telemarketers Just Beginning to Answer Their Calling," *Washington Post*, 31 August 1997, p. H-1.
18. "What Happened to Advertising?" *Business Week*, 23 September 1991, p. 68.
19. Anthony Smith, *Goodbye, Gutenberg*, p. 112.
20. "Rethinking Newspapers," *New York Times*, 6 January 1991, p. C-6.
21. American Society of Newspaper Editors, *Keys to Our Survival*, Reston, VA, July 1991.
22. "Internet News Takes Off," Pew Research Center Biennial News Consumption Survey. Pew Research Center for the People and the Press, Washington, DC, June 1998, p. 14.
23. "Slicing, Dicing News to Attract the Young," *Washington Post*, 6 January 1991, p. A-1.
24. "Rethinking Newspapers," *New York Times*, 6 January 1991, p. C-6.

25. Veronis, Suhler, *Communications Industry Forecast*, October 1998, p. 275.

26. "The Murdoch of the North," *Business Week*, 2 August 1998, p. 64.

27. See Ben Bagdikian, *Media Monopoly*. 2d ed. Boston: Beacon, 1987; Ellis Cose, *The Press*. New York: William Morrow, 1989; Frank Denton and Howard Kurtz, *Reinventing the Newspaper*. New York: Twentieth Century Fund, 1993.

28. David Pearce Demers, "Corporate Structure and Emphasis on Profit and Product Quality at U.S. Daily Newspapers," *Journalism Quarterly* 68, no. 1–2 (Spring–Summer 1991): pp. 15–26.

29. "A New Censor?" *Economist* (London), 18 October 1997, p. 30.

30. Ben Bagdikian, "In the Time Deal, the Public Is the Loser," *New York Times*, 19 June 1989, p. D-6.

31. Richard Harwood, "Thinking Small," *Washington Post*, 26 March 1995, p. A-23.

32. "Publishers Are Trying New Techniques to Win Over Loyal Readers," *New York Times*, 4 January 1999, p. C-20.

33. Katherine Corcoran, "Power Journalists," *Washington Journalism Review* 13, no. 11, November 1991, pp. 28–34. See also Jean Ward and Kathleen Hansen, "Journalist and Librarian Roles: Information Technologies and Newsmaking," *Journalism Quarterly* 68, no. 3 (Fall 1991): pp. 491–498; and "Quantum Leaps: Computer Journalism Takes Off," *Columbia Journalism Review* 31, no. 1 May–June 1992, pp. 61–63.

34. "The Gray Lady Shows a Healthy Flush," *Business Week*, 6 October 1997, p. 78.

35. "Good News For McPaper," *Washington Post*, Washington Business supplement. 11 August 1997, p. 12.

36. "We Want News, McPaper Discovers," *Washington Post*, 26 December 1991, p. A-1.

37. For a description of early efforts at electronic publishing, see Walter S. Baer and Martin Greenberger, "Consumer Electronic Publishing in a Competitive Environment," *Journal of Communication* 37, no. 1. Winter 1987, pp. 49–63.

38. "First U.S. Experiments in Electronic Newspapers Begin in Two Communities," *New York Times*, 7 July 1980, p. B-13.

39. "Post Co., Seven Media Firms Enter On-line Alliance," *Washington Post*, 20 April 1995, p. B-10.

40. "New Media Meltdown," *Business Week*, 23 March 1998, p. 70.

41. "Local Becomes Focal on the Web," *Interactive Week*, 8 December 1997, p. 59.

42. "In Dow Jones' Locker," *Economist* (London), 24 October 1998, p. 73.

43. "Futurist Newspaper Forced to Downsize," *Interactive Week*, 13 March 1995, p. 40.

44. "M.A.I.D. Serves Up Online Info in Dialog with Knight-Ridder," *Cowles/Simba Media Daily*, 10 March 1997.

45. "Looking at the Future," *Communications News*, 1 May 1989, p. 4.

46. "Newspaper Publishers Unite to Do New Classifieds," *Cowles/Simba Media Daily*, 28 December 1997.

47. "Can General Motors Learn to Love the Net?" *Business 2.0*, September 1998, p. 46.

48. "Microsoft Expands Sidewalk Online Guide," *Washington Post*, 21 October 1998, p. C-11.

49. "A Media Pioneer's Quest: Portable Electronic Newspapers," *New York Times*, 28 June 1992, p. F-11.

50. William B. Blankenburg, "The Viability of the Comprehensive Newspaper," research paper presented at the Association for Education in Journalism and Mass Communications annual conference, Montreal, Canada, August 1992, p. 7.

51. "Save the Front Page," *Economist* (London), 3 September 1994, pp. 27–28.

52. Quoted in Richard Clurman, *To the End of Time*. New York: Simon & Schuster, 1992, p. 33.

53. "Turn, Turn, Turn: Gleanings From That Magazine Jungle Out There," *New York Times*, 26 April 1998, p. WK-7.
54. "A Magazine Seeks to Push the On-line Envelope," *New York Times*, 31 October 1994, p. D-6.
55. "Magazines Raise Reliance on Circulation," *New York Times*, 8 May 1989, p. D-11.
56. "Even Titles Are Flexible as U.S. Magazines Adapt to Foreign Ways," *New York Times*. 4 August 1997, p. D-9.
57. "The Cosmo Naut," *Washington Post*, 22 February 1995, p. D-1.
58. "U.S. Trade Journals Go Abroad for New Growth," *New York Times*, 3 February 1992, p. D-8.
59. "Magazine Advertising: Up Close and Personal," *Washington Post*, 29 December 1989, p. F-1.
60. "Conde Nast to Jump into Cyberspace," *New York Times*, 1 May 1995, p. D-10.
61. "Detour From the Superhighway," *Financial Times* (London), 28 March 1995, p. 15.
62. "An American at Pearson Shakes Up the Status Quo," *New York Times*, 20 May 1998, p. D-2.
63. "Making a Mark, *Economist* (London), 10 October 1998, p. 69.
64. "Random Thoughts," *Economist* (London), 28 March 1998, p. 58.
65. "The Impossible Business," *New Yorker*, 6 October 1997, p. 50.
66. "News Corp. Finance Chief Offers Kind Words for HarperCollins," *Cowles/Simba Media Daily*, 29 December 1997.
67. "Is the Electronic Book Closer Than You Think?" *New York Times*, 18 May 1992, p. D-1.
68. "Voyager: The Weird Get Wired," *Interactive Week*, 30 January 1995, p. 40.
69. "Broderbund Casts Itself as a Studio," *New York Times*, 9 September 1995, p. D-7.
70. "Dusting off the Britannica," *Business Week*, 20 October 1997, p. 143.
71. "Paperless Papers," *Economist* (London), 16 December 1995, p. 78.
72. "A University Adapts Books from the Page to the Screen," *New York Times*, 24 August 1997, p. 27.
73. "Book Publishers Worry About Threat of Internet," *New York Times*, 18 March 1997, p. D-1.
74. "Amazon.com: The Wild World of E-Commerce," *Business Week*, 14 December 1998, p. 106.
75. "The Net Is Open For Business—Big Time," *Business Week*, 31 August 1998, p. 108. See also: "Does Amazon Equal 2 Barnes & Nobles?" *New York Times*, 19 July 1998, p. BU-4.
76. "In Hopes That Experience Speaks Volumes," *Washington Post*, Washington Business supplement, 20 July 1998, p. 13.
77. "The Time's Right for Books Now," *Interactive Week*, 8 December 1997, p. 57.
78. "Plugged-in Publishing," *Washington Post*, 6 May 1992, p. F-2.
79. "A New Chapter for E-Books," *Business Week*, 2 November 1998, p. 19.
80. "Digital Ink," *Wired*, May 1997, p. 162.
81. Quoted in Robert Coover, "The End of Books," *New York Times Book Review*, 21 June 1992, p. 1.

The Open-Ended Future

Mass communications in the United States are clearly in the middle of a massive transition. The older media face wrenching changes as they adapt to advancing technologies, changing audiences, and challenges by the Internet and other new computer-based channels.

This shift has been under way, in fits and starts, for decades. The difference now is that the pace is accelerating. The pressures put on the media by computers and other advanced technologies are no longer fringe phenomena. They are the dominant force reshaping the media industries. In turn, this media transformation is altering the form and direction of U.S. society: how we see ourselves, what we think is important, and where we get the information that affects our daily decisions and activities.

We are still at the edge of this change, but it is already possible to identify its general characteristics. Predicting future media patterns is a risky business. Anyone doing so twenty-five years ago would have had little or no forewarning of such developments as satellite broadcasting networks, multimedia cable TV, compact discs, videocassettes, personal computers, and the Internet, among other innovations that are setting the pace for current media developments.[1] We also need to avoid illusions about the new media, what French sociologist Jacques Ellul calls "the technological bluff." The introduction of new technologies always exacts a price, Ellul reminds us; each innovation adds something on one hand and subtracts something else on the other. Moreover, he adds, all such innovations have unforeseeable consequences.[2]

The current transition to a new media environment differs from past experiences when technologies were phased in slowly. The introductions of older media technologies such as the printing press, radio, and TV were more orderly. Sufficient time elapsed between one and the next to sort out the economic and social consequences of the changes. Now, however, the media industries must cope with a convergence of many technologies arriving at a speed and with an urgency that allow little time to assess how they can best be fitted into an already complex media pattern. This much is clear: Technology is opening a wide range of options for both media producers and consumers—a welcome challenge for a democratic society that values choice and variety, particularly in information matters.[3]

LOOKING AT THE OPTIONS

These technological options will be sorted out eventually, primarily through trial-and-error testing in the marketplace. As that occurs, a vastly different pattern of packaging and distributing information products will emerge. That pattern will be shaped by political and economic elements as well as by technological factors. It is this restructuring of the basic communications network that is, for the present, forcing change in media patterns. The next two decades will see the completion of a universal information utility, a resource that can be compared roughly to the networks that supply us with electricity, gas, and water. The new facility will be a high-tech extension of the telephone network, with capabilities extending far beyond voice telephony to include a full range of video, graphics, and print services. Originally designed to serve big business and government needs, the new network is now reaching into private homes and other consumer locations, part of the steady massification of advanced information services, including the media.[4]

Until recently, the media have operated separately from public communications utilities. Although they used the networks—especially the telephone system—for their internal operations, they issued their own products in traditional formats—print, nitrate film, videotape, and the like. Now these separate media products are merging into a single electronic "pipe," the nervous system of the evolving information utility, where print, video, or sound products become digital blips, indistinguishable from one another. The old media are being integrated into a larger, expanding system: the advanced electronic information network.[5]

This prospect causes considerable hand-wringing in some quarters about the decline of mass media, the rise of megamedia conglomerates, and the beginnings of electronic Big Brotherism. There are, indeed, troubling aspects to the electronic merging of the media. There could be greater centralized control of media and other information resources by government and/or powerful private economic interests.

In fact, the probable scenario is more optimistic. Electronic production and delivery of information open vast opportunities not only for the traditional media but for new competitors as well. Old ideas about the appropriate role of the media will have to be adjusted accordingly.[6] Mass communications have traditionally been defined as the industrialized production, reproduction, and multiple distribution of messages through technological devices.[7] The focus has been on information products produced in a relatively few centralized locations and distributed through separate one-way channels to large groups of consumers. The new technologies change this. Old distinctions disappear. Facsimile machines combine printed text and telephones. Interactive compact discs bring together the resources of personal computers, television, and printing devices. The telephone system becomes something else, used increasingly for nonvoice transmissions between information machines rather than for person-to-person conversations.[8]

THREE EMERGING MEDIA PATTERNS

Media resources are being reassembled in a new pattern, with three main parts. The first is the traditional mass media that will continue to be for a long time the most important element in the pattern in terms of their reach and influence. The second consists of the advanced electronic mass media, operating primarily within the new information utility, and competing increasingly with older media services. Finally, there are newer forms of personal electronic media, formed by clusters of like-minded people to fulfill their own professional or individual information needs. Internet chat rooms and personalized Web pages are fast-expanding examples of this development. Each of these parts of the evolving mass-communications pattern deserves separate scrutiny.

First, let's examine the traditional media—broadcast TV, film, radio, and print. Collectively, they are a formidable presence, with annual revenues of over $500 billion in the United States.[9] These services will continue to grow, particularly in international markets. In a survey of global media prospects, the London *Economist* sees major gains for the U.S. media industries:

> Entertainment is America's second-biggest export earner, after aerospace. Thanks to technology, the media industry is also merging with the (even bigger) global information business, which includes computers and telecoms. In 1990, that combined total was worth $1.3 trillion. By 2000 it may reach $3 trillion—or roughly $1 out of every $6 of global GNP.[10]

The traditional media are a continuing link in the transition to a new mass communications environment. As we have seen in our survey, media industries are surviving by facing up to changes in how they produce and distribute their wares. It is not just a matter of marketing old products in new ways. The contents and functions of the products themselves are changing. What is the daily newspaper's role in an information-saturated environment? How do television and cable TV deal with the fragmented information and entertainment demands of their viewers? How does the book business come to terms with the fact that its primary function—the assembling of ideas and facts into small packets—can often be performed more efficiently by computerized data banks held in the palm of the hand?

The second part of the new media pattern involves electronic mass-communications services: consumer data banks, multimedia computers, the

Internet, and so forth. At present, they make up a relatively small part of the pattern, but that is changing. Electronic production and distribution of information is still focused primarily on the needs of large organizations, public and private. The trend, however, is toward mass consumerization of computer-based information resources, with the potential for dramatically strengthening democratic values. Writing about the Internet, Supreme Court Justice John Paul Stevens notes:

> Any person with a phone line can become a town crier with a voice that resonates further than it could from any soapbox. Through the use of Web pages, mail exploders and news groups, the same individual can become a pamphleteer.[11]

The first computer literate generation is already moving into the media marketplace. They are young men and women who are at ease with keyboards, data disks, and video monitors. Their skills, learned in schools and offices, are now being used at home. Consumer data services, such as America Online and the Microsoft Network, are flowing over ordinary telephone lines onto computer screens. Over 20 million homes now subscribe to these services—not as exotic innovations but as practical, taken-for-granted aids to daily living (see Table 9.1).

The resources that the new computer-based technologies provide for ordinary consumers are still mainly in print data formats. This is changing with the introduction of full multimedia capabilities, combining text, sound, and video services in one electronic package. These services can now be delivered to multimedia PCs or to telecomputers, the replacements for today's TV sets. These machines will be standard fixtures in most U.S. homes early in the new century, providing services supplied by traditional media organizations as well as by their new electronics-based competitors.[12]

Finally, we will see the emergence of personal electronic media as a new form of mass communications. These are networks put together by individuals and groups that bypass the whole range of commercial information and entertainment providers. The Internet is the most spectacular example of this new kind of networking. Its high-speed data communications grid links over 10,000 other networks, private and public, around the globe. Originally developed by the U.S.

TABLE 9.1   Growth of U.S. Consumer Onliner Spending

	Online Access	Consumer Spending on Online Content	Online Advertising	Total
1997 Expenditures ($ Millions)	$4,816	$230	$906	$5,952
1992–1997 Compound Annual Growth (%)	42.2%	—	—	48.3%
1997–2002 Projected Compound Annual Growth (%)	16.5%	22.4%	48.3%	24.0%
2002 Projected Expenditures ($ Millions)	$10,341	$632	$6,500	$17,473

SOURCES: Veronis, Suhler & Associates, Wilkofsky Gruen Associates, Internet Advertising Bureau, Jupiter Communications, Find/SVP, SIMBA Information

government for communications among domestic research institutes, the Internet has blossomed into the world's largest data exchange, with an over 100 million online users at the turn of the century. The Internet and other data highways have turned small computers into electronic meeting places. Once the exclusive toys of small groups of computer buffs, Web pages and e-mail are now available to a vast audience. In the late 1990s, America Online had at least a million personal pages available on its service, matching similar services such as Lycos Inc.'s Tripod and WhoWhere Inc.'s AngelFire.[13] These videotext services will soon be supplemented by video and audio services as a new generation of multimedia computers becomes available.[14]

THE NEW IMPORTANCE OF PERSONAL MEDIA

These Internet resources are an electronic extension of a long tradition of "small media" that have always operated around the fringes of the larger media services. The small media include amateur and citizen-band radio grids, facsimile networks, and a multitude of special-interest newsletters, magazines, and bulletins collectively serving tens of millions of people. These traditional small-media outlets will continue to flourish, but they are being supplemented, and perhaps eventually replaced, by computer-based alternatives.

The definition of mass media will have to be modified to fit this new pattern of consumer information facilities. Mass communications are undergoing mutations that are changing their modes of operation and their purposes. The new personal networks are taking on the characteristics of traditional mass media. Collectively, these networks serve large audiences with specific information needs, from the frivolous to the profound. They break down the general public into special-interest groups and thereby fractionalize mass media audiences. Personal networks are competing directly with the larger mass media as information resources.

The Internet is only part of this structure of electronic media resources. The new personal networks also include networking by Touch-tone and cellular phones, audio- and videocassettes, personal fax machines, small-group satellite conferencing, and low-powered television transmitters aimed at specialized audiences. Some of these technologies may fall by the wayside as more efficient alternatives replace them. It will be years before their whole effect can be known, given the imaginative, unpredictable ways they are used by individual groups, from nuclear disarmament activists to stamp collectors. Personal electronic networking is a present-day reality, and it is changing the information habits of millions of people. Only when we shuck off conventional ideas about the media can we recognize that these networks are a form of mass communications. They provide decentralized, interactive information resources that supplement and often take the place of traditional mass media services.

The new networking can enhance the democratic dimension of U.S. society. A generation ago, Marshall McLuhan, the Canadian media guru, sent out an early-warning signal when he declared that photocopiers would make Everyman his own publisher. McLuhan, however, could not have imagined the wider prospects opened by the Internet, personal computers, compact discs, videocassettes, and facsimile machines. Each of these offers variations on the theme of liberation of individuals and groups from reliance on centralized media. Together, they greatly expand the possibilities for personal initiative in creating, storing, and distributing information. They are tipping the balance of power in the control of information toward individual users. Bill Frezza, a founder of the online forum DigitalLiberty, sees a revolutionary shift in the balance of information power:

> Networked computers and the torrent of information they carry are inherently decentralized, destabilizing and uncontrollable—a virtual Ho Chi Minh trail of cyber-insurgency. The information revolution will transform the politics of power just as surely as the broadcast media did 70 years ago. Only this time, power will devolve back towards its sources, not inward towards demagogues seeking to gather it. The [Internet] will subvert the centralized economic and social control mechanisms that allowed the great welfare-warfare states of the 20th century to dominate our commerce, our psychic landscape, and even our definition of who we are.[15]

THE THREAT TO SOCIAL COHESION

The shift is not without its dangers. For all their faults, the mass media have constituted a critical social force within our democratic society. They have served not only as information providers but also as a kind of glue, binding people into a coherent sense of shared interests. The new personal electronic networks can also serve this purpose, but they also could erode it. As communications researcher Gladys Ganley notes:

> In free societies, access to information tends to be regarded as democratizing, and therefore desirable. But such instantaneous access on such a wide scale has never before been possible and could create such unsettling shifts that the overall results might not be all positive. . . . Spread to millions of individuals throughout the world, each literally following his or her own agenda, such power could remove the glue of social cohesion, provided by limited numbers of organizations and governments. . . . Power to the people could mean that nobody is in control, with unpredictable political consequences.[16]

In a society dedicated to the expansion of the marketplace of ideas, we have no choice but to accept the social risks of the new personal electronic networks. The telecommunications industry is already restructuring its facilities to serve this new market, making it easier to form individualized networks. Electronic mail and other networking arrangements are an everyday fact of life. A breakthrough occurred in 1991 when the MCI telephone network began marketing its Friends & Family service, which offered greatly reduced rates to individuals who wanted to form their own personalized network. The company signed up 5 million customers within a few months.[17] Clearly, MCI was responding to a consumer need that went beyond the fact that the Friends & Family service would save a few dollars on the monthly phone bill.

MEDIA IN THE INFORMATION SOCIETY

Given these developments, what will the new media pattern look like? Where will the traditional media fit in an electronic framework in which large providers and small consumers share networks? Predictions swing between extremes. At one end, there are visions of a democratic society where computerized access to vast information resources will be shared by everyone. At the other extreme are forebodings of a disconnected society where individuals and groups are fragmented into information islands, unable to relate to one another, unaware of common concerns, and lacking any shared cultural reference points. Most likely, our media future lies somewhere between. Michael Janeway of the Medill School of Journalism at Northwestern University points out that "any vision of achievement of a 21st Century Great Society via computerization must be iffy, if only because technologists' ability to predict human tastes and social behavior is so notoriously poor."[18]

Dean Janeway's point is important. The effects of the new media pattern are long term and erratic. Wherever it is going, the process of change is under way. Every day, uncounted numbers of decisions are being made that move us closer to a radically different communications structure. The passage will be bumpy for both traditional media organizations and their new challengers. They will have to be guided largely by the imperfect signals coming from the marketplace. What sells? What doesn't? What is the competition up to? Do we try something new or do we sit tight? The marketplace is still a useful indicator of social needs. However valuable a new product or service may appear to be, it does not become a viable choice until a seller puts a price on its value and gets a significant number of buyers to agree to pay it. The new media services are no exception to that process.[19]

Marketplace economics thus will help decide the shape and purposes of the new mass-communications structure. However, economic forces cannot in themselves guarantee a fully accessible system. There will be gaps, at least as many as there are in the present system. There are still several million U.S. households that do not have adequate phone services, much less the prospect of plugging into exotic new information resources.[20] At another level, public schools with the most minority students lag seriously in computer resources, according to a 1997 Educational Testing Service survey.[21]

NEEDED: A NEW PUBLIC CONSENSUS

A case can be made for directing public policy decisions in ways that assure high quality and broad access for this advanced information system. The historical record shows that public intervention at critical points in U.S. communications development has actively encouraged better facilities and wider access to them.[22] The best example of this was the national policy decision made over half a century ago to create the world's first interactive mass-communications network. It is the U.S. telephone network, which had been an elite resource in this country for fifty years after the telephone was invented. The network became universally accessible only as the result of a far-reaching social decision embodied in congressional legislation—the Communications Act of 1934. The act mandated a new democratic principle: the right of universal access by all citizens to electronic communications networks.

The 1934 law dealt only with the technologies of the time—telephone, telegraph, and radio broadcasting—but its applications were later broadened to cover newer technological developments such as television, cable TV, and satellite broadcasting. The result was a patchwork of laws and regulations that reflected the lobbying power of the major media industries more than any overarching public policy to promote citizen access to media resources. The telecommunications law passed by Congress in 1996 attempted to set a new course, but the legislation is seriously flawed. It represents an uneasy compromise between the interests of the telephone, cable TV, and broadcasting industries. The mandate of universal service, enshrined in the original 1934 Communications Act, was reduced to a rhetorical phrase. The new emphasis was almost totally on marketplace concerns.

Robust marketplace competition is a necessary element in the continued growth of American communications, including the media. This, however, is not in itself a guarantee of adequate access, meeting the needs of ordinary citizens to survive and thrive. Such a goal was easier to achieve a generation ago when it meant access to a telephone or a radio. It will be much harder to reach when it includes a vastly more complex range of computer-based technologies.[23] The 1996 law does not adequately address this need. Universal access remains a critical issue in a postindustrial, information-based society.[24]

What is needed, beyond legal prescriptions, is a strong national consensus on universal access to the advanced information structure now being built in the United States. The subject was given new prominence in the Clinton administration's "information highway" initiative under Vice President Al Gore's leadership. One of the more interesting and imaginative proposals, advanced by Columbia University communications scholar Eli Noam, is to define a set of general principles to guide future public policy in the communications and media fields. Specifically, Professor Noam suggests a twenty-first-century revision of the First Amendment, which would affirm the right of people to gather electronically (see Appendix for the full text). Another prospect, put forward by media analyst Peter Huber, is to cut back drastically on government communications regulations (specifically, the activities of the Federal Communications Commission) and rely instead on common-law procedures.[25]

These proposals to redefine electronic rights could be useful in setting a broad national agenda for the information environment. Admittedly, no general principles by themselves will ensure a satisfactory outcome. The process will also be driven by the ongoing push-pull of economic and political interests, involving a continuing series of compromises and accommodations. In the accepted American tradition, everyone concerned will get something; no one will get everything. A perennial consequence of the process is that public policy lags behind marketplace developments.[26]

A case in point is the competition between the telephone and cable TV industries to determine which industry will have the lead in providing high-capacity, multimedia links into U.S. homes. The outcome of that contest will make a difference to the future of the universal information utility in general and the future of the mass media industries in particular. Congress, the White House, and the courts have all been involved in attempts to define public policies on the issue. Their decisions, however useful or well meaning, will serve primarily to validate what is already happening in the marketplace. The cable and phone industries are already making their own deals, which, in effect, will divide the market between them. Some form of large-scale information utility will be built, with or without a coherent public consensus. Sooner or later, however, such a consensus must be considered, and it must address the question of how this resource can best serve everyone.

This transition to a new-media environment will not be easy for the old-line communications industries or their new competitors. Most of the old guidelines are being smudged or even wiped out. Media managers face difficult decisions on the pace at which they will adapt to technological changes. The temptation to stick with old products and practices will be strong, and it will be reinforced by the resistance that consumers have put up against adopting many of the new electronic services. For example, surveys of cable TV subscribers over the years have shown that most viewers limit themselves to five or six channels; the idea of 150 or more channels, now being installed in many cable systems, leaves many of them nonplussed.[27] Television and videocassettes gained almost instant consumer acceptance in past years because they were relatively cheap, easy to use, and delivered a recognizable, attractive service. Mass adoption of many of the new electronic services is proving to be slower, in large part because they are more expensive for industry to build and for consumers to buy.

OLD MEDIA, NEW CHALLENGES

Meanwhile, the media industries must deal with more immediate problems, including the fragmentation of their traditional audiences, in part because of changing national demographics. Population growth in the coming decade will take place overwhelmingly within the African American, Hispanic, and Asian communities. In the early years of the new century, Caucasian citizens in the bellwether state of California will probably be in the minority. Previous assumptions about leisure habits, cultural tastes, and spending patterns will have to be rethought by the media industries.[28]

As we have seen, these industries face the well-documented erosion of their audience among younger age groups, particularly in the film, newspaper, and magazine sectors. This erosion began in the 1960s with the generation whose attitudes were formed by Vietnam, Woodstock, and other symbols of alienation. The media industries assumed that the disaffection was temporary and that younger people would "come home" to the older information outlets in due course.

This has not happened. The erosion of younger audiences continues, particularly among news outlets. In the mid-1990s, a survey of media patterns by Times-Mirror Center for the People and the Press (now the Pew Center) reported that among young people 42 percent were nonusers of any kind of news media. Overall, the survey found that young Americans, aged eighteen to thirty, knew less and cared less about news and public affairs than any other generation of Americans in the past half-century. The report concluded:

> With the advent of satellite technology, CNN, and ever-longer local news broadcasts, one might expect that young people would know more than ever before. . . . The ultimate irony of the Times-Mirror findings is that the Information Age has spawned such an uninformed and uninvolved population.[29]

Hand-wringing over the shortcomings of young people is hardly new. The Times-Mirror survey, like most of its kind, tended to equate current-affairs literacy with use of traditional print media—newspapers, magazines, and books. More recent surveys indicate that technohip youth are turning to the Internet and other computer resources for news and other information.[30] These demographic changes are forcing the traditional media industries to reassess their product lines. What new computer-based products will sell in today's market? How much should we invest? Who are the audiences and how can we reach them? The answers to these questions will determine the corporate winners and losers in the new information environment.

THE ROLE OF THE MEDIA CONGLOMERATES

Current wisdom among many media observers suggests that the winners will be the new breed of big multimedia conglomerates, mainly because they will be best able to handle the diversity of new demands. These information packagers have evolved in two ways: by cross-ownership between media firms and by acquisition of media companies by nonmedia firms. Time Warner and Rupert Murdoch's News Corporation are typical examples of the former; the Sony and Matsushita takeovers of two major Hollywood studios are examples of the latter. The heyday of media mergers occurred in the mid-1980s. Seventy-seven major deals were carried out by thirteen large media firms between 1983 and 1987; more than half of the transactions involved European and Canadian companies.[31] A relatively small group of these megamedia firms now have an outsized influence on the pace and direction of the industry's development.[32]

Are these companies the media wave of the future? Perhaps they are not. Despite their size, they still represent a minority share of the total media market in the United States and abroad. The orthodox justification for media conglomerization is that news and entertainment companies must grow or die. They are industries with large fixed costs and high product risks. The classic examples of this are the Hollywood studios, most of whose films are financial failures.

For all their undoubted successes, the big multimedia firms have still not fully mastered the trick of producing best-sellers, hit records, or blockbuster films on a consistent basis. This is not due to bad management or other incompetence, although that occurs. It is because the success of the big firms' products depends on the erratic tastes of the consumer public.

Only media giants, the argument goes, can absorb failures and wait for the high returns from more successful products. This was the thinking that created the spree of media mergers and acquisitions in the 1980s and its renewal during the 1990s. It was bolstered by the idea that synergies among different media products could be exploited by vertically integrated companies: Books could beget films that could beget videocassette profits and so on.

The idea was both intriguing and simplistic. In the years since the merger mania, media synergies have had mixed results, at best. By and large, the prospects opened by media synergies have not been a decisive benefit for Rupert Murdoch or for other multimedia enthusiasts.

THE TIME WARNER EXAMPLE

Consider, for instance, the 1989 merger of Time Inc. and Warner Communications, which created the world's largest multimedia corporation. On paper it was the perfect media marriage, involving a full range of film, magazine, book, cable TV, and record resources. In the years since the merger, however, successful synergies among Time Warner products have been relatively few, generating a small percentage of the new firm's activities. Time Warner is a marriage of unequals. During a large part of the 1990s, Warner's operations were producing two-thirds of the firm's revenues. Moreover, the new company was saddled with a staggering debt as a result of the merger. Although the original merger proposal was to have been a simple debt-free exchange of stock, the negotiations ended up with Time's borrowing $14 billion to buy Warner outright. Managing the debt seriously hobbled Time Warner's ability to put its synergistic plans into practice. The firm did not make significant profits until the late 1990s.[33]

One reason is that the 1989 merger was something of a psychological mismatch. The somewhat buttoned-down attitudes of Time's New York managers did not mix readily with the open-shirt-and-gold-chain style of its new Hollywood partners. The two corporate cultures clashed, causing tensions at the upper-management levels and confusion in the lower ranks.[34] These tensions were heightened by the ostentatious way in which the firms' top managers compensated themselves at a time when lower-level employees were being fired. The late Steven J. Ross, who, as head of Warner Communications, was primarily responsible for the merger, received $78.2 million in salary and bonuses in 1990.

The Time Warner merger was not a typical megamerger deal, if only because of its sheer size. It provides a case history, however, of problems that also plague other corporate attempts to get synergy out of their multimedia resources. Like Time Warner, other information packagers are finding that individual media sectors—films, books, magazines, and so on—have operational styles that are not always easy to meld into winning combinations.

HOLLYWOOD'S CONGLOMERATES

Future expectations for the big-scale conglomerates will differ from sector to sector. Consider the film industry: Hollywood today, as in the past, is dominated by a half dozen major studios. Two of the biggest, Warner and Twentieth Century Fox, are controlled by large conglomerates, Time Warner and Rupert Murdoch's News Corporation. Although both studios are doing well as independent units, there is little evidence that they have contributed decisively to the synergistic multimedia strategies of their owners.

An instructive example was the attempt by two Japanese electronics companies, Sony and Matsushita, to integrate their studio properties, Columbia and MCA, into their overall corporate strategies. In each case, they wanted to strengthen their consumer equipment operations by ensuring a supply of entertainment software for videocassette recorders and similar products. In both cases these experiments in vertical integration of software and hardware products failed to work out in practice. Sony and Matsushita each experienced difficulties in reconciling Japanese corporate styles with the free-swinging fiscal practices of their new Hollywood affiliates. Both companies invested heavily in their film operations, with less than lucrative results. Matsushita bailed out of its MCA investment in 1995; Sony managed to retain control of its renamed Sony Pictures but only through massive infusions of money and a series of corporate reorganizations.

CHAIN PUBLISHING

In the publications industry, multimedia conglomerates have generally had only sporadic success in developing synergies between their print products and their other media holdings. Large newspaper and magazine firms have focused on buying up other publications, forming so-called chain ownership. The traditional argument against chain ownership is that it discourages diversity of news and editorial opinion at the local level. This has often happened in newspaper buyouts. The usual practice in chain publishing, however, is to leave editorial matters up to the local editors. If anything, this indifference has encouraged editorial blandness, a journalistic failure not limited to chain publishing.

Chain ownership of newspapers has reduced or eliminated competition in many cities. In general, this occurs because the large chains can finance and manage their properties more effectively. However, increases in one-newspaper towns cannot be blamed exclusively on the increase in chain ownership. Another reason is the well-documented decline in total U.S. newspaper readership, reflecting a general erosion of print journalism as a primary news source.[35]

CHANGING PATTERNS IN TELEVISION AND CABLE

In television broadcasting, dominance by the Big Three networks is ending. Thirty years ago, ABC, NBC, and CBS controlled, through direct ownership or affiliation, most local stations. They also produced most of the popular prime-time entertainment programming. Both of these advantages have been seriously eroded in recent years. The production of and profits from prime-time entertainment programs are now centered in the Hollywood studios. Meanwhile, local station affiliates are operating more independently of the networks. Cable TV has cut deeply into broadcast television's audience base. There is increasing competition from Fox Television and other new networks, as well as an increase in the number of independent stations. The outcome has been a greater quantity, although not necessarily a better quality, of broadcast television programming at both the national and local levels.[36]

In cable television, the trend toward conglomeration is striking. Here, a half dozen companies control most local cable networks under virtually monopolistic conditions. These conglomerates also have effective control over the most popular cable programming, particularly satellite-delivered services such as HBO, Showtime, and the sports networks. They have, moreover, tried to use this control to exclude competing program providers. This became a major issue as the big cable companies moved aggressively to supply hundreds of channels of multimedia services to U.S. homes.

Under circumstances of normal competition, such extended services would be a welcome development, contributing to greater diversity of information and entertainment. The circumstances are not, however, normal. Cable conglomerates have lobbied hard to preserve their control over local networks and the program services they supply. Their efforts are comparable to those that took place in the film and television broadcasting industries a generation ago. The big film studios controlled most Hollywood production, as well as the major theater chains through which their films were distributed. In television, ABC, CBS, and NBC had similar control over network programming and their affiliated local station outlets. This industry-wide vertical integration in films and television severely restricted outside competition. This did not change until the federal government stepped in under the antitrust laws, forcing the big studios to sell off their theater holdings. In television, the Big Three networks were required to open program acquisition to outside producers.

Although the cable TV industry's control over both programs and distribution outlets is similar to earlier experiences with films and television, there is an important difference. Vertical integration of production and distribution in films and television involved, in each case, a single media product. However, the cable industry's hold on vertical integration takes in all major media—film, television, radio, and print—that can be delivered electronically through high-capacity lines. The communications legislation passed by Congress in 1996 reduced somewhat the cable industry's ability to dominate the market for multimedia services to U.S. households.

The effects of this legislation will not be measurable for years. Meanwhile, the telephone companies are pressing for advantages in supplying multimedia services to U.S. homes. As we saw in Chapter 4, the cable and telephone industries have enlisted powerful political and economic resources to control high-capacity consumer circuits and the media resources that flow through them. The outcome of this contest is critical to the future of U.S. mass communications.

BACKLASH AGAINST BIGNESS

Media conglomeration may be affected by an opposite trend in America—namely, the backlash against big corporations in general. The assumption that megacorporations are efficient has held sway for most of this century; that notion is now questioned by eminent economists, both conservative and liberal. They argue for the disassembling of giant corporations into smaller, more efficient parts: the "unbundling of America," as communications analyst Peter Huber describes it.[37] Such restructuring has already begun throughout the economy. In the 1990s, two corporate giants, AT&T and ITT, both split themselves into smaller units. For the present, this has not been the case with the big media conglomerates. However, they may be prime candidates for unbundling in future years if they find themselves at a disadvantage as smaller, more innovative firms emerge that can deal more flexibly with technological innovations and with both the demographic and economic fragmentation that characterize all media audiences now.

This may not happen for some time. Until it does, large media organizations will continue to be a dominant factor on the U.S. media scene. There are recurrent proposals for curbing the power of megamedia firms in the interest of ensuring greater diversity of information from more sources. British communications scholar Anthony Smith has suggested that the alternative may be that "the democratic process itself is placed in thrall to a company or individual that may be pursuing, albeit quite legitimately, ends that are at variance with other objectives of a society."[38] The problem, as media critic Ben Bagdikian points out, is not that the big firms are evil media empires but that they tend to dominate the economics, operating styles, and product content of all the media sectors.

NEW CHALLENGES TO FIRST AMENDMENT RIGHTS

This conflict between individual rights and communal needs is, of course, a continuing one. The U.S. experience has been to avoid political controls over media and other information resources in the interests of diversity and individual expression. Fitting these principles into the new-media environment presents special difficulties. With the expansion of electronic channels, the possibilities for misusing them become more serious. Computer graphics technology has reached a point where it can create digitized representations of people and events that are fictional but virtually indistinguishable from reality. First Amendment rights in the new electronic environment are still unclear. Are the new computerized media networks akin to telephone networks with their assurance of privacy and open information exchange? On the other hand, are they the equivalents of electronic newspapers, where libel laws and other limitations apply? Confusingly, they can be both, and drawing the line between these choices is difficult.[39]

These First Amendment questions are now being raised with greater intensity as electronic networks expand. In a now-classic case, the Prodigy online network became involved a decade ago in a controversy challenging the right of electronic free speech. Prodigy's electronic mail network allowed subscribers to exchange views on a wide variety of subjects. One such exchange was a discussion as to whether the Holocaust of World War II was a hoax—an outlandish theory promoted by a small fringe group. The electronic exchanges included statements that were clearly anti-Semitic. After complaints by the Anti-Defamation League of B'nai B'rith, Prodigy's managers decided to allow the electronic exchange on the subject to continue. However, they also changed Prodigy's guidelines by banning statements that are "grossly repugnant expressions of bigotry and hate," an action that was challenged by the American Civil Liberties Union.

More recently, the Internet has been a target for those who want to limit its role as an open-access electronic platform, particularly its use as a channel for large dollops of pornography. In 1996, Congress passed the Communications Decency Act, which mandated penalties for sponsors of pornographic materials on the Internet. The law was challenged in the courts by a wide coalition of organizations from the American Civil Liberties Union to the American Library Associations. It was eventually declared unconstitutional by the Supreme Court. This did not stop Congress from trying to resuscitate the law in a slightly different form in the late 1990s.[40]

CENSORSHIP IN AN ELECTRONIC AGE

Outright censorship is not the only problem. Censorship usually involves an overt action that can be debated and resolved. Other issues raise more difficult questions about the suppression or alteration of the flow of information through electronic networks. Some of these techniques involve direct electronic manipulation of media messages. Other practices are more subtle, hidden in a complex pattern of conventional information. Control mechanisms can invade networks softly and invisibly without, so to speak, leaving fingerprints or other incriminating evidence. Such intrusions are hard to identify and even harder to prevent, since they often involve routine electronic functions whose threat to personal liberties is not obvious.[41]

Such practices are not the only barriers to full utilization of the new electronic media networks. Thirty years ago, political scientist Karl Deutsch proposed that advanced information resources must be made universally available if modern democratic societies are to thrive and survive. Information is power, he pointed out, and, more important, it is a multiplier of power. The problem is complicated by a rising flood of media messages and other information that pushes us toward the limit of human capacity to cope with them. The solution, Professor Deutsch suggested, is a new approach to what he called "intelligence amplification," taking advantage of new information technologies in ways that permit more effective access to the information we need to function individually and as members of an advanced democratic society.[42]

BARRIERS TO UNIVERSAL INFORMATION ACCESS

Access to media and other information resources in the United States is unequal for many reasons. Not the least of these reasons is that tens of millions of Americans are functionally illiterate. Illiteracy is both a cause and an effect of economic disparities. Millions of families do not have the financial means to plug into cable TV systems, much less take advantage of the Internet and other advanced services.

Economist Robert Reich has underscored the impact that this information gap has on U.S. society: "No longer are Americans rising or falling together, as if in one large boat. We are, increasingly, in different, smaller boats." If present trends continue into the next generation, he calculates, the top 20 percent of U.S. earners will account for more than 60 percent of all earned income; the bottom fifth, for 2 percent.[43] Increasingly, the factor that separates U.S. economic classes is information access and control. Media critic Terry Curtis thinks that we may be moving toward a computer-generated caste system. At the top of the scale are the information elite, who prosper because they know how to use the new resources. Farther down the scale are the information Lumpenproletariat, who lack the skills and the will to cope with advanced technologies.[44]

This is nearly an information-age version of Darwin's survival of the fittest, except that the information poor will not become extinct. They have the political and social power to strike back. Communications technologies have augmented the ability of disadvantaged groups to demonstrate their grievances—witness the impact of TV reportage of inner-city riots and similar events. America's disenfranchised are now less willing to accept second-class status until economic and social benefits, including those promised by advanced information services, trickle down to them through the market system. In an interdependent postindustrial society, the risks of excluding these groups from the new resources are dangerous.

THE MEDIA AS MEDIATOR

The mass media have an important mediating role to play both in documenting the new realities and in providing a forum for discussing them. Will the new media services accept that role so necessary to our individual and collective survival in the new postindustrial environment? There are powerful forces, inside and outside the industry, favoring greater trivialization of information. Infotainment is the buzzword among media producers and advertising executives these days as they grapple with the problem of retaining their audiences in highly competitive markets. Gresham's Law, defining how the bad drives out the good, operates as readily in the media business as in any other. Will we, in media critic Neil Postman's scathing phrase, find that we are "amusing ourselves to death" in the new communications environment?[45]

These issues are part of the larger question of how advanced information technologies change the ways we see ourselves and how we relate to the world around us. We communicate primarily to tell stories. These stories both reflect and re-form our self-images and our communal values. For most of human history, these concepts were passed on by storytellers to small groups of listeners gathered in a village square or by a fireside. It is only in the past 500 years that the role of the storyteller began to be replaced by a machine-produced resource—the printed book. Now we are moving through the age of image communications: first photography, then film and television, and now multimedia computing.[46] These resources deliver powerful messages to enormously expanded audiences. Battered by their drumbeat pervasiveness, our defenses against them begin to break down. The result, too often, is a loss of the purposes and interconnectedness by which we are sustained—personally and as a community.[47] Neil Postman explains:

> The problem is not that we don't have enough information. The problem lies elsewhere. People don't know what to do with the information. They have no organizing principle—what I would call a transcending narrative.[48]

As we have seen throughout this book, the media industries are being transformed by powerful technological, economic, and social forces. Those forces can either reinforce the centralized, corporate-dominated influence of the older media or disperse it in new, more democratic ways. The options are still open. Too much of what the media produces today reflects narcissistic and escapist trends in U.S. society rather than giving us information on and insights into the problems and opportunities before us.

The good news is that this pattern is being challenged. The new communications technologies can widen and diversify the control of information, giving more power to individual users and groups. If this happens, we will be well served. An advanced information utility, providing universal access, can add a dramatic new dimension both to democratic information resources and to the shape and purpose of American society in the new century.

NOTES

1. The perils of technological prediction in the electronics field are documented in Carolyn Marvin, *When Old Technologies Were New*, New York: Oxford University Press, 1988. See also John Rennie, "The Uncertainties of Technological Innovation," *Scientific American* 273, no. 3, September 1995, pp. 56–58.
2. Jacques Ellul, "The Technological Order," *Technology and Culture* 3, no. 4 (Fall 1962): p. 394.
3. "Where Is the Digital Highway Really Heading?" *Wired*, July/August 1993, p. 53.
4. *Universal Telephone Service: Ready for the 21st Century?* Annual review of the Institute for Information Studies. Queenstown, MD: Aspen Institute, 1991.
5. These changes are described in "The Death of Distance: A Survey of Telecommunications," special supplement, *Economist* (London), 30 September 1995.
6. For a useful discussion of these prospects, see Ellen Hume, *Tabloids, Talk Radio and the Future of News* (Washington, DC: Annenberg Washington Program of Northwestern University, 1995).
7. The relationship between mass media and mass communications is discussed in Joseph Turow, *Media Systems in Society*. New York: Longman, 1992, pp. 9–10.
8. David Bollier, ed., *The Information Evolution: How New Information Technologies Are Spurring Complex Patterns of Change*. Washington, DC: Communications & Society Program, Aspen Institute, 1993.
9. Veronis, Suhler & Associates, *Communications Industry Forecast*, October 1998, p. 39.
10. "The Media Mess," *Economist* (London), 29 February 1992, p. 17.
11. "Everyman's Electronic Soapbox," *Interactive Week*, 21 July 1997, p. 48.
12. Frederick Williams, "Network Information Services as a New Public Medium," *Media Studies Journal* 5, no. 4 (Fall 1991): pp. 137–151.

13. "AOL To Offer Web-Based Home Page Publishing," *Interactive Week,* 13 July 1998, p. 8.
14. For a useful discussion of the implications of this change, see Sherry Turkle, *Life on the Screen: Identity in the Age of the Internet.* New York: Touchstone Press, 1997.
15. Bill Frezza, "Internet: Killer Virus of the State," *Interactive Age,* 5 June 1995, p. 13.
16. Gladys D. Ganley, "Power to the People via Personal Electronic Media," *Washington Quarterly* 10, no. 3 (Spring 1991): p. 20.
17. "MCI's Winning Pitch," *Business Week,* 23 March 1992, p. 36.
18. Michael C. Janeway, "Power and Weakness of the Press," *Media Studies Journal* 5, no. 4 (Fall 1991): p. 11.
19. For a spirited defense of the marketplace as a reliable arbiter for media industries, see Mark Fowler and Daniel Brenner, "A Marketplace Approach to Broadcast Regulation," *Texas Law Review* 60, no. 2: pp. 207–257.
20. Herbert S. Dordick, "Towards a Universal Definition of Universal Service," in *Universal Telephone Service,* Institute for Information Studies annual review, 1991, p. 120.
21. "Poor, Minority Students Lack Access to Computers," *Washington Post,* 15 May 1997, p. A-13.
22. For a thoughtful review of the relationship between marketplace realities and wider public needs, see Robert M. Entman and Steven S. Wildman, "Reconciling Economic and Non-Economic Perspectives on Media Policy: Transcending the 'Marketplace of Ideas,'" *Journal of Communications* 42, no. 1 (Winter 1992): pp. 5–18.
23. "Déjà Vu All Over Again," *Wired,* May 1995, p. 175.
24. Wilson Dizard, *The Coming Information Age,* 3d ed. New York: Longman, 1989, pp. 166–168.
25. Peter Huber, *Law and Disorder in Cyberspace: Abolish the FCC and Let Common Law Rule the Telecosm,* New York: Oxford University Press, 1997.
26. Jeffrey Abramson, Christopher Arterton, and Garry Orren, *The Electronic Commonwealth: The Impact of New Communications Technologies on Democratic Politics.* New York: Basic Books, 1988.
27. "Quantity Time on Cable," *Washington Post,* 12 February 1992, p. C-1.
28. For a discussion of this issue, see Dorothy Butler Gilliam, "Media Diversity: Harnessing the Assets of a Multicultural Future," *Media Studies Journal* 5, no. 4 (Fall 1991): pp. 127–135.
29. "The Age of Indifference: A Study of Young Americans and How They View the News," Times-Mirror Center for the People and the Press, Washington, DC, June 1990, pp. 1, 3.
30. "Internet News Takes Off." Pew Research Center Biennial News Consumption Survey. Pew Research Center for the People and the Press, Washington, DC, June 1998.
31. Greg MacDonald, *The Emergence of Multi-Media Conglomerates,* working paper 70, Multinational Enterprises Program, International Labor Organization, Geneva, Switzerland, 1990, p. 13.
32. For a useful summary of the major media mergers in recent years, see "Media Mergers: First Step in a New Shift of Antitrust Analysis," *Federal Communications Law Journal,* vol. 49, no. 3, May 1997, pp. 675-700.
33. "Time Warner's Magic Kingdom," *New York Times,* 2 November 1998, p. C-1.
34. The Time Warner merger and its aftermath are documented in Richard Clurman, *To the End of Time.* New York: Simon & Schuster, 1992.
35. For a survey of print journalism's prospects, see David Bartlett, "The Soul of a News Machine: Electronic Journalism in the Twenty-first Century," *Federal Communications Law Journal* 47, no. 1 (September 1994): pp. 1–29. See also "Media and Public Life: A Retrospective," special issue, *Media Studies Journal* 9, no. 1 (Winter 1995).

36. These changes in the networks' fortunes are recorded in Ken Auletta, *Three Blind Mice*. New York: Random House, 1991.

37. Peter Huber, "The Unbundling of America," *Forbes*, 13 April 1992, p. 118.

38. Anthony Smith, *The Age of Behemoths: The Globalization of Mass Media Firms*. New York: Priority, 1991, p. 71.

39. The debate on media freedoms in the electronic age is lively and growing. See Fred H. Cate, ed., *Visions of the First Amendment for a New Millennium*. Washington, DC: Annenberg Washington Program, 1992; "The First Amendment—the Third Century," special issue, *Journalism Quarterly* 69, no. 1 (Spring 1992); "Celebrating the First Amendment," *Columbia Journalism Review* 30, no. 4 (November–December 1991): pp. 41–55; Charles M. Firestone and Jorge Reina Schement, *Towards an Information Bill of Rights and Responsibilities* (Washington, DC: Communications & Society Program, Aspen Institute, 1995).

40. Senate's Internet Legislation Under Fire," *New York Times*, 27 July 1998, p. D-5.

41. For a comprehensive review of civil liberties issues in cyberspace, see "Law and Order Comes to Cyberspace," *Technology Review*, October 1995, pp. 24–33.

42. Karl Deutsch, *The Nerves of Government*. New York: Free Press of Glencoe, 1963.

43. Robert Reich, *The Work of Nations*. New York: Alfred A. Knopf, 1991, p. 302.

44. Terry Curtis, "The Information Society: A Computer-Generated Caste System," in *The Political Economy of Information*. Edited by Vincent Mosco and Janet Wasko. Madison: University of Wisconsin Press, 1988, pp. 95–107.

45. For a review of these issues, see Everette Dennis, *The Race for Content on the Information Superhighway*, occasional paper, Freedom Forum Media Studies Center, New York, 1994.

46. "The New Storytellers," *Newmedia*, 22 September 1997, p. 39.

47. The point is argued persuasively in Neil Postman, *Technology: The Surrender of Culture to Technology*. New York: Alfred A. Knopf, 1992.

48. Quoted in "Summer Musings," *New York Times Magazine*, 25 June 1995, p. 24.

PRINCIPLES FOR THE COMMUNICATIONS ACT OF 2034

A proposal made by Dr. Eli M. Noam, director of Columbia University's Institute for Tele-Information, that would establish a new legal basis for protecting citizen rights in the new electronic information environment. Dr. Noam's restatement of First Amendment principles was presented at the Massachusetts Institute of Technology in October 1991.

1. Preamble

We, the people, in order to create a more perfect union of various transmission and content media, have established principles by which all electronic communications should be governed, with the goals of encouraging the production of information of many types, sources, and destinations; ensuring the existence of multiple pathways of information; encouraging their spread across society, the economy, and the world, and advancing social and economic well-being, technology, and education.

2. Freedoms of Speech and Transmission

Freedom of content is technology neutral. Government shall not prohibit the free exercise of communications or abridge the freedom of electronic speech or of the content provided by the electronic press or of the right of the people to peaceably assemble electronically.

3. Common Carriage

All electrons and photons are created equal. Carriers operating as a common carrier must be neutral as to content, use, and users. The transmission of lawful communications shall not be restricted by a common carrier. Common carriers are not liable for the use to which their conduit is put.

Where no competition exists in a conduit, it must be offered on a common carrier basis on at least *part* of the capacity. Competitive transmission segments need not be common carriers. *But* if a transmission segment interconnects with or accesses other networks by taking advantage of common carrier access rights, then it must offer such rights reciprocally on part of its capacity, without discriminatory terms or conditions of service.

Any party complying with a conduit's reasonable technical specification may interconnect into, access, or exit any common carrier conduit segments at interface points, which must be provided at technologically and economically reasonable intervals.

4. Market Structure

Government shall make no law establishing a network privileged in terms of territory, function, or national origin. Nor shall it burden any network more than its competitors', except with compensation.

A conduit may offer carriage of any type of service over its conduit and may interconnect with any type of carrier. Monopolistic conduit segments can be accessed by their own content services only where adequate capacity is available for common carrier access and subject to antitrust principles.

Competitive conduits and all content can be priced freely. Prices for noncompetitive conduit segments are presumptively regulated where their increase exceeds inflation, taking into account other important factors, too. Prices for noncompetitive conduit segments cannot be set such that they distort competition for nonmonopolistic services.

For competitive conditions in a market segment to be said to exist, three or more offerers of substantially similar or equivalent services constitute a rebuttable presumption. With two, evidence of vigorous price competition is necessary.

Spectrum use is a property right that is sold or leased out by the government and can be used flexibly. Frequency zoning for the clustering of services may be instituted.

5. Privacy

Electronic information cannot be searched and seized arbitrarily by the state.

Electronic information is the property of its creators or assignees. Where information is created by a transaction involving two parties, they normally hold the property jointly, and the consent of both is needed for the use of the information. Each party should disclose jeopardies of privacy to the other.

6. Subsidized Services

Financial support for some users (e.g., universal service) and to content providers, contents, or technologies, where instituted by government, must be generated and allocated explicitly and the burden of such support be placed on general revenue or equally on all competitors.

Where the development of new communications services or technologies requires coordination efforts and the creation of a critical mass of users, and where the service in question is of clear societal benefit, government may support such efforts in their infancy stage.

7. Jurisdiction

Information must move freely across interstate and international borders, without unreasonable burdens by state or national jurisdictions. No content or carrier should be treated in a country more restrictively than domestic providers are. But the right to equivalent treatment in another country requires reciprocity at home.

Federal jurisdiction (in the United States) sets basic national telecommunications policy where it deems national solutions to be clearly necessary. It may delegate flexibility in application and implementation to lower-level governmental bodies, which may also set policy for functions of clearly local nature.

Where a non-common carrier serves horizontal groupings of users in the same industry, its exclusion of other users is subject to antitrust principles.

Glossary

A NEW-MEDIA DICTIONARY

Addressability. The function in a cable television system that allows a subscriber to contact, through keypad input, the system's central office in order to receive special programs (e.g., pay-per-view entertainment).

America Online (AOL). In the late 1990s, the largest of the consumer-oriented online services available to personal computer users.

Amplitude modulation (AM). In broadcasting, a method of modulating electrical impulses in which the amplitude (power) is varied and the frequency remains constant. AM is used in the radio broadcast band (540 to 1,605 kilohertz), in the picture portion of television transmissions, and in shortwave broadcasting.

Analog. In telecommunications transmissions, the representation of numerical or alpha-numerical values by physical variables (e.g., voltage, current). *See* Digital.

Anonymous FTP. An anonymous File Transfer Protocol allows an Internet user to retrieve documents, files, programs, and other archived material at any point on the Internet without having to establish a password. It allows the user to bypass local security checks and to access publicly accessible files on the remote system.

Artificial intelligence. A computer's capability to perform functions normally associated with human intelligence (i.e., reasoning and learning). Early attempts to replicate human thought have been overtaken by more limited but practical applications, such as neural networking.

Aspect ratio. The ratio of a television screen's width to its height. Current television sets have a 4:3 aspect ratio. High-definition television sets will have aspect ratios that will allow a wider screen.

Associated Press (AP) principle. A modern restatement of First Amendment media freedoms, stemming from a 1945 court decision in which the AP was held to be in violation of antitrust laws for prohibiting service to nonmembers and allowing members to blackball competitors for membership.

Automated number information system. The process by which cable TV systems can provide interactive services (e.g., pay-per-view television).

Baby Bells. The seven regional telephone companies created as a result of the 1984 divestiture of AT&T's local telephone holdings. The Baby Bells, known more formally as the Regional Bell Holding Companies, will be primary suppliers of phone company information and entertainment services to homes once their legal right to do so is clarified.

Bandwidth. The range within a band of wavelengths, frequencies, or energies.

Basic services. A Federal Communications Commission designation for transmission capacity offered by a common carrier (e.g., phone companies) to move information between two or more points. *See* Value-added network.

Baud. A measure of signaling speed in a digital communications circuit. The speed in baud is the number of signal elements per second.

BCNU. Internet shorthand for "be seeing you."

Betamax. The videocassette standard supported by Sony in the 1980s, which was superseded by Matsushita's VHS standard. Although Betamax faded as a standard for home VCRs, it continues to be used for other applications within the media industries.

Birds of a feather (BOF). On the Internet, a BOF is an informal discussion group, usually formed ad hoc to discuss a specific issue.

Bit. A contraction of *binary digit*, a bit is the smallest unit of information that a computer recognizes. A bit is represented by the presence or absence of an electronic impulse, usually symbolized by a 0 or a figure 1.

Bookmark. User-definable disks that allow a person to easily display a certain location within a document or a page on the World Wide Web. Mouse-clicking a bookmark usually calls up the location it references. Bookmarks are often used in connection with Web browsing programs such as Microsoft Internet Explorer. The lists let users point and click on names and locations instead of typing addresses or paging through screens of text.

Broadband. A signal that requires a large bandwidth to be transmitted, alternately applied to equipment that must be capable of receiving or transmitting accurately a signal with a large bandwidth.

Browser. An application that allows users to download World Wide Web pages and view them on their own computers. A key aspect of browsers such as Netscape Navigator and Microsoft Internet Explorer is that they all display the Hypertext Markup Language (HTML) code in which Web pages are commonly written.

Buffer. A temporary storage area in a computer's memory, usually random-access memory, that holds recent changes to files and other information to be written later to the hard-drive.

Byte. A group of adjacent binary digits (often shorter than a word) that a computer processes as a unit. Usually, one byte is eight bits long.

Cable antenna television (CATV). The original name for cable television systems that provided coaxial cable retransmission of over-the-air television. The name was dropped after the introduction of national satellite-delivered channels in the 1970s.

Cable-telco debate. The political and economic contest between telephone companies and the cable TV industry to gain the upper hand in supplying multimedia information and entertainment services to U.S. households.

Chapter. One independent, self-contained segment of a computer program or an interactive video program.

Chip. A silicon-based device on which microscopic electronic circuitry is printed photographically to create passive and active devices, circuit paths, and device connections within the solid structure.

Coaxial cable. Insulated cable used to transmit telephone and television signals in a high-frequency mode. "Coax" has been the standard channel carrier for cable TV.

Coder/decoder (CODEC). A series of integrated circuits that perform a specific analog-to-digital conversion, such as the conversion of an analog voice signal to a digital bit stream or an analog television signal to a digital format.

Common carrier. The provision of transmission capability over a telecommunications network. A common carrier company offers public communications services. It is subject to regulation by federal and state regulatory bodies that establish operating rules and tariffs in order to make the services available at a fair price and on a nondiscriminatory basis. Telephone companies are common carriers.

Communications Act of 1934. The basic national legislation that regulated the use of electronic communications for over sixty years. The act mandated a national telephone system, the first such legislation to recognize the importance of telecommunications for social and economic growth. It is currently being superseded by new congressional legislation that incorporates regulatory changes made necessary by the introduction of advanced telecommunications and media technologies.

Compact disc. An optical storage medium, used for music, computer data, and other services.

Compact disc audio (CD-A). A popular compact disc format for high-fidelity digital music. Each disc offers up to seventy-five minutes of programmable sound with no degradation of quality during playback.

Compact disc interactive (CD-I). A disc storage medium for interactive audio, video, and text information. Pioneered by Sony and Philips, CD-I was originally developed for business training uses. It is currently being introduced into the home market, with marketing efforts focused on consumer information and entertainment applications.

Compact disc–read-only memory (CD-ROM). A prerecorded, nonerasable disc that stores up to 600 megabytes of digital data. On the market since the late 1980s, early applications have focused on reference materials, databases, and audio and video files.

Compression. The reduction of certain parameters of a signal while preserving the basic information content. The result is to improve overall transmission efficiency and to reduce cost. In media operations, the most extensive use of compression techniques is in cable TV coaxial cable, where compression can double or triple the number of available channels.

Compunications. A description, proposed by Harvard professor Anthony Oettinger, of the convergence of computer and telecommunications technology that results in an integrated information network.

Customer premises equipment (CPE). Any advanced telecommunications network equipment located on the premises of the customer (e.g., Private Branch Exchange telephone device). The phrase is also used by telephone companies to refer to customer-provided (as opposed to company-provided) equipment in offices and homes.

Cyberspace. A computer-generated artificial environment designed to maximize the user's freedom of movement and imagination. The term was coined by William Gibson in his fantasy novel *Neuromancer*.

Data. Alphabetical or numerical representations of facts or concepts in a manner suitable for communication, interpretation, or processing by human or automatic means.

Data communications, The transfer, reception, and validation of data between a source and a receiver via one or more data links, using appropriate code conversions or protocols.

Desktop publishing. The editing and layout of newspapers and other publications on small computers, using specialized software. Text, photos, and graphics are assembled electronically, then transmitted for final printing.

Digital. A method of signal representation by a set of discrete numerical values (1s and 0s), as opposed to a continuously fluctuating current or voltage. *See* Analog.

Digital audio broadcasting (DAB). Digital transmission of sound signals by cable, terrestrial microwave, or communications satellites. DAB will eventually replace AM and FM technology in radio broadcasting.

Digital audio tape (DAT). A tape format for storing digital audio signals. Each tape can store more than 2.5 gigabytes of data. DAT is often used as a computer storage backup system.

Digital video interactive (DVI). A technology for compressing and decompressing video and audio to create multimedia applications. DVI can store up to seventy-two minutes of full-motion video on a compact disc. Using DVI, a viewer can interact with the image being shown. As an example, a viewer may "walk" through a computer-generated building, seeing details of the interior from any angle.

Direct-broadcast satellite (DBS). A communications satellite whose signal both radiates over a large area and is capable of being picked up by small earth stations. DBS technology has been used in recent years to deliver information and entertainment services to homes and other locations.

Direct-read-after-draw. An optical disc technology that allows a user to record material that cannot be erased. A high-powered laser "burns" pits into a heat-sensitive layer beneath the surface of a recordable disc. The information is then read by a lower-power laser.

Disk. A flat, circular, rotating platter that can store and replay various types of information, both analog and digital. *Disk* is often used when describing magnetic storage media. *Disc* usually refers to optical storage media.

Divestiture Agreement. The plan, finalized in 1984, in which AT&T and the federal government set the terms for AT&T's relinquishment of control over its local phone companies in exchange for permission to enter the information services market. The resultant document is also called the Modified Final Judgment.

Domain Name System (DNS). On the Internet, the DNS is a general-purpose distributed, replicated, data query service. Host names on the Internet are called *domain names*, because they are the style of names used to look up anything in the DNS. Some of the more common domains are .com (commercial), .edu (educational) and .gov (government). Countries also have a domain designation, for example, .us (United States) and .au (Australia).

Dynabook. A concept advanced by MIT researcher Alan Key to describe an all-purpose handheld computer that would store vast amounts of data as well as have the capability to access other data sources.

Dynamic random access memory (DRAM). A type of computer memory in which information can be stored and retrieved in miscellaneous order but that must be "maintained" or refreshed by a periodic electrical charge if the memory is not read out or used immediately.

Electronic data interchange (EDI). Networks that eliminate intermediate steps in processes that rely on transmission of paper-based instructions and documents by performing them electronically, computer to computer. EDI networking is growing rapidly in the United States.

Electronic mail (e-mail). The forwarding, storage, and retrieval of messages by electronic transmission systems, usually using digital techniques.

Electronic manuscript management. In book production, computerized tracking of the preparation of the book on a day-by-day basis, including keeping current tallies on costs, work hours, and production scheduling.

Electronic news gathering (ENG). In broadcasting, coverage of events outside the studio through the use of satellite-dish-equipped trucks, providing live or taped coverage.

Electronic publishing. Replaces traditional means of delivering and storing text information by using computerized delivery. The information is held in a storage device for delivery to computer screens rather than printed on paper.

E-mail address. The domain-based address that is used to send electronic mail to a specified destination.

Encoding. The process of transforming an analog signal into a digital signal or a digital signal into another digital format.

Enhanced-definition television (EDTV). A variation on high-definition television, providing a better picture than current TV sets but offering less resolution than high-definition technology. *See* High-definition television.

Enhanced services. A telecommunications category established by the Federal Communications Commission to describe services that result in additional, different, or restructured transmitted information or that involve user interaction with stored information, whether voice or data. *See* Basic services.

Erasable rewritable optical disc (EROD). A read/write storage medium that uses a laser and reflected light to store and retrieve data on an optical disc. The discs can store more than one gigabyte of data and are generally used to replace a hard drive.

Facsimile (fax). A form of electronic mail or remote copying. Also, the document resulting from a fax transmission.

FAQ. Frequently asked questions. An Internet acronym, designed to guide new users through the intricacies of the system.

Federal Communications Commission (FCC). The federal independent regulatory agency that licenses and sets standards for telecommunications and electronic media. FCC deregulatory policies in recent decades have had a major impact on U.S. media patterns by expanding the range of delivery services available.

Femtosecond. A millionth of a billionth of a second. The capabilities of optical-fiber systems now under development will be measured in femtoseconds (i.e., millions of times the capacity of present systems).

Fiber optics. The technology of guiding and transmitting light for use as a communications medium. Modulated light-wave signals, generated by a laser or a light-emitting diode, are propagated along a silicon-based waveguide and then demodulated back into electrical signals by a light-sensitive receiver. The bandwidth capacity of fiber-optic wire is substantially greater than that of coaxial cable or copper wire.

File transfer protocol (FTP). A protocol that allows a user on one host to access and transfer files to and from another host over the Internet or other network. FTP is also used as the name of the program the user selects to execute the protocol.

First Amendment. The Bill of Rights provision that is the ideological base, and protector, of information freedoms in the United States.

Flame. On the Internet, a strong opinion or criticism, often inflammatory, in an electronic mail message. Such a message can lead to "flame wars," in which users fire electronic volleys against the flamers.

Flash-memory chip. A recent major advance in chip technology. Flash-memory chips retain information when a computer is turned off, unlike earlier chips. The result is to eliminate the need for disk-drive storage systems, permitting much smaller, lighter computers.

Freenet. Community-based bulletin board system that often includes e-mail, information services, interactive communications, and conferencing. Freenets are usually funded and operated by individuals and volunteers.

Frequency modulation (FM). In broadcasting, a method of modulation in which the frequency is varied and the amplitude (power) remains constant. In addition to its radio uses, FM is used in the sound portion of TV transmissions. *See* Amplitude modulation (AM).

Generator. Any device that facilitates a computer task such as text, graphics, or program design.

Gigabit. A measure of the quantity of binary digits. A gigabit equals one billion bits per second.

Gopher. A distributed information service that makes available hierarchical collections of information across the Internet. A Gopher client can access information from any accessible Gopher server, providing the user with a single "Gopher space" of information. Gopher derives its name from the fact that it was begun by a group at the University of Minnesota. In the late 1990s, Gopher was being displaced by newer, more efficient ways of accessing the Internet.

Headend. A cable TV system's control center where program signals from satellites and other sources are transferred to the system's network.

High-definition television (HDTV). A group of technical systems, each of which can encode, transmit, and display greatly enhanced levels of information compared to conventional TV, making possible a sharper video picture, improved color fidelity, and the use of stereophonic sound. HDTV is scheduled for large-scale adoption in the United States, Europe, and Japan early in the new century.

Host. A computer that allows users to communicate with other host computers on a network.

Hypertext. Computer software that allows users to link information together through a variety of paths or connections. Users can randomly organize the information in a manner that conforms to their own needs. Hypercard programs (*stacks*) are made up of *cards*, which, when activated, allow users to move to another part of the material they are working with. Hypercard programs are written in *hypertalk*, a simple, object-oriented programming language.

Hyperlink. An icon, graphic, or word in a file that, when mouse-clicked, automatically opens another file for viewing

Icon. In computer operations, a symbolic, pictorial representation of any function or task.

Image technology. A general category of computer applications that convert documents, illustrations, photographs, and other images into data that can be stored, distributed, accessed, and processed by computers and special-purpose workstations.

IMHO. Internetese for "in my humble opinion."

Information utility. The concept of a national, and eventually global, electronic network, which will supply a full range of media and other information resources to all locations (comparable to water and electricity utility networks).

Integrated services digital network (ISDN). A long-term plan for the transition of the world's telecommunications systems from analog to digital technology, permitting the integrated transmission of any combination of voice, video, graphics, and text over a common electronic "information pipe." ISDN is a software standard that will eliminate present technical incompatibilities between telecommunications systems and allow uninterrupted transfer of traffic between them.

Interactive media. Media resources that involve the user in providing the content and duration of a message, permitting individualized program material. Also, they are used to describe media production operations that take maximum advantage of random-access, computer-controlled videotape, and videodisc players.

Interactive video. A combination of video and computer technology in which programs run in tandem under the control of the user. The user's choices and decisions directly affect the ways in which the program unfolds.

Interactive Video Data Service (IVDS). A service authorized by the Federal Communications Commission in 1992 that allows home viewers to use their television sets for interactive video links to a variety of resources from home shopping services to educational courses.

Interface. The point or boundary at which hardware or software systems interact (e.g., the connection between a computer and a terminal).

International Telecommunications Union (ITU). A United Nations agency that sets the technical and administrative standards for the global telecommunications network. The ITU has been a leader in promoting digital standardization. Its headquarters are in Geneva, Switzerland.

internet. A small-i internet usually refers to a collection of networks interconnected with routers, the devices that forward traffic between networks.

Internet. The largest inter-networking system in the world. It is a multilevel hierarchy, composed of backbone networks (e.g., NSFNET), midlevel networks, and subnetworks.

Internet Protocol address. The address of a computer on a Transmission Control Protocol/Internet Protocol (TCP/IP) network. IP addresses are written as four groups of up to three digits each, separated by periods.

Internet Society (ISOC). A nonprofit, professional membership organization with headquarters in Reston, Virginia. ISOC facilitates and supports the technical evolution of the Internet and promotes the development of new applications of the system. Its work in developing technical standards has been supported by funds from a U.S. government group, the Corporation for National Research Initiatives. In recent years, similar Internet societies have been established abroad.

Interoperability. The ability of software and hardware on multiple machines from multiple vendors to communicate meaningfully.

KA band. The new frontier of the radio-frequency spectrum. Located in the 20 to 30 gigahertz frequency bands, KA is, for the present, the upper limit of spectrum use for media and other normal communications needs. The KA frequencies are capable of handling enormous amounts of information. The other high-capacity bands currently in use are **C band** and **KU band**, both used extensively for satellite and terrestrial microwave transmissions.

Karaoke. Japanese for "empty orchestra." A videodisc-based form of entertainment that provides musical and video accompaniment for amateur singers.

Laser. Technically, *light amplification by stimulated emission of radiation*. Lasers amplify and generate energy in the optical, or light, region of the spectrum above the radio frequencies. In a typical media application, lasers are used to read the micropits on a videodisc, which contain video or sound signals.

Light-emitting diode (LED). A semiconductor device that changes electrical energy into light energy.

Light guide. An extremely clear, thin glass fiber that is to light what copper wire is to electricity. It is synonymous with optical fiber.

Low-powered television (LPTV). Small television stations, licensed by the Federal Communications Commission, using low transmitter power. LPTV stations cover relatively small geographic areas.

Media composing. A high-tech variation on desktop publishing that incorporates sound and video resources with print and still-graphics materials.

Media Lab. A unit of the Massachusetts Institute of Technology that has done much of the pioneering research on applying advanced technologies to media uses.

Megabit. One million binary digits or bits.

Microprocessor. An electronic circuit, usually on a single microchip, that performs arithmetic, logic, and control operations, customarily with the assistance of a small internal memory also on the chip.

Microsoft Network (MSN). A consumer-oriented database established in 1995 by Microsoft Corp. to compete with America Online, Prodigy, and similar services.

Minitel. A national information-retrieval network in France, which supplies thousands of data services to millions of homes.

Modem. A device that makes possible the linkage of a digital computer to the analog telephone system. As digital telecommunications networks evolve, modems will become obsolete.

Multichannel microwave system (MMDS). Television delivery system that uses line-of-sight microwave circuits to transmit programs similar to those supplied on cable TV. MMDS systems have limited channel capacity, however, compared with cable systems. MMDS is often referred to as "wireless cable."

Multimedia. Information delivery systems that combine different content formats (e.g., text, video, sound) and storage facilities (e.g., videotape, audiotape, magnetic disks, optical discs).

Multiple-system operators (MSO). Large cable TV companies, each controlling many local cable TV systems across the country.

Multiplexing. A technique that allows handling of multiple messages over a single channel. It is accomplished by varying either the speed at which the messages are sent (time division multiplexing) or by splitting the frequency band (frequency division multiplex).

Multi-User Dungeon. Adventure, role-playing games, or simulations played on the Internet. The games can feature, among other possibilities, fantasy combat, booby traps, and magic, with players interacting in real time.

National Association of Broadcasters. The Washington trade association whose membership includes most of the television and radio stations in the country.

National Cable Television Association. The Washington trade association of the cable television industry.

National information infrastructure. A phrase coined by Michael Dertouzos, chief of the computer research lab at MIT, to describe the eventual development of an integrated multimedia telecommunications system. *See* Information utility.

National Science Foundation. A U.S. government-funded agency whose purpose is to fund the advancement of science. It has been instrumental in promoting the use of the Internet for scientific and academic purposes. *See* NSFNET.

National Television Systems Committee (NTSC). In the 1940s, this committee formulated the U.S. television standard of 525 horizontal lines per frame at 30 frames per second. The NTSC standard will eventually be phased out with the introduction of high-definition television, which offers twice as many horizontal lines.

Newbies. New Internet users. Sometimes used derisively to distinguish them from long-time Internet buffs.

NSFNET. A "network of networks" that is part of the Internet. It is hierarchical in nature and funded by the National Science Foundation. At the highest level, it is a high-speed backbone network, spanning the United States. Attached to that are midlevel networks, and attached to the midlevels are campus and local networks. NSFNET has connections with networks throughout the world.

Optical memory. Technology that deals with information storage devices that use light (generally laser based) to record, read, or decode data.

Overlay. The technique of superimposing computer-generated text or graphics or both onto motion or still video.

Packet. The unit of data sent across a network.

Packet switching. The transfer of data by means of addressed blocks (*packets*) of information in which a telecommunications channel is occupied only for the time of transmission of the packet. This allows more efficient use of channels, which ordinarily have periods of low use.

Pay-per-view (PPV). Program services purchased by cable TV subscribers on a per-program rather than per-month basis.

Peripheral equipment. Equipment that works in conjunction with a communications system or a computer but that is not integral to them (e.g., computer printers).

Personal electronic media. Networks serving the specialized information needs of their users, usually through electronic-mail exchanges. Eventually such personal networking will incorporate video capabilities.

Photon. The fundamental unit of light and other forms of electromagnetic energy. Photons are to optical fibers what electrons are to copper wires; like electrons, they have a wave motion.

Prodigy. A consumer-oriented network based on personal computers, originally developed by IBM and Sears Roebuck. Although it has been eclipsed by America Online and the Microsoft Network in recent years, Prodigy is a viable consumer information-services provider.

Protocol. A set of rules that defines procedures for the transfer of information in a communications system.

Qube. An interactive cable TV system developed in the 1980s by American Express and Warner Communications in Columbus, Ohio. Although unsuccessful at the time, it demonstrated the potential of interactive programming to homes.

Quicktime. A computer file format that enables Macintosh computers to compress and play digitized video without additional hardware.

Random-access memory (RAM). A computer memory, the contents of which can be altered at any time. It is the most commonly used method of defining computer capability (e.g., 64K RAM).

Read-only memory (ROM). A computer chip that stores data and instructions in a form that cannot be altered. It is thus distinguished from random-access memory, the contents of which can be changed.

Router. The par of a communications network that receives transmissions and forwards them to their destinations using the shortest route available. Data may travel through multiple routers on the way to its destination.

Satellite master antenna television (SMATV). Broadcasting satellite systems designed to serve apartment houses and hotels.

Search engine. A program that lets users locate specified information from a database or mass of data.

Semiconductor. A material (e.g., silicon, germanium, gallium arsenide) with properties between those of conductors and insulators. Semiconductors are used to manufacture solid-state devices such as diodes, transistors, integrated circuits, injection lasers, and light-emitting diodes.

Server. *See* Web server.

Snail mail. A pejorative term used primarily by computer buffs to describe the U.S. Postal Service.

Software. The detailed instructions or programs that tell the computer what to do byte by byte.

Squarial. A small earth terminal that is square or rectangular in shape and designed to be attached to the roofs or sides of houses and other, smaller structures.

TCP/IP. *See* Transmission Control Protocol/Internet Protocol.

Telecomputer. A combined television receiver and computer, which may be the central information and entertainment unit of homes in the new multimedia environment.

Teletext. One-way broadcast transmissions that piggyback digital data onto the regular television broadcasting signal by inserting their messages into unused lines of the vertical blanking interval.

Television receive-only (TVRO) terminal. A small earth station that receives video signals from a space satellite.

Transmission Control Protocol/Internet Protocol (TCP/IP). This is the language governing communications among all computers on the Internet. TCP/IP is two separate protocols that are used together. The Internet Protocol dictates how packets of information are sent out over networks. It has a packet-addressing method that lets any computer on the Internet forward a packet to another computer that is a step (or more) closer to the packet's recipient. The TC ensures the reliability of data transmissions across Internet-connected networks. It checks packets for errors and submits requests for retransmission if errors are found. It also returns the multiple packets of a message into their proper original sequence when the message reaches its destination.

Transponder. A component in a satellite that receives and transmits television or data signals.

Ultra-high frequency (UHF). The radio spectrum from 300 megahertz to 3 gigahertz. It is the frequency band that includes TV channels 14 to 83, as well as cellular radio frequencies.

Universal Resource Locator (URL). A standardized naming, or "addressing," system for documents and media accessible over the Internet.

Value-added network (VAN). Data processing done as part of a transmission service package.

Very high frequency (VHF). The radio spectrum from 30 to 300 megahertz, which includes TV channels 2 to 13, the FM broadcast band, and various specialized services.

Very small aperture terminal (VSAT). A range of small earth station designs that are capable, due to advanced semiconductor technology, of receiving signals from space satellites. A newer generation of VSATS can also transmit signals to the satellites.

VHS. The technical standard that dominates videocassette use, following an epochal marketing battle with the Betamax standard in the 1980s.

Videotext. The transmission of information by television channels, FM frequencies, or telephone circuits to a TV or computer monitor. There are many variations of videotext services, the most advanced of which is full two-way transmission, in which a television receiver is equipped to function as a computer terminal.

Videotext publishing. An increasingly important market for supplying videotext materials from large databases to home computers and other terminals. Many newspapers and magazines now offer their printed products electronically in this manner.

Virtual reality. Software that produces multidimensional visual images. The computerized images can create "realities," which are manipulated in many different formats by a user wearing computerized gloves or helmet.

Virus. A destructive program that replicates itself on computer systems by incorporating itself into other programs that are shared among computer systems.

Web server. A computer where a certain set of Web pages resides. A server may be dedicated, meaning its sole purpose is to be the server, or nondedicated, meaning that it can be used for basic computing in addition to acting as a server.

Wireless cable. *See* Multichannel microwave distribution system.

World Wide Web (WWW). A hypertext-based, distributed information system on which Internet users may create, edit, or browse hypertext documents. The Web was created by researchers at CERN, the European nuclear research facility near Geneva, Switzerland.

Write once, read many (WORM). An optical storage medium that becomes readable only after data are written into the disk. It can store large amounts of information and has a long shelf life. Some WORM disks are analog and some are digital.

WYSWYG. Pronounced "wizzywig." Internetese for "what you see is what you get."

Selected Bibliography

Abramson, Jeffrey B., Christopher Arterton, and Gary Orren, eds. *The Electronic Commonwealth*, New York: Basic Books, 1988.

American Newspaper Publishers Association. *The Media Landscape: The Next Five Years*, Reston, VA, 1989.

———. *Newspaper Electronic Information Services Directory*. Reston, VA, 1991.

American Society of Newspaper Editors. *Keys to Our Survival*. Reston, VA, July 1991.

Aspen Institute Program on Communications and Society. *Shaping the Future Telecommunications Structure*. Queenstown, MD, 1991.

———. *Electronic Media Regulation and the First Amendment*. Forum report 14. Queenstown, MD, 1991.

———. *Universal Telephone Service: Ready for the 21st Century?* Queenstown, MD, 1991.

———. *The Knowledge Economy: The Nature of Information in the 21st Century*. Queenstown, MD, 1994.

———. *Crossroads on the Information Highway: Convergence and Diversity in Communications Technologies*. Queenstown, MD, 1995.

———. *The Global Advance of Electronic Commerce*, Queenstown, MD, 1998.

Auletta, Ken. *Three Blind Mice: How the TV Networks Lost Their Way*. New York: Vintage Books, 1992.

———. *The Highwaymen: Warriors of the Information Superhighway*, New York: Random House, 1997.

Aziz, A. M. A. *A Pakistani Journalist Looks at America*. Dacca: Al-Helat, 1960.

Baer, Walter S. *Technology's Challenge to the First Amendment*. Report P-7773. Santa Monica, CA: Rand Corporation, 1992.

Bagdikian, Ben. *Media Monopoly*. Boston: Beacon, 1987.

Baldwin, Thomas, D. Stevens McVoy, and Charles Steinfield. *Convergence: Integrating Media, Information & Communication*. Newbury Park, CA: Sage Publications, 1996.

Barnouw, Erik. *Tube of Plenty: The Evolution of American Television*, 2d ed. New York: Oxford University Press, 1990.

Bart, Peter. *The Calamitous Final Days of MGM*. New York: William Morrow, 1990.

Bell, Daniel. *The Coming of Post-Industrial Society*. New York: Basic Books, 1973.

Beniger, James. *The Control Revolution*. Cambridge, MA: Harvard University Press, 1986.

Benjamin, Gerald, ed. *The Communications Revolution in Politics*. New York: Academy of Political Science, 1982.

Bennett, W. Lance. *The Governing Crisis: Media, Money and Marketing in American Elections*. New York: St. Martin's, 1982.

Berger, Arthur Asa. *Media USA*. New York: Longman, 1991.

Besen, Stanley. *Misregulating Television: Network Dominance and the FCC*. Chicago: University of Chicago Press, 1984.

Bibb, Porter. *It Ain't as Easy as It Looks: Ted Turner's Amazing Story*. New York: Crown Publishers, 1993.

Birkerts, Sven. *The Gutenberg Elegies: The Fate of Reading in an Electronic Age*. Boston: Faber and Faber, 1994.

Bogart, Leo. *The American Media System and Its Commercial Culture*. Occasional paper, Gannett Foundation Media Center, New York, March 1991.

Bolling, George H. *AT&T: Aftermath of Antitrust*. Washington, DC: National Defense University Press, 1983.

Brand, Stewart. *The Media Lab: Inventing the Future at MIT*. New York: Penguin Books, 1988.

Branscomb, Anne. *Who Owns Information? From Privacy to Public Access*. New York: Basic Books, 1994.

Brown, Richard D. *Knowledge Is Power: The Diffusion of Information in Early America*. New York: Oxford University Press, 1989.

Burnett, Robert. *The Global Jukebox: The International Music Industry*. New York: Routledge, 1996.

Cairncross, Frances. *The Death of Distance: How the Communications Revolution Will Change Our Lives*. Cambridge, MA: Harvard Business School Press, 1997.

Carpentier, Michel, Sylviane Farnoux-Toporkoff, and Garric Christian. *Telecommunications in Transition*. New York: John Wiley & Sons, 1992.

Carter, Thomas. *The First Amendment and the Fifth Estate*, 2d ed. Mineola, NY: Foundation, 1988.

Cate, Fred, ed. *Visions of the First Amendment for a New Millennium*. Occasional paper, Annenberg Washington Program, Washington, DC, 1992.

Clarke, Neville, and Edwin Riddell. *The Sky Barons: The Men Who Control the Global Media*. London: Methuen, 1992.

Clurman, Richard. *To the End of Time*. New York: Simon & Schuster, 1992.

Cohen, Stephen S., and John Zyzman. *Manufacturing Matters: The Myth of the Post-Industrial Economy*. New York: Basic Books, 1987.

Collins, Richard. *New Media, New Policies: Media and Communications Strategy for the Future*. New York: Polity Press, 1996.

Cook, Philip, Douglas Gomery, and Lawrence Lichty, eds. *The Future of the News*. Washington, DC: Woodrow Wilson Center, 1992. Distributed by Johns Hopkins University Press.

Corner, John, Philip Schlesinger, and Roger Silverstone, eds. *International Media Research: A Critical Survey*. New York: Routledge, 1997.

Corporation for Public Broadcasting. *Strategies for Public Television in a Multi-Channel Environment*. Washington, DC, March 1991.

Cose, Ellis. *The Press*. New York: William Morrow, 1989.

Crandall, Robert W. *After the Breakup: U.S. Telecommunications in a More Competitive Era*. Washington, DC: Brookings Institution, 1991.

Czitrom, Daniel J. *Media and the American Mind: From Morse to McLuhan*. Chapel Hill: University of North Carolina Press, 1982.

Dahlgren, Peter. *Television and the Public Sphere*. Thousand Oaks, CA: Sage, 1995.

Dahlgren, Peter, and Colin Sparks. *Journalism and Popular Culture*. Newbury Park, CA: Sage, 1992.

Dates, Jannette L., and William Barlow. *Split Image: African Americans in the Mass Media*. Washington, DC: Howard University Press, 1990.

Davis, L.J. *The Billionaire Shell Game: How Cable Baron John Malone and Assorted Corporate Titans Invented a Future Nobody Wanted*. New York: Doubleday, 1998.

Dennis, Everette E. *Of Media and People*. Newbury Park, CA: Sage, 1992.

Dennis, Everette E., and John Merrill. *Media Debates: Issues in Mass Communication*. New York: Longman, 1991.

Dennis, Everette, and Edward C. Pease, eds. *Media and Public Life*. Newbury Park, CA: Sage Publications, 1997.

Dennis, Everette, Craig L. LeMay, and Edward C. Pease, eds. *Publishing Books*. Newbury Park, CA: Sage Publications, 1996.

Denton, Frank, and Howard Kurtz. *Reinventing the Newspaper*. New York: Twentieth Century Fund, 1993.

Dertouzos, Michael. *What Will Be: How the New World of Information Will Change Our Lives*. San Francisco, CA: Harper San Francisco, 1997.

Dertouzos, Michael, and Joel Moses. *The Computer Age*. Cambridge, MA: Massachusetts Institute of Technology Press, 1979.

DeSonne, Marcia. *Spectrum of New Broadcast/Media Technologies*. National Association of Broadcasters, Washington, DC, March 1990.

Deutsch, Karl. *The Nerves of Government*. New York: Free Press of Glencoe, 1963.

Dizard, Wilson P. *Television: A World View*. Syracuse, NY: Syracuse University Press, 1966.

———. *The Coming Information Age*, 3d ed. New York: Longman, 1989.

———. *Meganet: How Global Communications Will Connect Everyone on Earth*. Boulder CO: Westview, 1997.

Dizard, Wilson P., and Blake Swensrud. *Gorbachev's Information Revolution: Controlling Glasnost in a New Electronic Era*. Colorado Springs, CO: Westview, 1987.

Donlan, Thomas G., *Supertech*. Homewood, IL: Business One Irwin, 1991.

Dorfman, Ariel. *The Emperor's Old Clothes*. New York: Pantheon Books, 1983.

Downing, John, Ali Mohammidi, and Annabelle Sreberny-Mohammadi. *Questioning the Media*, 2d ed. Thousand Oaks, CA: Sage, 1995.

Drake, William, ed. *The New Information Infrastructure: Strategies for U.S. Policy*. New York: Twentieth Century Fund, 1995.

Dutton, William, Jay Blumler, and Kenneth Kraemer, eds. *Wired Cities: Shaping the Future of Communications*. Boston: G. K. Hall, 1987.

Dye, Thomas R., Harmon Ziegler, S. Robert Lichter, and L. Harmon Ziegler. *American Politics in the Media Age*. New York: Brooks/Cole Publishers, 1997.

Dyson, Esther. *Release 2.0: A Design for Living in the Digital Age*. New York: Broadway Books, 1997.

Economist (London). Special reports on communications and mass media: "The Entertainment Industry," 23 December 1989; "Netting the Future," 10 March 1990; "The New Boys," 5 October 1991; "End of the Line: a Survey of Telecommunications," 23 October 1993; "The Third Age: a Survey of the Computer Industry," 17 September 1994; "The Accidental Highway: A Survey of the Internet," 1 July 1995; "The Death of Distance," 30 September 1995; "Future Perfect: a Survey of Silicon Valley," 29 March 1997; and "A Connected World: a Survey of Telecommunications," 13 September 1997.

Egan, Bruce L. *Information Superhighways: The Economics of Advanced Public Communications Networks*, Norwood, MA: Artech House, 1991.

Eisenstein, Elizabeth. *The Printing Press as an Agent for Change*. New York: Cambridge University Press, 1980.

Ellul, Jacques. *The Technological Society*. New York: Alfred A. Knopf, 1964.

———. *Propaganda*. New York: Alfred A. Knopf, 1968.

Elton, Martin C. J. *Integrated Broadband Networks: The Public Policy Issues*. Amsterdam, Netherlands: Elsevier Science Publishers, 1991.

Entman, Robert M., and Charles M. Firestone. *Strategic Alliances and Telecommunications Policy*. Program in Communications and Society, Aspen Institute, 1995.

Etheredge, Lloyd. *Politics in Wired Nations: Selected Writings of Ithiel de Sola Pool*. Newbury Park, CA: Sage Publications, 1997.

Fellows, James. *Breaking the News: How the Media Undermine American Democracy*. New York: Vintage Books, 1997.

Fidler, Roger. *Mediamorphosis: Understanding the New Media*. Thousand Oaks, CA: Pine Forge Press, 1997.

Firestone, Charles, and Jorge Reina Schement. *Toward an Information Bill of Rights and Responsibilities*. Program in Communications and Society, Aspen Institute, 1995.

Fischer, Claude S. *America Calling: A Social History of the Telephone to 1940*. Berkeley: University of California Press, 1992.

Flamm, Kenneth. *Creating the Computer: Government, Industry and High Technology*. Washington, DC: Brookings Institution, 1988.

Flournoy, Don M. *CNN World Report: Ted Turner's International News Coup*. Acamedia research monograph 9. London: John Libbey, 1992.

Fortner, Robert S. *International Communication*. Belmont, CA: Wadsworth, 1993.

Fowles, Jib. *Why Viewers Watch*. Newbury Park, CA: Sage, 1992.

Frantzich, Stephen. *The C-Span Revolution*. Norman, OK: University of Oklahoma Press, 1996.

Frederick, Howard. *Global Communication and International Relations*. Belmont, CA: Wadsworth, 1993.

Freedom Forum Media Studies Center. *Media at the Millennium*. Report of the First Fellows Symposium on the Future of the Media and Media Studies. New York, 1992.

Gates, Bill. *The Road Ahead*. New York: Viking, 1995.

Geller, Henry. *Fiber Optics: An Opportunity for a New Policy?* Annenberg Washington Program, Washington, DC, 1991.

Gilder, George. *Life after Television*. New York: W. W. Norton, 1992.

Goldman, William. *Adventures in the Screen Trade*. New York: Warner Books, 1983.

Gooler, Dennis D. *The Education Utility: The Power to Revitalize Education and Society*. Englewood Cliffs, NJ: Prentice-Hall, 1986.

Graham, Gordon, and Richard Abel, eds. *The Book in the United States Today*. Newbury Park, CA: Sage Publications, 1997.

Grossman, Lawrence K. *The Electronic Republic: Reshaping Democracy in the Information Age*. New York: Viking, 1995.

Grover, Ron. *The Disney Touch: How a Disney Management Team Revived an Entertainment Empire*. New York: Business One Irwin, 1991.

Gumpert, Gary. *Talking Tombstones & Other Tales of the Media Age*, New York: Oxford University Press, 1987.

Hafner, Katie, and Matthew Lyon. *Where Wizards Stay Up Late: The Origins of the Internet*. New York: Touchstone Press, 1998.

Hamelink, Cees J. *The Politics of World Communication*. Thousand Oaks, CA: Sage, 1994.

Harlow, Alvin F. *Old Wires and New Waves*. New York: Appleton Century, 1936.

Harper, Christopher. *And That's the Way It Will Be: News and Information in a Digital World*. New York: New York University Press, 1998.

Henderson, Albert. *Electronic Databases and Publishing*. Newbury Park, CA: Sage Publications, 1997.

Hiaasen, Carl. *Team Rodent: How Disney Devours the World*. New York: Ballantine Books, 1998.

Horowitz, Irving Louis. *Communicating Ideas: The Politics of Publishing in a Post-Industrial Society*. New Brunswick, NJ: Transaction, 1991.

Horowitz, Robert. *The Irony of Regulatory Reform: The Deregulation of American Telecommunications*. New York: Oxford University Press, 1989.

Hume, Ellen. *Tabloids, Talk Radio and the Future of News*. Occasional paper, Annenberg Washington Program of Northwestern University, Washington, DC, 1995.

Innis, Harold A. *Empire and Communications*. Toronto: University of Toronto Press, 1972.

International Encyclopaedia of Communications. 4 vols. New York: Oxford University Press, 1989.

Jackson, Charles, Harry Shooshan, and Jane Wilson. *Newspapers and Videotex. How Free a Press?* Modern Media Institute, St. Petersburg, FL, 1981.

Johnson, Craig, ed. *The International Cable-Telco Tango*. International Communications Studies Program, Center for Strategic and International Studies, Washington, DC, March 1991.

Johnson, Leland. *Development of High-Definition Television: A Study in US-Japan Trade Relations*. Report R-3921-CUSJR. Santa Monica, CA: Rand Corporation, 1991.

Johnson, Leland, and Deborah Castleman. *Direct Satellites: A Comparative Alternative to Cable Television*. Report R-4047-MF-RL. Santa Monica, CA: Rand Corporation, 1991.

Johnson, Leland, and David Read. *Residential Broadband Services by Telephone Companies? Technology, Economics and Public Policy*. Report R-3906-MF-RL. Santa Monica, CA: Rand Corporation, June 1990.

Johnson, Steven. *Interface Culture: How New Technology Transforms the Way We Create and Communicate*. San Francisco, CA: Harper San Francisco, 1997.

Johnston, Carla Brooks. *Winning the Global News Game*. New York: Focal Press, 1995.

Jones, Glenn. *Making All America a School: Mind Extension University*. Englewood, CO: Jones 21st Century Inc., 1990.

Jones, Steven, ed. *Cybersociety: Computer-Mediated Communication and Community*. Thousand Oaks, CA: Sage, 1995.

Jowett, Garth. *Movies as Mass Communication*. 2d ed. Newbury Park, CA: Sage, 1989.

Kellner, Douglas. *Television and the Crisis of Democracy*. Boulder, CO: Westview, 1990.

Kern, Montague. *30-Second Politics*. New York: Praeger, 1989.

Keyworth, George, and Bruce Abell. *Competitiveness and Communications: America's Economic Future—The House-to-House Digital Fiber Optic Network*. Hudson Institute, Indianapolis, IN, 1990.

Kobrak, Fred, and Beth Leuy, eds. *The Structure of International Publishing in the 1990s*. New Brunswick, NJ: Transaction, 1991.

Koch, Tom. *Journalism for the 21st Century: Online Information, Electronic Databases and the News*. New York: Praeger, 1991.

Koelich, Frank. *The Information Revolution*. New York: McGraw-Hill, 1995.

Kurtz, Howard. *Media Circus: The Trouble With America's Newspapers.* New York: New York Times Books, 1994.

———. *Hot Air: All Talk, All the Time.* New York: Random House, 1996.

———. *Spin Cycle: Inside the Clinton Propaganda Machine.* New York: Free Press, 1998.

Laurie, Peter. *The Micro Revolution.* New York: Basic Books, 1980.

Leaming, Barbara. *Orson Welles: A Biography.* New York: Viking Penguin, 1985.

Lensen, Anton. *Concentration in the Media Industry: The European Community and Mass Media Regulation.* Washington Annenberg Program, Washington, DC, 1992.

Levy, Mark, and Barrie Gunter. *Home Video and the Changing Nature of the Television Audience.* IBA Television research monograph. London: John Libbey, 1988

Lichtenberg, Judith. *Democracy and the Mass Media.* New York: Cambridge University Press, 1990.

Lippmann, Walter. *Public Opinion.* New York: Harcourt Brace, 1922.

Loader, Brian, ed. *Convergence of Cyberspace: Politics, Technology and Global Restructuring.* New York: Routledge, 1997.

Lowenstein, Ralph, and John Merrill. *Macromedia: Mission, Message, Morality.* New York: Longman, 1990.

Lubar, Steven. *Infoculture: The Smithsonian Book of Information Age Inventions.* Boston: Houghton Mifflin, 1993.

Lweebaert, Derek. *The Future of the Electronic Marketplace.* Cambridge MA: MIT Press, 1998.

MacDonald, Greg. *The Emergence of Global Multi-Media Conglomerates.* Working paper 70. International Labor Organization, Geneva, Switzerland, 1990.

MacDonald, J. Fred. *One Nation under Television: The Rise and Decline of Network TV.* New York: Pantheon Books, 1990.

Maney, Kevin. *Megamedia Shakeout: The Inside Story of the Leaders and the Losers in the Exploding Communications Industry.* New York: John Wiley & Sons, 1995.

McGannon Communications Research Center. *Fiber Optics in the Home: What Does the Public Want and Need?* Fordham University Department of Communications, New York, May 1989.

Machlup, Fritz. *The Production and Distribution of Information in the United States.* Princeton, NJ: Princeton University Press, 1962.

McLuhan, Marshall. *The Gutenberg Galaxy.* Toronto: University of Toronto Press. 1962.

———. *Understanding Media,* 2d ed. New York: New American Library, 1964.

McQuail, Denis. *Media Performance: Mass Communications and the Public Interest.* Newbury Park, CA: Sage, 1992.

Mandel, Michael J. *The High-Risk Society: Peril and Promise.* New York: Times Business Books, 1996.

Maney, Kevin. *Megamedia Shakeout: The Inside Story of the Leaders and Losers in the Exploding Communications Industry.* New York: John Wiley & Sons, 1995.

Manheim, Jarol B. *All the People, All the Time.* Armonk, NY: M. E. Sharpe, 1991.

Marvin, Carolyn. *When Old Technologies Were New.* New York: Oxford University Press, 1988.

Marx, Leo. *The Machine in the Garden.* New York: Oxford University Press, 1964.

Masuda, Yoneji. *The Information Society as Post-Industrial Society.* Tokyo: Institute for the Information Society, 1980. Reprinted in the United States by the World Future Society, Bethesda, MD, 1981.

Meyer, Martin. *Whatever Happened to Madison Avenue?* Boston: Little Brown, 1991.

Miller, Nod, and Rod Allen. *It's Live—But Is It Real?* Current Debates in Broadcasting 2. London: John Libbey, 1992.

Minow, Newton. *How Vast the Wasteland Now?* Freedom Forum Media Studies Center, Columbia University, August 1991.

Mintz, Morton, and Jerry S. Cohen. *American Inc.: Who Owns and Operates the United States?* New York: Dell, 1972.

Morrison, David E. *Television and the Gulf War.* Acamedia research monograph 7. London: John Libbey, 1992.

Mosco, Vincent. *The Pay-Per Society: Computers and Communications in the Information Age.* Norwood, NJ: Ablex, 1989.

Mosco, Vincent, and Janet Wasco. *The Political Economy of Information.* Madison: University of Wisconsin Press, 1988.

Moskin, Robert, ed. *Toward the Year 2000: New Faces in Publishing.* Gutersloh, Germany: Bertelsmann Foundation, 1989.

Mougayer, Walid. *Opening Digital Markets: Battle Plans and Business Strategies for Internet Commerce.* New York: McGraw Hill, 1998.

Naisbitt, John. *Megatrends.* New York: Warner Books, 1984.

Nava, Mica, Andrew Blake, Iain Macrury, and Barry Richards, eds. *Buy This Book: Studies in Advertising and Consumption.* New York: Routledge, 1997.

Negroponte, Nicholas. *Being Digital.* New York: Alfred A. Knopf, 1995.

Neuman, W. Russell. *The Future of the Mass Audience.* New York: Cambridge University Press, 1992.

Noam, Eli. *Television in Europe.* New York: Oxford University Press, 1991.

Nora, Simon, and Alain Minc. *The Computerization of Society.* Cambridge, MA: Massachusetts Institute of Technology Press, 1981.

Orlik, Peter B. *The Electronic Media: An Introduction to the Profession.* Ames, IA: Iowa State University Press, 1997.

Owen, Bruce. *The Internet Challenge to Television.* Cambridge, MA: Harvard University Press, 1999.

Owen, Bruce, and Steven Wildman. *Video Economics.* Cambridge, MA: Harvard University Press, 1992.

Penzias, Arnold. *Ideas and Information.* New York: W. W. Norton, 1989.

Pew Research Center for the People and the Press. *Internet News Takes Off.* Washington, DC: June 1998.

Pool, Ithiel de Sola. *Technologies of Freedom.* Cambridge, MA: Harvard University Press, 1983.

———. *Technologies without Boundaries.* Cambridge, MA: Harvard University Press, 1990.

———, ed. *The Social Impact of the Telephone.* Cambridge, MA: Massachusetts Institute of Technology Press, 1977.

Porter, David, ed. *Internet Culture.* New York: Routledge, 1997.

Postman, Neil. *Amusing Ourselves to Death.* New York: Penguin Books, 1986.

———. *Technology: The Surrender of Culture to Technology.* New York: Alfred A. Knopf, 1992.

Postman, Neil, and Steve Powers. *How to Watch TV News.* New York: Penguin Books, 1992.

Quester, George. *The International Politics of Television.* New York: Lexington Books, 1990.

Read, William. *America's Mass-Media Merchants.* Baltimore: Johns Hopkins University Press, 1976.

Real, Michael R. *Super Media.* Newbury Park, CA: Sage, 1989.

Reich, Robert. *The Work of Nations.* New York: Alfred A. Knopf, 1991.

Reid, T. R. *The Chip*. New York: Simon & Schuster, 1984.

Rheingold, Howard. *Virtual Reality*. New York: Summit Books, 1991.

Rochlin, Gene I. *Trapped in the Net: The Unanticipated Consequences of Computerization*. Princeton, NJ: Princeton University Press, 1997.

Roof, Dana, Denise Trauth, and John Huffman. *In Pursuit of Diversity: An Argument for Structural Regulation of the Cable Television Industry*. School of Mass Communications, Bowling Green State University, Bowling Green, KY, August 1991.

Rosen, Jay, and Paul Taylor. *The New News and the Old News: The Press and Politics in the 1990s*. Twentieth Century Fund, New York, 1992.

Rubin, Michael R., and Mary T. Huber. *The Knowledge Industry in the United States, 1960–1980*. Princeton, NJ: Princeton University Press, 1986.

Sabato, Larry J. *Feeding Frenzy: How Attack Journalism Has Transformed American Politics*. New York: Free Press, 1994.

Scientific American. "Communications, Computers and Networks." Special issue. September 1991; "Key Technologies for the 21st Century." Special issue. September 1995; "Telecommunications for the Twenty-first Century." Special issue, April 1998.

Setzer, Florence, and Jonathan Levy. *Broadcast Television in a Multichannel Marketplace*. Office of Policy and Plans working paper 26. Federal Communications Commission, Washington, DC, June 1991.

Shaughnessy, Haydn, and Carmen Fuente Cobo. *The Cultural Obligations of Broadcasting*. Media monograph 12. European Media Institute, University of Manchester, Great Britain, 1990.

Shawcross, William. *Rupert Murdoch: Ringmaster of the Information Circus*. London: Chatto & Windus, 1992.

Shenk, David. *Data Smog: Surviving the Information Glut*. San Francisco, CA: Harper San Francisco, 1997.

Sirois, Charles, and Claude E. Forget. *The Medium and the Muse: Culture, Telecommunications and the Information Highway*. Montreal: Institute for Research on Public Policy, 1995.

Slack, Jennifer D., and Fred Fejes, eds. *The Ideology of the Information Age*. Norwood, NJ: Ablex, 1987.

Smith, Anthony. *The Geopolitics of Information*. New York: Oxford University Press, 1980.

———. *Goodbye, Gutenberg*. New York: Oxford University Press, 1980.

———. *The Age of Behemoths: The Globalization of Mass Media Firms*. Report for the Twentieth Century Fund. New York: Priority, 1991.

Smith, Sally Bedell. *In All His Glory*. New York: Simon & Schuster, 1990.

Squires, James D. *Read All About It! The Corporate Takeover of America's Newspapers*. New York: Times Books, 1993.

Stefik, Mark. *Internet Dreams: Archetypes, Myths and Metaphors*. Cambridge MA: MIT Press, 1996.

Sterling, Christopher, and John Kitross. *Stay Tuned: A Concise History of American Broadcasting*. Belmont, CA: Wadsworth, 1990.

Stevenson, Robert L. *Global Communication in the Twenty-First Century*. New York: Longman, 1994.

Stoll, Clifford. *Silicon Snake Oil: Second Thoughts on the Information Highway*. New York: Doubleday, 1995.

Stonier, Tom. *The Wealth of Information*. London: Thomas Methuen, 1983.

Straubhaar, Joseph, and Robert LaRose. *Communications Media in the Information Society*. Belmont, CA: Wadsworth, 1996.

Sussman, Gerald. *Communications Technology and Politics in the Information Age*. Newbury Park, CA: Sage Publications, 1997.

Sussman, Leonard. *Power, the Press and the Technology of Freedom: The Coming Age of ISDN*. Lanham, MD: University Press of America, 1990.

Swisher, Kara. *AOL.Com: How Steve Case Beat Bill Gates in the War for the Web*. New York: Times Business/Random House, 1998.

Times-Mirror Center for the People and the Press. *The Age of Indifference: A Study of Young Americans and How They View the News*. Washington, DC, June 1990.

———. *Technology in the American Household: Americans Going Online*. Washington, DC, October 1995.

Toffler, Alvin. *The Third Wave*. New York: William Morrow, 1980.

Traber, Michael. *The Myth of the Information Revolution: Social and Ethical Implications of Information Technology*. Newbury Park, CA: Sage, 1988.

Turkle, Sherry. *Life on the Screen: Identity in the Age of the Internet*. New York: Touchstone Books, 1997.

Turow, Joseph. *Media Systems in Society*. New York: Longman, 1992.

Ulloth, Dana R., ed. *Communications Technology: A Survey*. Lanham, MD: University Press of America, 1991.

Underwood, Doug. *When MBAs Rule the Newsroom: How Marketers and Managers Are Reshaping Today's Media*. New York: Columbia University Press. 1993.

U.S. Congress. House of Representatives. *Options Papers*. Prepared by the staff of the Subcommittee on Communications, Committee on Interstate and Foreign Commerce, 95th Congress, 1st Session. Committee Print 95-13. Washington, DC, May 1977.

———. Office of Technology Assessment. *Critical Connections: Communications for the Future*. OTA Publication OTA-CIT-407. Washington, DC, January 1990.

———. Office of Technology Assessment. *The Big Picture: HDTV and High-Resolution Systems*. Report OTA-BP-CIT-64. Washington, DC, June 1990.

U.S. Department of Commerce. National Telecommunications and Information Administration. *Telecom 2000*. Washington, DC: 1989.

———. *The Globalization of Mass Media Firms*. Washington, DC, 1993.

U.S. Department of Commerce. Office of Telecommunications. *The Information Economy*. Special publication 77-12. Washington, DC, 1977.

———. International Trade Administration. *1992 Industrial Outlook*. Washington, DC, January 1992.

U.S. Department of Justice. Anti-Trust Division. *The Geodesic Network: Report on Competition in the Telephone Industry*. Washington, DC, January 1987.

United States Institute of Peace. *Peaceworks: Keynote Addresses from the Virtual Diplomacy Conference*. Washington, DC, September 1997.

Veronis, Suhler & Associates. *Communications Industry Forecast*. New York, October 1998.

Walker, James R., and Douglas A. Ferguson. *The Broadcast Television Industry*. New York: Allyn & Bacon, 1998.

Watts, Steven. *The Magic Kingdom: Walt Disney and the American Way of Life*. Boston: Houghton Mifflin, 1998.

Webster, Frank. *Theories of the Information Society*. New York: Routledge, 1995.

Wildman, S. S., and S. E. Siwek. *International Trade in Films and Television Programs*. Cambridge, MA: Ballinger Books, 1988.

Wilhelm, Donald. *Global Communications and Political Power*. New Brunswick, NJ: Transaction, 1990.

Williams, Frederick, ed. *Measuring the Information Society*. Newbury Park, CA: Sage, 1988.

Wired. "Scenarios: The Future of the Future." Special issue. October 1995.

Woolf, Michael. *Burn Rate*. New York: Simon & Schuster, 1997.

Wriston, Walter B. *The Twilight of Sovereignty: How the Information Revolution Is Transforming Our World*. New York: Scribner, 1992.

Yergin, Daniel, and Joseph Stanislaw. *Commanding Heights: The Battle Between Government and the Marketplace That Is Remaking the Modern World*. New York: Simon & Schuster, 1998.

Zeff, Robbin Lee, and Brad Aronson. *Advertising on the Internet*. New York: John Wiley & Sons, 1997.

Index

About the Author

Wilson Dizard, Jr. is a senior associate in the communications policy program at the Center for Strategic & International Studies in Washington, DC. For twenty years, he taught in the communications program at Georgetown University. In addition to over sixty scholarly articles, research reports, and monographs on communications subjects, his books include *The Strategy of Truth, Television—A World View, Gorbachev's Information Revolution, The Coming Information Age*, and *Meganet: How the Global Communications Network Will Connect Everyone on Earth*. His current project is a study of the impact of advanced information technologies on the conduct of American foreign policy.